175

187-88 Objective
Burma

133 Bengal Lancer

{ 178 Miniver/Dover
{ 196

61 Novello

57 Mountbatten

4 flag

5. chaplin

Tales From The Hollywood Raj

Tales From The Hollywood Raj

The British, the Movies, and Tinseltown

SHERIDAN MORLEY

THE VIKING PRESS   NEW YORK

All rights reserved
Published in 1984 by The Viking Press
40 West 23rd Street, New York, N.Y. 10010
Published simultaneously in Canada by
Penguin Books Canada Limited

The author and publishers are grateful for permission to reprint copyrighted
material from the following sources: Article by Nora Laing, *Hollywood
Reporter*, November 1932; *Hollywood by Starlight*, R. J. Minney; article
by J. B. Priestley, *New Statesman*, 1947; *Victorian in Orbit*, Cedric Hardwicke,
Methuen, 1961; *Harlequinade*, Constance Collier, Bodley Head, 1929; *My Life
in Pictures*, Charles Chaplin, Bodley Head, 1974; *Confessions of an Actor*,
Laurence Olivier, Weidenfeld & Nicolson, 1982; *Round the Room*, Edward
Knoblock, Chapman & Hall, 1939; articles by Sir Herbert Beerbohm Tree,
The Times, 1917; articles by George Grossmith, *Listener*, 1938; *The Glass
Ladder*, June Hillman, Heinemann, 1960.

LIBRARY OF CONGRESS CATALOGING IN PUBLICATION DATA
Morley, Sheridan, 1941–
   Tales from the Hollywood Raj.
   Includes index.
   1. Moving-picture industry—California—Hollywood—Anecdotes, facetiae,
satire, etc.   2. Entertainers—California—Hollywood—Anecdotes, facetiae,
satire, etc.   I. Title.
PN1993.5.U65M67   1984   384'.8'0979494   83-40214
ISBN 0-670-69162-3

Printed in the United States of America
Set in Devinne

For Peter Bull, with love

Contents

Illustrations

'Hollywood is a chain gang and we lose the will to escape; the links of our chain are forged not of cruelties but of luxuries: we are pelted with orchids and roses; we are overpaid and underworked.'
Clive Brook, 1933

'God felt sorry for actors, so he gave them a place in the sun and a swimming-pool; all they had to sacrifice was their talent.'
Cedric Hardwicke, 1935

'They are a very decent, generous lot of people out here and they don't expect you to listen. Always remember that, dear boy. It's the secret of social ease in this country. They talk entirely for their own pleasure. Nothing they say is designed to be heard.'
Sir Francis Hinsley in Evelyn Waugh's The Loved One, *1948*

'It's no good explaining to people why one lives here – either they understand it's the only place, or they don't.'
Christopher Isherwood, 1966

'The British are coming.'
Colin Welland, at the 1982 Oscar-winning ceremony for Chariots of Fire, *made just a century after the British first arrived in California*

Acknowledgements

For the last five years, between other assignments, I have been assembling this book in jigsaw fashion; it is intentionally written much in the style of a radio or television documentary script, for the ground it covers seems by its very nature to require that kind of approach: seven decades of Hollywood on- and off-screen history seen through the eyes of the expatriate British who helped to make and shape it.

Many of the actors, actresses, writers and directors involved have been dead for several years, and in writing about them I have drawn not only on their own published or private memoirs but also on the often more accurate memories of their friends and families. Many others are still happily very much alive and have been invaluable in their spoken and written help. Credits will be found in the body of the text: a list of books consulted here would read like a complete catalogue of the British Film Institute's superlative library (both its chained and public sections) and a list of people consulted over the years would simply be an alphabetical index of those dozens of British actors who have worked in Hollywood and been kind enough to talk to me about some aspect of it. They will be found in the main index and it will be clear from any reading of the book precisely who they are.

I would additionally like to thank Tony Richardson, Douglas Fairbanks, Vincent Price and Anna Lee for giving up a great deal of their time to answer my questions while I was completing the book, and the staffs of the BFI Information Library in London and of the Library of the Academy of Motion Picture Arts and Sciences in Hollywood for their constant and patient help. I am also extremely grateful to the owner of the Cinema Bookshop in London for letting me use it as a third reference library. Finally I am grateful to three men (quite apart from my ever encouraging publishers at Weidenfeld and Viking) without whom this book would have happened even more slowly than it did: one is Colin Webb, who finally over a lunch gave shape to an idea that had been living at the back of both our minds for several years; the second is Steve Bottomore, whose initial research got me started; and the third is my editor at *Punch*, Alan Coren, who once again was kind enough to give me the time to finish a book which would otherwise have remained forever incomplete.

I also have to thank the original editors, writers and publishers of the following newspapers and magazines, some of them alas long since defunct, from which I have drawn both direct and indirect quotations: *Cinema, Film Spectator, Photoplay, Picturegoer, Picture Show, Vanity Fair, Sight and Sound, Films and Filming, The New Yorker, Punch, Kine Weekly, Harper's Bazaar, Motion Picture, Moving Picture Classic, Film Weekly, Moving Picture World, Variety, The Stage*, the Los Angeles, New York and London *Times, Literary Digest, Movie* and *The Movie*.

For illustrations I am indebted to all those who are credited in the list on pages ix and x.

Sheridan Morley

Tales From The Hollywood Raj

1:
The British Are Coming

Though there have been countless histories of Hollywood and its professional inhabitants, not one has ever considered in isolation the extraordinary feat of colonization achieved there by the British from the coming of sound through fifty years to the final destruction of the old studio structures by television.

It was India all over again and a century later: the British arrived as an invading army of expert settlers (they, after all, could speak the English language at a time when many silent film stars were still having trouble mastering basic American) who formed themselves rapidly into polo clubs and cricket teams and gave tea parties for each other on Sunday afternoons. 'Darling,' I once heard Robert Coote call across to my grandmother Gladys Cooper in tones of some disapproval during one of these weekly gatherings, 'there seems to be an American on your lawn.'

The fact that the lawn was in Pacific Palisades, not a mile away from where Ronald Reagan was then setting up home in the course of his 1940s career as a B-movie star, and the fact that the American was a director no less distinguished than George Cukor, did not seem to strike anyone as odd.

Although it has been twelve years now since Gladys died, twenty since she tore up her deep Hollywood roots and came home to Oxfordshire, I find that I still think of California in terms of her own unshakably English attitude towards it. A child of the Victorians, born in 1888, she belonged to that C. Aubrey Smith generation who colonized Beverly Hills as surely as their parents had once colonized Africa and Australia. The Americans, though for two decades her MGM-contract employers, were also her natives; they were there to be taught the English language, to be encouraged towards a more European way of life, to be civilized if possible and dealt with if not. They were to be spoken to loudly and tersely and clearly; they were to be urged into the war, off the drink and out into the fresh air.

They were not to be mocked, or patronized, or cheated; but neither were they to be treated as equals, exactly, even if their wealth and their lives and their weather were vastly superior to anything Gladys had known back home in England. It was not precisely the Americans' fault that they could not be born and die (as did Gladys) by the banks of the Thames, but they should not be allowed to forget it either. Then there was Nanny Marshall, whose name wasn't really Marshall at all; it just so happened that she'd been taken out to California by Edna Best and Herbert Marshall early in the 1930s to look after their baby, and following the London tradition of the time she'd acquired the family surname along with the job. Nanny Marshall had stayed on in Hollywood, taking care not only of other film-star offspring but also of the other English nannies who were later brought out West on similar child-minding missions by affluent local families. Such families thought that prestige, tone or at the very least security might be added to their life-styles by a lady who looked and sounded as though she had once wheeled a coroneted pram around the Peter Pan statue in Kensington Gardens.

Nanny Marshall, therefore, found herself at the head of a powerful nanny mafia; in return for 'filling in' on her compatriots' various days off, she acquired an enviable store of Hollywood backstairs gossip. If you wanted to know about the Chaplin marriage or the Sinatra divorce, you asked Nanny Marshall. Nanny Marshall knew it all and had a memory that must have been the envy of both Hedda Hopper and Louella Parsons. Once, just after the war when I was living with Gladys in California, word came that Greta Garbo was expected for tea. Gladys rather liked her, especially as she always volunteered to wash up afterwards, but I asked Gladys if the great Swede was truly expected: 'Certainly,' came the reply, 'but so too is Nanny Marshall and she is far more important, so kindly be on your best behaviour.' Garbo may have been the world's greatest movie star but Nanny Marshall was English, and that, even in the California of 1949, was still what really counted.

The British who had begun to arrive in California twenty years earlier were often refugees from the Broadway or London stage, actors who realized that on home territory their careers might prove unexciting, but who had discovered (often on some prolonged American stage tour) this magical place in the sun where just to be English and an actor was already enough.

The early arrivals, like those in India, had to be prepared to put up with the heat, separation from nearest and sometimes dearest, and a long five-day rail trek out from New York, which itself was at least another five days by boat from London. Some, like Elizabeth Taylor, arrived at such an early age that they went native without discernible difficulty; others, like Cedric Hardwicke and C. Aubrey Smith, realized that their success would lie in their ability to become more and more English the longer they stayed in California, so that they ended up on screen as caricatures of the colonels they might in other circumstances so easily have become.

Later arrivals, like Harrison and Niven, tended to colonize by stealth, but here too there was a remarkable air of colonial settlers: many brought furniture and nannies and children out by boat and train from the old country. For those of us lucky enough to have been children there after the war, California was a magical land where you could swim and buy bananas and not have to go to school too often. For the nannies, it was still a posting abroad. Deborah Kerr met hers at Los Angeles station off the train that in five marvellous days and nights crossed the vast hinterlands of the mid-West and the Grand Canyon.

'Well, Nanny,' she asked on the platform, 'what did you think?'

'Of what, Madam? If you mean America, I did not care for it. All those open spaces.'

By the time I got there, during the last heyday of that particular Californian Raj, a lot of the flags were already coming down and the younger actors, those who had not already gone home for the war, were beginning to become uneasily aware that for the 1950s in Hollywood it was no longer going to be quite enough just to be English. But others could never go back; they were too old, too rich, too comfortable or sometimes just still too nervous – the wartime British press campaign known as 'Gone With The Wind Up' and directed at those who had declined to come home in 1939 had left scars which had not fully healed a decade later.

A few, like my grandmother, stayed on into the early 1960s, picking up useful work as dowagers in television series and waiting for the occasional Anglophile blockbuster like Separate Tables or My Fair Lady; but even she, with her passionate love of the California sun, began spending more and more of her time at home in England, where the work and the family now tended to be, and if you go back to California today, traces of a British settlement are limited to the occasional mock-Tudor pub in Santa Monica or a friendly accent in a used-car showroom specializing in the Rolls-Royce status symbols which seem to change hands rapidly in a still volatile local economy.

Now the British actor in California tends to be out there on a short-term contract, for a single movie or television series, and the coming of the ten-hour flight across the Pole from London has made Los Angeles just one more location stop where before it was a way of life. Even the once valuable English accent is now a problem for world audiences who have become used to an all-purpose mid-Atlantic neutrality of speech.

Yet there is one building that still flies the Union Jack in the heart of Hollywood today. Just above the Sunset Boulevard that has always been the main thoroughfare of the celluloid dream, and now resembles nothing so much as the decaying central street of a town from which the parade has definitely passed on, runs North Doheny Drive, and about halfway up it, in a house decorated with more flags than you will see outside Windsor Castle during the average royal wedding, lives the last doyenne of the Hollywood British.

She is Anna Lee, and at the age of sixty-nine she's one of the few survivors of the generation of British actors who settled in Hollywood during the 1930s. Born Joanna Winnifrith, she had started out in the London theatre, gone under contract to Gaumont-British and then followed her husband, the director Robert Stevenson (who later made the Orson Welles *Jane Eyre* and seventeen of the most successful Disney features), out west:

> I only ever really meant to come for a holiday, but in those days Hollywood was quite a lovely place; the air was clean and you could see the snow-capped mountains and there were no freeways and I thought perhaps I'd stay for a while. Then the war came and I was trapped; Bob wasn't about to go home and they wouldn't give me a visa on my own because I had a young child, so Bob joined the American army and I went up to Canada and got into the Red Cross and somehow I never managed to live in England again.

Instead she brought a hunk of England to California: married now for the third time, to the veteran American author and poet Robert Nathan, she lives in a house that appears to have been designed by Harrods and provisioned by Fortnum's, surrounded by paintings of the Duke of Wellington and signed photographs of the Queen Mother, these last being the trophies gained from a series of charity banquets arranged in Hollywood by Miss Lee to benefit the National Trust. Were we still in need of food parcels, she would doubtless be first in line at the Sunset Boulevard post office; as it is, she declares her almost fanatical devotion to England on all possible occasions and often at considerable personal risk. During a recent spate of Ulster bombings she raised a banner from her roof on St Patrick's Day reading GOD SAVE THE QUEEN AND DEATH TO THE IRA, only to awake the next morning to find her front door smeared with blood.

Though still best known for the John Ford classic *How Green Was My Valley* (and a fleeting appearance as a nun in *The Sound of Music*), Anna Lee now makes a comfortable living as one of the stars of a daytime American television soap opera called *General Hospital*. More than half her life and three-quarters of her career have been totally American, yet she remains deeply and defiantly homesick: 'The thing I most dread now is dying in America; I really can't bear the idea of Forest Lawn. I want an English country churchyard and a tombstone with moss growing on it.'

Meantime, dressed in Ingrid Bergman's breastplate from *St Joan* and Charlton Heston's helmet from *Ben-Hur*, she rides as Britannia in Los Angeles parades and remembers a somewhat different Hollywood:

When I first arrived here there were very few women stars from England, and most of the men were already thinking about going home to fight or at the very least they were going off to join the Eagle Squadron in Canada. The first film I ever starred in here was *My Life With Caroline*, in which I played opposite Ronald Colman, and he insisted the writers should add a bulldog called Winston to the script. But the really disgusting thing at that time, before Pearl Harbor, was that Hollywood was full of Germans, and I remember one at a cocktail party proposing a toast to the fall of France, so I threw a lot of glasses at him and they told me to behave because America was still supposedly neutral. One or two people did behave really appallingly; I remember Chaplin claiming that the war in Europe wasn't 'our war' and that we shouldn't join it, so I told him never to forget he had been born English, and that seemed to surprise him. Aubrey Smith and Nigel Bruce used to go around presenting one-way tickets home to England to young British actors they found hanging around the studios. They were a bit old themselves for the fighting, but most of the younger ones like Niven and Olivier behaved very well and went home as soon as they could, though there was always a good deal of doubt surrounding Hitchcock.

But then of course Pearl Harbor happened and suddenly it was everybody's war, and then it was really all right and we got a lot of American help with Bundles for Britain and knitting balaclava helmets, though some of the English thought they'd done their bit with a terrible film called *Forever and a Day* which was made for war charities without any salaries. I always thought the balaclavas were a lot more useful, but Americans are very curious, you know; there was utter panic in Santa Monica when the Japanese reached Hawaii, even though it was still thousands of miles away. I used to tell all my neighbours that if the English could stand the Battle of Britain, then they should be able to manage not to worry about the Japanese way out in the Pacific.

By the time the war ended, the British community here had already begun to disintegrate; the vogue for English costume dramas was already passing, the best of the actors had gone home, those that were left began to get very nervous of the new (often temporary) arrivals from London, the smog began to descend, television caught on and then suddenly it was all over.

Those of us left here now are just staying on, hanging on, waiting for the end because it's too late to go home. After Greer Garson they stopped bothering to make English stars out here; nowadays everybody looks interchangeably international and they all sound more or less the same. It's a different world; the English in Hollywood today are more likely to be used car salesmen or television comedy writers than actors.

And, one suspects, are less likely to get invited to share the Fortnum's imported tea along North Doheny Drive; but Anna Lee was not, of course, the first expatriate of her kind. The Hollywood British began almost as early as Hollywood itself, with the London music-hall comedians Stan Laurel and Charles Chaplin, and they lasted way into the post-war years, though admittedly with a much lower and less overtly British profile. Some of the best-known of the Hollywood British had never been British at all: Errol Flynn, who defeated the Armada and led the *Charge of the Light Brigade*, in fact hailed from Australia; George Sanders was Russian; Laurence Harvey was Lithuanian; Leslie Howard was Hungarian. Yet somehow they all managed to symbolize something utterly English that Hollywood felt was unavailable locally. The Scots and the Welsh seem to have made markedly fewer inroads into California even in the heyday of actors' immigration, though the Irish (thanks largely to John Ford's interest in the Abbey Theatre players of the 1930s) were always much in demand for crinkly character work. It was indeed with a real Irishman that the whole British invasion of California first got under way.

2:
Wilde Times

'Here, from the uttermost end of the great world, I send you love and greeting,' wrote Oscar Wilde in a letter from California to Norman Forbes-Robertson on 29 March 1882.

The British had not been slow in discovering California; some, of course, pioneers and sons of pioneers, had rolled west with the wagon trains. Actors followed, actors from New York and Chicago but also, as I've indicated, actors from London on extensive American tours. The mid-west, which for most of the nineteenth century had been where all touring from Europe stopped, suddenly became a halfway-house on the route to California, so that by 1905 a young and ecstatic Sybil Thorndike, born in the year Wilde sent that letter to Forbes-Robertson, was writing home to her mother (between performances of *Hamlet*, in which, for Ben Greet, she was understudying Ophelia) of the 'glory of California; you can't imagine the smell of the air – something the sun does to the air – it's sort of intoxicating.'

Curiously, in a career which was to continue for another seventy years and include twenty-one film appearances, Sybil Thorndike never went back to California; but then she was never especially interested in what California was best at. Oscar Wilde had already discovered that; California was best at making you famous.

It was, somewhat surprisingly, Gilbert and Sullivan who were responsible for Wilde's arrival in California; in the April of 1881, when the vogue for satirizing 'the aesthete' had been at its height, Richard d'Oyly Carte had presented a new comic opera at the Opéra Comique in London. Called *Patience*, and written by Gilbert and Sullivan, it included a character called Bunthorne, important enough to have his name in the opera's subtitle: 'Bunthorne's Bride'. Modelled partly on Rossetti, partly on Swinburne and perhaps fractionally also on the young Wilde, Bunthorne is the 'perfectly precious' young aesthete who in the story eventually loses the girl he loves for being, in a contemporary word, too camp.

After its considerable London success, d'Oyly Carte decided that *Patience* was strong enough to survive an Atlantic crossing, and made plans for its American presentation under the auspices of Colonel W.F. Morse, an astute American manager and publicist whose view it was that the show would go down rather better in America if someone could alert its audiences to the existence of the 'aesthetes' in advance. Otherwise, he wrote to d'Oyly Carte, the whole production would be liable to die a terrible death, since very few Americans of the time had the remotest idea of what an aesthete actually was, let alone why Gilbert and Sullivan should have gone to the trouble of creating an entire opera in order to mock one.

Accordingly, Morse sent a cable to Wilde in Chelsea asking if he would consider a personal-appearance tour, making fifty speeches across the length and breadth of America in advance of the touring *Patience* company. Oscar's reply was both immediate and typical: 'Yes, if offer good.' The deal was that he would get all his expenses paid plus one-third of the box-office takings in each of the towns that he and *Patience* played, and after the exchange of a series of letters Oscar set sail aboard the *Arizona* for the New World on Christmas Eve 1881.

America brought out the best and worst in Wilde; for the first (and perhaps the last) time in his life he was being paid to do the one thing he really enjoyed, which was to be himself only more so. He was following in the footsteps of Charles Dickens, a considerably more familiar name in America when he began his dramatic readings there in 1867, and blazing a trail for Dylan Thomas and Brendan Behan in that line of distinguished British authors who have barnstormed their way across America in search of money, alcohol, fame or combinations of all three.

Mercifully for Oscar, whose star at home was currently none too bright, America was to supply him with a whole new series of targets: 'Everybody here seems in a hurry to catch a train. This is a state of things which is not favourable to poetry or romance. ... In America life is one long expectoration. ... There are no trappings here, no pageants, no gorgeous ceremonies. I have seen only two processions: one was the Fire Brigade preceded by the Police, the other was the Police preceded by the Fire Brigade.'

By the end of March 1882, however, when he was writing to Forbes-Robertson, he had discovered California. More importantly, it had discovered him:

There were 4,000 people waiting at the 'depot' to see me, open carriage, four horses, an audience at my lecture of the most cultivated people in 'Frisco, charming folk. I lecture here again tonight, also twice next week; as you see I am really appreciated by the cultured classes. The railway have offered me a special train and private car to go down the coast to Los Angeles, a sort of Naples here, and I am feted and entertained to my heart's content from the chill winter of the mountains down into eternal summer here, groves of orange trees in fruit and flower, green fields and purple hills, a very Italy without its art ...

Fame, fortune, sunshine, oranges: four years before the name Hollywood was first conferred on a ranch in the Cahuenga Valley, twenty-seven years before the first film was shot there, Oscar Wilde had neatly summarized the reasons why hundreds if not thousands of his fellow-countrymen were, across the next century, to follow him out to California and create in performance, much as he had done, extensions of themselves which could cause queues to form at box-offices around both the nation and the world.

Curiously, however, the first traveller from London who decided to make Los Angeles a show-business home instead of just another stopover on an American tour was the one who, on first arrival, hadn't cared for it at all: 'Los Angeles was an ugly city, hot and oppressive, and the people looked sallow and anaemic,' wrote Charles Chaplin when recalling, half a century later, his first impression of the city he was visiting in 1910 as a twenty-one-year-old member of the Fred Karno *Wow-Wows*. This was, in fact, a crucial year in the history of Hollywood, since it was the year that the new municipality there voted (for reasons largely to do with the piping of water) to become a part of greater Los Angeles; but Chaplin was not there because of anything even remotely to do with the making of films.

The child of once affluent music-hall performers, he (like many who followed his footsteps into Californian exile) had grown up amid considerable poverty in London at the turn of the century. His father, a baritone, had abandoned his mother and taken to drink, leaving her with so little money that in 1896 Charles, his mother and her son by an earlier alliance, Sydney, all entered the work-house in Lambeth, where they spent the next eighteen months. Chaplin escaped to become one of the Eight Lancashire Lads doing a clog-dance act round the music-halls, and then, while his mother retreated into a madhouse, he spent five years as Billy the newspaper boy in Frohman's long-running melodrama *Sherlock Holmes*, the play that was in its myriad later film variants to prove one of the most constant and fruitful employment areas for the rest of the Hollywood English. In 1906, thanks to his brother Sydney, he got an audition for Fred Karno, who then had more than thirty comedy troupes playing the British provincial halls, and it was with a Karno company that he first toured America in that summer of 1910.

Hollywood had been in existence since 1886, and incorporated as a municipality in its own independent right since 1903. It owed its name to Mrs Harvey Henderson Wilcox, wife of a wealthy local real-estate developer, who named her ranch there in memory of an estate called Hollywood which she had once visited near Chicago. By 1897 it had become a village, complete with its own post office, which was to be found in Sackett's Hotel on the corner of its two main streets, Cahuenga and Hollywood Boulevards. It also had a general store, opened by an English dry-goods clerk called John Watts in 1886 at the corner of Vine Street, but soon taken over by an American family after Mr Watts returned to Liverpool, indignant (so contemporary reports said) at the local practice whereby customers in need of ready money felt entitled to ransack his cash register, leaving promissory notes in place of the dollars they had 'borrowed'.

By 1903 Hollywood had 177 registered male voters living in the village and in that year ninety-four of them – a working majority – voted to incorporate themselves and their community as 'the City of Hollywood in a sector of Los Angeles County containing not more than 3,000 persons'. Their first mayor was a retired millionaire meat-packer from Indiana, who forbade the carrying of concealed weapons and 'the driving of more than two thousand sheep, goats or hogs through city streets at any time unless accompanied by eight competent men'.

Amateur theatricals were first observed at the Hollywood Club in 1904, a bank opened in 1905 and the first (1907) Hollywood census revealed a population of just under 3,500, of whom 615 owned homes of their own in the area. It also revealed that living in Hollywood at the time were 103 immigrants from England, 102 from Germany, 86 from Canada, 20 from France, 28 from Ireland and 24 from Scotland. There were also 158 New Yorkers and a man from Chicago called Francis Boggs. Mr Boggs was a film director attached to the Selig Polyscope studios in Chicago and when, a year later, their production of *The Count of Monte Cristo* was beset by a particularly hard Illinois winter, he remembered the warmth of Hollywood, moved cast and crew out there and finished the production near Laguna Beach, thereby earning his place in the reference books as the first director to shoot at least part of a film in California.

In May 1909, Boggs was again back in California, this time because the actor due to star in his *The Power of the Sultan*, Hobart Bosworth, was suffering from tuberculosis and had been ordered to seek the sun; accordingly, Boggs again moved his unit west and shot the film in three days on a site he rented next to a Chinese laundry in downtown Los Angeles. This, therefore, became the first film using actors to be made in California, and Mr Boggs would have undoubtedly gone on to a profitable career as Hollywood's founder-director had he not unfortunately been murdered three years later by a mad Japanese studio gardener in the first of the scandals that were soon to make the locality as famous as its films.

By 1910, therefore, when Chaplin first arrived in Los Angeles as a stage comedian, the notion of Hollywood as a home for the American movie had begun to take root.

Fragmentary Vitascope films by Thomas Alva Edison had been on show in New York as early as 1894, though four years earlier, reported the *New York Sun*, friends of Mrs Edison were entertained by being allowed to peer through a one-inch hole in a small pine box in the Edison workshop : 'There, as they looked through the hole, they saw the picture of a man. It was a most marvellous picture. It bowed and smiled and waved its hands and took off its hat with the most perfect naturalness and grace. Every motion was perfect.'

In 1892 William Dickson had developed the vertical-feed camera, and by 1895 the industry had advanced to the point where four-minute films were regularly being screened on Broadway to paying customers. That year commercial film shows were also offered at the Atlanta Cotton States Exposition, so the establishment of a film colony in Hollywood came in fact fully fifteen years after the start of regular film production in the east.

Over the next half-century, the British were to go to California much as they had once travelled to the farther outposts of their own empire, and for many of the same reasons. Some went to seek a fortune, others to escape a failed career or a mistaken marriage back home, or just because the weather looked better and there seemed to be a lot going on. Like Africa and India at the end of the nineteenth century, California at the start of the twentieth century was a place where to be English, or at the very least British, was nearly enough.

True, the British didn't get themselves into positions of comparable power; where they once had been colonial administrators they now had to live as actors and writers and (occasionally) directors, while the rather more dedicated and ambitious middle-Europeans took charge of studios and production. But they were still in the front line, hired for much the same reason that, in the 1960s, New York banks and Madison Avenue advertising agencies would hire English secretaries and tele-phonists and receptionists: they brought a touch of distinction to an otherwise rough-and-ready business.

The curious thing about the British in Hollywood was their ability to survive and prosper in what was then the newest of media simply by clinging to a world that had already vanished. The bits of old England that were brought to Hollywood by men like Aubrey Smith and George Arliss were seldom reflections of their own time, of the 1920s or 1930s. Instead, they were bringing to America an England of about 1870: the England of Kipling and Queen Victoria, never that of Jarrow or George v. Post-1914 Britain was of remarkably little interest to Hollywood in its heyday; you can go almost from *Journey's End* to *Mrs Miniver*, from mid-First World War to mid-Second World War, without finding a major Hollywood film about contemporary Britain.

So the Hollywood British were out of their time as well as out of their place; they survived in a remarkable historic and geographic limbo, like the curators of a stately home suddenly transported (as in *The Ghost Goes West*) to another continent, complete with furniture and fittings. Some of them, of course, couldn't take it: a thoughtful, introspective, stage-trained actor like Leslie Howard was forever trying to get back to England even at the height of his *Gone With The Wind* fame, while many others took sizeable cuts in living standards and career prospects to return to a world where acting meant something more than the per-petuation of often crude colonial-nationalist stereotypes. Of those who did stay, some managed full and satisfactory careers; but these were very often the kind of character actors who, back home, would never have left the middle ranks of a good repertory company. Those who achieved a Cary Grant–Michael Caine level of superstardom often had to tone down their Englishness to an acceptable mid-Atlantic neutrality, and the current British acting community in what is left of Hollywood is scrupulously careful never to be thought of as anything but Anglo-American.

Up in the hills above Santa Monica, often in somewhat reduced circumstances, it is still possible to find a few surviving members of the old Hollywood British community today; but they, like Paul Scott's British community in India, are now only Staying On, blood thinned by the western instead of the eastern sun, and unable to get back to where many of them have almost forgotten they once belonged.

3:
California Cockneys

In technical terms, the very first of the Hollywood English was also the man without whom there might have been no Hollywood: Eadweard Muybridge, inventor of the moving picture. A considerable eccentric (like many of the later California exiles), Muybridge was born Edward James Muggeridge on 9 April 1830 at Kingston-on-Thames. His father was a corn chandler; Muggeridge, apparently determined early upon a more exotic life, took the name Eadweard after the Saxon martyr king whose statue stood in Kingston's market place, and converted Muggeridge to Muybridge according to early Anglo-Saxon spelling traditions. In 1852, three years after news of the California Gold Rush reached Kingston, he sailed for America, returning to Kingston in 1860 after being seriously injured in a stage-coach accident.

By 1867, however, he was back in California, billing himself as 'Helios the Flying Camera' and offering a collection of Yosemite Valley photographs for sale at twenty dollars; a year later he had become Director of Photographic Surveys for the US Government, and was already in Alaska photographing ports and harbours for the US army at the time when that territory was purchased from Russia.

Then, in 1872, two American millionaires (Leland Stanford and Fred McCrellish) found themselves deeply embroiled in an argument, which soon became a wager, about whether a trotting horse ever lifts all four hooves simultaneously. Muybridge was asked to settle the matter once and for all with his camera; technical difficulties were at the time prodigious, and the early shots proved both blurred and disappointing. But after five years of experiment and improvement (largely funded first by Stanford, an ex Governor of California, and later by the University of Pennsylvania) Muybridge did come up with a clear photograph of a horse galloping at more than twenty miles an hour; this in turn led to a series of photographs of animals and humans in motion, and then to the world's first-ever moving picture, the projection of a horse's movements achieved by lining up twelve cameras along a racetrack and then printing their individual shots onto a revolving disc.

In the meantime, and again true to the pattern of the Hollywood that indirectly he had helped to invent, Muybridge was involved in a massive personal scandal: having in 1872 married a young divorcée little more than half his forty-two years, Muybridge returned home from a photographic assignment at the Modoc Indian War to find Flora with a child that he reckoned could not possibly have been his. Accordingly he went out and shot her lover, another Englishman named Harry Larkyns; in October 1874 he was arrested and charged with murder, and the following February a jury found him not guilty, though apparently not before his hair and beard had turned totally white. Flora tried twice thereafter to sue him unsuccessfully for divorce on the grounds of his 'extreme cruelty'; this charge was also thrown out by the court and she died a year later, though their son lived on in San Francisco, where he worked as a gardener until being knocked down and killed by a car in Sacramento on 1 February 1944.

Muybridge senior, unaware of the industry to which he had given birth (and ignoring the child to which he had apparently not), started a worldwide series of lecture tours on the art of still photography and returned to Kingston in 1900; he died there four years later at the age of seventy-four, leaving his slides to the Science Museum in London and his photographic equipment to the local library. This included the Zoopraxiscope, a remarkable device which he had shown at the Chicago World's Fair in 1893, though to a distinct lack of public interest. The forerunner of Edison's Kinetoscope, it was in effect the world's first projector, though able to show only very short sequences of photographs to create the illusion of movement. He had first displayed it during a lecture on 4 May 1880 at the San Francisco Art Association rooms; that night he became the first man in the world to project moving photographs on to a screen in front of an audience. The movie was born that night, a couple of hundred miles north of Hollywood; and its father was an Englishman.

Yet Muybridge had pioneered a machine, not an industry, and for the next thirty years there seemed little point in other Englishmen following him out to California unless they were in search of more immediate gold than even movies could ever provide. The film industry as such had its birth in the east, in New York and Europe, and did not get back to its Californian roots for another thirty years. But British actors were not in the meantime inclined totally to ignore the US. In the wake of Dickens and Wilde, a number of them – not least Henry Irving – had discovered that New York, Chicago and Boston could prove lucrative additional dates to a British provincial touring schedule, and by 1906 an actor called Donald Crisp had already settled in America – the same actor who was also to work as an assistant to D.W.Griffith from 1910 and then turn in a final film portrayal as a crusty old Scot fully half a century later.

Though by no means the most charismatic of the Hollywood British community (he was born in 1880 in Aberfeldy, Scotland), Crisp probably deserved its long-service medal. After Eton and Oxford he served in the Boer War, reached Biograph in 1910, turned up as General Grant in *Birth of a Nation* (1915), directed some of the best of the elder Fairbanks' and Keaton's movies of the 1920s, won an Oscar in Ford's *How Green Was My Valley* (1941) and made his final appearance in *Spencer's Mountain* in 1963 – eleven years before his death, in Hollywood, at the ripe old age of ninety-four. In terms of its key movies, and the men and women he made them with, Donald Crisp's career (one which started in New York with stills for 'What the Butler Saw' machines) was in itself a history of silent and talking Hollywood. Yet because he was not always immediately recognizable as the cricket-playing colonel, or perhaps just because Hollywood Scots were somehow never as much in demand as Hollywood English, or maybe just because as a director himself he knew too much about the perils of instant type-casting, Crisp never attained the immediate audience identification of an Aubrey Smith or even a Basil Rathbone. Crisp looked too often as though he belonged in California, as though he might even actually live there; part of the essence of the Hollywood British was to look like visiting dignitaries who might at any moment be called away from mere studio shooting to serve as ambassador or general in some far-flung out-post of the Empire where natives could not be calmed by anything as simple as a cinema projector.

But the celluloid aristocracy came later; the first to establish a British presence in Hollywood were in fact the two star Cockney members of Fred Karno's army, Stan Laurel and Charles Chaplin. Born within a year of each other (Chaplin in London in 1889, Laurel as Arthur Stanley Jefferson at Ulverston in Lancashire in 1890) they were both music-hall trained by Karno: 'He didn't teach Charlie and me all we know about comedy,' said Laurel later, 'but he taught us most of it. If I had to pick an adjective to fit Karno it would be supple; that's what he was, mentally and physically. And precise; he taught us to be precise. Out of all that endless rehearsal and performance came Charlie, the most supple and precise comedian of our time.'

In that sense it was perhaps Karno, rather than Mack Sennett, who deserved the credit for the original creation of screen slapstick, for what were Chaplin's and Laurel's earliest films but faithful records of their old stage routines? Yet Karno was, ironically, to become one of the great failures among the Hollywood English; like another great European stage impresario, André Charlot, he left his arrival about twenty years too late, only to find when he did get to California that the men he had made stars were faintly embarrassed by his presence; Chaplin treated him to a two-hour organ recital, and although Laurel got him a job for $1,000 per week as an 'advisor' to Hal Roach, Karno rapidly alienated himself by pointing out that the studio was still using routines which he'd abandoned on Victorian music-hall tours of the 1890s.

That was 1930, and memories were already short; in any case neither Chaplin nor Laurel were in the empire-building business, not at any rate in nationalist terms. Unlike the 'legitimate' actors who followed them they did not especially wish to create their own colony in California to which like-minded but non-threatening entertainers could later be welcomed; they were, like all great music-hall artists, traditional loners who saw an allegiance only to their own routines. Chaplin and Laurel first visited America on a Karno tour in 1910; Chaplin made his first film there in 1914 and only left California at the time of the shameful McCarthy witch-hunt of 1951; Laurel made his first film there in 1917, teamed up with Oliver Hardy ten years later and remained in California until his death nearly forty years after. So Laurel spent fifty years in California, Chaplin almost forty; both achieved early silent fame, considerable wealth and a way of life unknown to even the most triumphant Victorian touring vaudeville comedians from whose ranks they had emerged. Laurel, in the end, went into a vastly steeper and more painful decline than did the more astute Chaplin, whose instinct for survival ensured him a quarter-century of elegant if embittered Swiss semi-retirement. Though taken together their careers add up to almost a hundred years of Hollywood comic history, they left surprisingly little mark on the community around them; California did not become a haven for other music-hall comedians when the music halls started to close during the 1920s and 1930s. Partly perhaps this was because neither Chaplin nor Laurel exactly encouraged others to follow in their footsteps; mainly it was that they (unlike the straight actors) reached Hollywood while still young enough to learn, and indeed condition, the rules of a new medium. They were not simply repeating on celluloid the tricks that had made them successful on stage, though that was certainly how they started; they were also pioneering a new form of entertainment, one which was in fact to destroy the very music halls where they had begun their careers with Karno.

Precisely because they were in at this new beginning, and because they had also seen the music halls fall to something below the peak of their popularity even before the coming of the cinema, neither Chaplin nor Laurel carried around the studios with them the faint sense of guilt which was to beset many of the actors who came after them. The actors had, after all, left behind them in Britain a legitimate theatre which was still thriving and was to continue to do so throughout and well beyond the heyday of the cinema. For an actor working in Hollywood, there was always the faint feeling that perhaps he should have been at the Old Vic giving his Lear or learning his trade by the ritual spear-carrying recommended to all drama students. For a comic like Chaplin or Laurel, there was only the memory of increasingly seedy provincial tours, bad money and no fame; anything that Hollywood had to offer was likely to be an improvement.

Not that Chaplin saw it quite like that from the beginning. After his initial touring visit to Los Angeles in 1910 with Karno's *Wow-Wows*, he returned with that vaudeville troupe to New York. William Morris booked them to play *A Night in an English Music Hall* for six weeks at a theatre on Eighth Avenue and it was while they were there that Mack Sennett, then working as an actor for D.W. Griffith's Biograph Studios, first saw his future star: 'I was more than impressed – stunned might be a good word. I think I was so struck by him because he was everything I wasn't: a little fellow who could move like a ballet dancer. The next week I couldn't remember his name, but I sure as hell never forgot that easy grace of movement.'

Stan Laurel, also in that company on the American tour, seems to have made less of an impression on Sennett, but has left us a vivid early account of Chaplin:

I was Charlie's room-mate on that tour and he was fascinating to watch. People through the years have talked about how eccentric he became, but he was a very eccentric person then. He was very moody and often very shabby in appearance. Then suddenly he would astonish us all by getting dressed to kill. It seemed that every once in a while he would get an urge to look very smart. At these times he would wear a derby hat (an expensive one), gloves, smart suit, fancy vest, two-tone side-button shoes and carry a cane. ... I remember that he drank only once in a while, and then it was port. He read books incessantly. One time he was trying to study Greek but he gave it up after a few days and started to study yoga. A part of this yoga business was what was called 'the water cure' – so for a few days after that he ate nothing, just drank water for his meals. He carried his violin wherever he could. Had the strings reversed so he could play left-handed, and he would practise for hours. He bought a cello once and used to carry it round with him. At these times he would always dress like a musician, a long fawn-coloured overcoat with green velvet cuffs and a collar and a slouch hat. And he'd let his hair grow long in back. We never knew what he was going to do next. He was unpredictable.

The Karno company, still complete with Laurel and Chaplin, then did another twenty-week tour of America during which Charlie got a firm offer from Sid Grauman, the owner of the Empress Theater in San Francisco, to leave Karno and create his own American vaudeville team. Considering that Chaplin had only a few months earlier been considering total retirement from the music hall to run a pig farm, things were definitely looking up.

It was in May 1913 that Chaplin got his real break: he and the Karno company were playing the Nixon Theater in Philadelphia when Alf Reeves, the tour manager, received a telegram from Kessel and Baumann of 24 Longacre Building on Broadway: 'Is there', it read, 'a man named Chaffin in your company or something like that stop if so will he communicate.' Remembering that he had a rich aunt somewhere in the US, Chaplin thought that he had come into a fortune; in fact he had, though not by means of a will. Kessel and Baumann were not lawyers but partners in one of the earliest film production companies, one which in fact owned Keystone, where the director, Mack Sennett (remembering his visit to the Karno show but not the name of the comic he wanted), had told them to locate 'the old man who does the drunk scene in the box'. Sennett was already turning out three comedy silent shorts a week, and in no mood to hang around; Keystone offered Chaplin a year's contract at $125 a week, roughly twice what Karno was then paying him; Chaplin, remembering the advice of his brother and business manager Syd, held out for rather more and in fact got $200, as well as the agreement that Keystone would wait for him until his Karno tour closed in Kansas at the end of the following November.

'Eager and anxious', as he described himself later, Chaplin then took the train to Los Angeles and booked into a small hotel:

The following morning I boarded a street car for Edendale, a suburb of Los Angeles. It was an anomalous-looking place that could not make up its mind whether to be a humble residential district or a semi-industrial one. It had small junk-yards and lumber-yards, and abandoned-looking small farms on which were built one or two shacky wooden stores that fronted the road. After many enquiries, I found myself opposite the Keystone Studio. It was a dilapidated affair with a green fence round it, one hundred and fifty feet square. The entrance to it was up a garden path through an old bungalow – the whole place looked just as anomalous as Edendale itself. I stood gazing at it from the opposite side of the road, debating whether to go in or not.

In the event, he decided not to:

I was seized with shyness and walked quickly to the corner at a safe distance, looking to see if Mr Sennett or Mabel Normand would come out of the bungalow, but they did not appear. For half an hour I stood there, then decided to go back to the hotel. The problem of entering the studio and facing all those people became an insuperable one. For two days I arrived outside the studio, but I had not the courage to go in. The third day Mr Sennett telephoned and wanted to know why I had not shown up. I made some sort of excuse. 'Come down right away, we'll be waiting for you,' he said. So I went down and boldly marched into the bungalow and asked for Mr Sennett.

In that somewhat diffident manner, the first star of the Hollywood British arrived to stake his claim to celluloid immortality. Laurel, meanwhile, was still with Karno's stage army, though this was now rapidly beating some sort of a retreat as gradually its troops deserted for more lucrative American employment on the vaudeville circuit. But the Hollywood limelight into which Chaplin backed with such caution in 1913 was already considerably brighter than it had been during his first visit to Los Angeles three short years earlier. In the interim D. W. Griffith had made the first major Hollywood film (*In Old California*, Biograph 1910) and apart from Sennett (who started Keystone at Edendale in 1912, a year before Chaplin's arrival there) Vitagraph had opened a western branch of their New York film studios in 1911, while a group of other studios – Universal, Eclair and Lasky – had opened up around Sunset Boulevard.

Charles Chaplin, unlike many of the more classically trained actors who followed him out to California from London, knew precisely what he was running away from, and even had a hazy idea of what he was running towards. Always an astute observer of his own professional chances, he had noticed music-hall audiences already in decline and knew that artistically it was time to move on; but he also had little real affection for the London he was leaving behind (despite later sentimental journeys back to the slums of his childhood) – so little indeed that in early Hollywood interviews he took to claiming that he'd been born in the French town of Fontainebleau, presumably because even in those days mimes were meant to come from the other side of the Channel.

Given a reasonably common language, and a shared artistic and bloodline heritage, it was of course inevitable that the American cinema was going to be closer to the British cinema than to that of any other nation in Europe, at least in terms of plot origins. Just as the American theatre had, since the early 1800s, drawn on London for its writers and often for its actors too, so now would Hollywood; but, as early as 1910, doubts were already beginning to occur on both sides of the Atlantic about the precise nature of this nitrate alliance. By then, American film-makers (largely in New York) had already released one-reel dramas drawn from Dickens, Shakespeare and Walter Scott, and there had even been a 1909 silent of Wilkie Collins's *The Moonstone*, while the big hit of 1909 had been a Selig-Polyscope comedy called *The Tenderfoot*, all about an English aristocrat and his faithful valet taking over a ranch in the Wild West and doing comic battle with the local Red Indians.

The following year Vitagraph in New York released a film of Tennyson's *Becket*, using as scenario the dramatization by Henry Irving; just five years earlier, the great Victorian actor had died in Bradford after a performance of this very play (in which he'd toured America in 1893–4), and the Victorian theatre had effectively died with him, only to be almost immediately recreated on screen. Not content with the usual murder in the cathedral, Vitagraph added for New York patrons an interesting sub-plot wherein King Henry falls in love with the Fair Rosamond, only to have to kill one of the priests who objected to this alliance before the said priest could get on to the main business of killing Becket.

By this time Vitagraph had also made films of *Macbeth* ('worse than the bloodiest melodrama,' said the Chicago police censor before banning it), *Richard III*, *Othello*, *Romeo and Juliet*, *King Lear*, *Julius Caesar*, *Antony and Cleopatra*, *The Merchant of Venice*, *Twelfth Night* and *A Midsummer Night's Dream*, as well as a *Comedy of Errors*, for which they borrowed the title from Shakespeare but decided, perhaps under-standably, to supply their own plot. All these were filmed in the period 1908–10, each was only around ten minutes in length, and Vitagraph were accustomed to make at least four other films in any given week.

All were shown in England within months of their first American release, and the first faint stirrings of patriotic unease, of a kind which was to persist way into the 1960s and 1970s, can be found in an anonymous letter written to the *Moving Picture World* of 23 July 1910, evidently by an Englishman in New York:

We have always wanted to see the British picture take a place of prominence in the American market and secure its share of American business, just as the American picture is securing a share – and a very large share – of British business, which the American pictures obtain on their merits. But the British-made picture is not on its merits entitled to a share of American business. Its photography is below that of the highest American standard, dramatic subjects are undramatic, and even in Britain the British picture holds a secondary place, whilst in the United States and other countries it is barely tolerated. This is a melancholy fact, reflecting little or no credit on English manufacturers of films, who are trailing the procession with a vengeance. In other words they are years behind their French, German, Italian and American competitors.

And that wasn't all; 'there are', noted the writer,

English film-makers living and even working within a few miles of Canterbury Cathedral. Yet not one of them seems to have seized upon the opportunity of making a *Becket* picture; that was left to Vitagraph in the suburbs of New York. American film-makers have already illustrated Dickens and Scott as well as Shakespeare. They are even planning to illustrate the Bible. They are ransacking the world of literature, poetry and art for suitable subjects. What are the British makers doing – those British makers who have such a beautiful world of subjects at their very doors? What are they doing to uphold the best aspects of the picture? Absolutely nothing. As we write this, the hum of progress is heard in this land; American business is on the boom. Licensed film manufacturers are doubling the size of their plants; the Independent manufacturers are plunging into the great competition of quality. In England people are writing to the trade magazines and asking, 'Where is the English film?' And only echo answers.

Already, then, English actors and writers and directors had one strong inducement to follow Chaplin out west, the inducement of domestic inactivity in British films that was to remain, in one form or another, across the next half-century. If American film-makers couldn't be beaten, they would have to be joined.

4:
Tree in the Backwoods

One of the first and most detailed reports of the life of an English film actor in California appeared in *The Times* of 8 September 1916 from Sir Herbert Beerbohm Tree, the celebrated actor-manager who, in his middle sixties, had gone out to Hollywood to make a film of *Macbeth*. Under the heading 'Impressions of America: Not Bad For A Young Country', Sir Herbert, whose illegitimate descendants were to include both Carol and Oliver Reed, wrote extensively if faintly patronizingly about a California that was clearly of more interest and relevance to him than it was to any other of his stage-bound London generation.

Though he came of the Victorian world of Irving, Alexander and Forbes-Robertson, and though the major part of his working life was spent like theirs in running London theatres (most notably the one he built in the Haymarket, Her Majesty's, which remains his monument), Tree was, in fact, one of the great bridges linking the modern to the ancient world of acting. As early as 1899 he was to be found striding along the Embankment dressed as *King John* for the making of the first-ever Shakespearian film, one largely based on productions of the play that he had been doing at Her Majesty's and before that at the Crystal Palace. It was suitable and perhaps unsurprising that Tree, with his celebrated love for scenic flamboyance and elaborate effects, should have been the first British actor to latch onto the unique possibilities of film, though for a long time he was on his own. Indeed as late as 1916, while he was shooting his Hollywood *Macbeth*, the playwright J. M. Barrie was, in a Stratford speech, mocking the very notion that Shakespeare and the cinema might be suited for each other.

Six years after that first and primitive *King John*, Tree persuaded the inventor of the Bioscope, Charles Urban, to photograph the complex ship scene from *The Tempest* so that when the Tree company went on tour they could save themselves the expense of travelling a stage ship from town to town, the idea being that when that point in the action was reached the actors would retire from the stage and the audience would then watch what followed on a screen lowered to the back of the set. There is, alas, no evidence that this ever happened as planned, but Urban did take his film to America and show it there 'through the courtesy of Mr Beerbohm Tree by special and exclusive arrangement', and Urban's sales catalogue noted that:

This remarkable picture, taken under the ordinary conditions of stage lighting during an actual performance, illustrates the great advances in animated photography which the motion camera has rendered possible. The shipwreck with all its intense realism is reproduced with startling detail. The lightnings flash, the billows leap and roll and break, until on the tossing ship (where the terror-stricken voyagers can be seen wildly rushing about) the mast snaps and crashes to the deck. Three views are given in the film, each from a more distant point as the wreck recedes, and as the film is issued tinted to the suitably weird moonlight color, the effect obtained is very fine.

The film ran just under two minutes, featured Tree's daughter Viola as Ariel (Tree himself, playing Caliban, was of course not yet to be seen) and rented to American distributors for just thirteen dollars.

So Tree, the first man to make Shaw into a commercial success with *Pygmalion*, the first West End manager to stage Ibsen, the man who memorably described the stage spectacle *Chu Chin Chow* as 'more navel than millinery' and the man who said of himself, 'I cannot help being exceptional,' was also (a fact curiously under-rated by his many biographers) the British actor who more than any other pioneered the cinema. In 1911 he made a remarkable deal with a commercial traveller turned film producer called Will Barker, whereby for a thousand pounds Tree would allow Barker to film his famous *Henry VIII* production. Only twenty prints were to be made, however, ten for London cinemas and ten for the provinces, and these were not to be sold to cinema managers as usual but rather to be leased out for special exhibition as 'an exclusive'. Then, after six weeks, all the prints were to be called in and destroyed by fire, so that they would not interfere with live theatre ticket sales during Tree's future tours.

Other actors then began, somewhat cautiously, to follow where Tree had led (in 1913 Arthur Bourchier made a British silent *Macbeth* and Sir Johnston Forbes-Robertson committed his *Hamlet* to film), and by 1916 the notion of Shakespeare on film was so well and thoroughly established that it could even be parodied; in that year a number of English actors, led by A.E.Matthews and featuring such later stalwarts of the

Hollywood British as Edmund Gwenn and Gladys Cooper, made for First War charities a J.M.Barrie spoof of *Macbeth* called *The Real Thing At Last*, purporting to show how Hollywood would treat *Macbeth*. The cast list included four murderers, two murdered, one willing to murder, one afterwards murdered, one nearly murdered, one not worth murdering but murdered and three murder specialists, and one of its best moments allowed A.E.Matthews (as an unbilled messenger) to gallop up to Gwenn (as Macbeth) with a note reading, 'If Birnam Wood moves, it's a cinch!'

A letter from Lady Macbeth to her murderous husband read, 'Dear Macbeth, the King has gotten old and silly, slay him. Yours sincerely, Lady M,' and an early subtitle read, 'The elegant home of the Macbeths is no longer a happy one,' while the final one added, 'The Macbeths repent and all ends happily.'

The whole affair was subtitled 'The *Macbeth* Murder Mystery', thereby predating Thurber by about thirty years, but whether or not its makers were aware that Sir Herbert Beerbohm Tree was already en route for Hollywood and a real film *Macbeth* has never been satisfactorily established; my grandmother Gladys maintained that they all meant it as a generalized spoof with no particular reference to Tree, then regarded as the head of the profession and unmockable. Knowing A.E.Matthews's lifelong devotion to irreverent schoolboy humour of a somewhat more specific kind, I am inclined, all the same, to believe that he at least well knew at whom *The Real Thing* was aimed.

Tree, meanwhile, was already in New York, setting up a Shakespeare season at the New Amsterdam Theater, when the summons came from D.W.Griffith. At first it was somewhat vague: Tree was merely asked to sign a contract for $10,000, in return for which he would travel to California and make a Shakespeare film, at first thought to be either *The Tempest* or *The Merchant of Venice*, the latter to be shot 'on the canals of Santa Monica' near that other, Californian Venice. Then, however, John Emerson, who was to script and direct for Griffith, decided that Californian locations could also well double for Scotland:

> You can't successfully produce Shakespeare on the small scale; there is too much meat in his plots, so it has been decided to make *Macbeth* in nine reels and thereby avoid omitting any essentials ... we can also add scenes merely described in the play, for instance the fight between Macbeth and Cawdor, and the Coronation, which will be one of the biggest scenes in the picture. In the film are also shown some wild dances of the highlanders, and at great rental expense we have secured some special large greyhounds ...

for the 'catalogue' speech to the murderers, presumably; already the spirit of Cecil B. de Mille was abroad in filmland.

Tree now had to think about the casting. Griffith already had a reliable company of experienced screen players for the minor roles, and by the greatest good fortune one of Sir Herbert's most constant and distinguished leading ladies in both public and private life was already living and working in California. Constance Collier had crossed the Atlantic in 1915, at the height of the submarine scare and only a few weeks after the sinking of the *Lusitania*; she had gone to New York to be with her husband, Julian l'Estrange, failed to realize that by working in California she would in fact be almost as far removed from him as if she had stayed at home in England, but travelled on nevertheless, secure in a promise from Griffith that she could play in his forthcoming *Intolerance*. As she recalled a decade later:

On into the sun of California. You pull up at Los Angeles after those five days' journey on the train, dazed and giddy when the motion ceases. You get out opposite an ostrich farm. ... Hollywood was still a village, with farms that had not yet been built over, and the surly farmers were furious at the advent of the picture folk. ... In those days there was one main street and a little hotel. The 'stars' either lived there or in a few bungalows that had been built up quickly. The studios were about five miles outside Los Angeles, and when you had finished your day's work you were generally too tired to go there, so you would go home, have a bath, change your clothes and meet the same people over again, their faces now white instead of yellow with make-up ... but I felt like a prisoner of war in Hollywood. Not that I did not adore the people and the place, but the fact that there was nothing else to do and nowhere else to go, and the sun never left off shining, and the Pacific Ocean never had a wave on it, was stultifying; I longed for a good London drizzle and a bit of fog; but each day was as radiant as the day before, and the sky as blue.

Not surprisingly, Miss Collier rapidly found an ally in her fellow-exile from the London fogs, Charles Chaplin:

He used to come to dinner with me very often and we would talk about London and the Lambeth Road and Kennington and all the places we had known in our youth. He was a strange, morbid, romantic creature, seemingly totally unconscious of the greatness that was in him. How he loved England! And yet the years he spent there had been so bitter and full of poverty and sorrow. America had given him all, and his allegiance belonged to her, but in our talks one felt his longing, sometimes, to see the twisted streets and misty days and hear Big Ben chiming over London. ... Sometimes we would have a meal at a cafeteria and

Charlie would wait on me, fetching me coffee and thick sandwiches or bread and cheese, and we would talk for hours. He was happier this way. It was impossible to go to any big restaurant, as the minute he appeared he was mobbed. Besides, he said he couldn't bear the masses of knives and forks on the table, and the magnificence of the head waiters gave him a feeling of inferiority.

Having introduced Mr Chaplin to another of her new Hollywood friends, Douglas Fairbanks Sr (whose Anglophilia was already so well-developed that he treated both her and Chaplin like the royalty he was eventually to net at Pickfair), and thereby indirectly paved the way for United Artists, the company Chaplin and Fairbanks were to form with Mary Pickford and D.W. Griffith in 1919, Miss Collier turned her attention back to her old Haymarket partner:

I had already made two pictures in California when Sir Herbert Tree cabled me that he had an offer to do the picture of *Macbeth* and asking if I would play Lady Macbeth. He said he was coming out with his daughter Iris, so I wrote glowing accounts of Los Angeles and the wonderful Californian sun and filled them with such enthusiasm that they were impatient of everything until they could start. I chose them a bungalow with a lovely tennis court and pretty garden round it and I begged them to bring bathing dresses and told Iris she must have nothing but the lightest summer dresses. The day they arrived the floods started and never stopped for two months. The rain poured down. The tennis court was a tank. Water came through the roof. They froze with cold.

Nevertheless the *Macbeth* film was made: 'perfect weather for the blasted heath,' noted Tree, who also became firm friends with Chaplin during this damp Californian summer. Sometimes, after the shooting, they would all meet for dinner, and some nights along Sunset Boulevard it was possible to see a bowler-hatted tramp, a man in a long wig, beard and dress, and a woman with a crown and black hair down to her knees all sheltering under raincoats as they awaited a chauffeur. Nothing about Hollywood seemed to surprise Tree, but then years of British and American touring had taught him that it was just another date:

At Los Angeles station the Mayor welcomes me and I am asked to a banquet given by the *Los Angeles Examiner*, to which the leading citizens were invited. Then to the Studio, where as our car stops we are surrounded by a motley crowd, all painted and costumed, among whom are Red Indians, cavaliers, moderns, gorgeous Babylonians and cowboys. Suddenly there is a terrific explosion as a dozen cowboys fire their pistols in the air. Finding myself happily unwounded, I raise my hat to the cheering crowd. My instinct tells me I am in the midst of a democratic society. At that moment a fair-haired little boy of five approached. He is, as I afterwards discovered, one of the most popular film actors. The Infant Phenomenon wore a long garment on which was sewn in large letters the word WELCOME, and coming towards me with extended hand at once put me at my ease by saying, 'Pleased to meet you, Sir Tree.' By way of conversation I ventured, 'And how has the world been using you these last few years?' With a world-weary shrug of the shoulders, it replied, 'Well, I guess this world's good enough for me.' Truly this is a land of many babies but few children.

No Victorian explorer dealing with African natives could have behaved better than Tree in California in 1916; they were shooting at the Fine Art studios, 'situated at Hollywood,' noted Tree, 'a suburb some seven miles out of Los Angeles,' and on an adjacent stage could be seen the beginnings of *Intolerance*. Tree became its very first fan:

I turned my eyes towards a stage of many acres on which was raised the City of Babylon. Yes, there, solidly built . . . you can wander up a great street peopled by thousands of actors and stage employees, all clad in the costumes of the period. Life-size elephants decorate the buildings and huge images of gods and goddesses confront you at every turn. Not only are the actors expert and daring riders – the horses, too, are marvellously trained for this kind of work. Chariots gallop past at full tilt followed by hundreds of soldiers on horseback, the populace escaping miraculously from the menacing hoofs and wheels. The wonder is how few accidents occur.

At the centre of it all, Tree recognized a producer after his own extravagant heart:

It will be remembered that D.W.Griffith was responsible for *The Birth of a Nation*; but this new picture of his beggars all description – it has taken two years to prepare, and its cost must be between £150,000 and £200,000. Mr Griffith is an imaginative artist, his energy is amazing, and he apparently has a supreme indifference to money. To be a spectator of his latest work is like having gold flung in one's face, but I imagine that this will be the high-water mark in the way of film production.

Tree completed this first letter home from California to *The Times* by a sharp counter-attack on what he already saw as an unfortunate and snobbish English tendency to deride Hollywood:

We in England have no conception of the vast influence of the moving picture industry in America, where it has become part of the national life of the people. There is at home the habit of sneering at serious work undertaken by such striving artists as Mr Griffith . . . it is the invariable fate of any new movement to be ignored until it has taken root among the great necessities. Steam, electricity, telegraphy, wireless telegraphy, the motor car and the airship were all scoffed at until they became part of the daily life of the people.

Yet for all that enthusiasm, Tree was still inclined to be cautious in his bets over the long-term future of the cinema:

Huge sums are frequently lost in film enterprises, and it is probable that the present prodigality of outlay will not be of long duration. I believe the art of the moving picture has not yet found its feet. It has hitherto been largely imitative of the theatre. ... I believe that its future use will be largely educational, and that in coming generations both history and geography will be taught through this fascinating medium. On the other hand I do not think that in the great cities the vogue of the cinema will be abiding . . .

although, he finished triumphantly, 'a taste for the regular theatre will have been created among the millions who daily witness these primitive dramas of the screen'.

One of which was now, of course, to be *Macbeth*:

When going on 'location' (there obtains in California a curious love of Latin words) our entire party are driven to the destination in motor-omnibuses. We would sometimes start for the mountains at midnight and proceed to a country inn, be dressed by 7 o'clock to catch the early sun and ride forth on horseback, all caparisoned and bewigged, towards the 'location' of the 'Blasted Heath', there to meet the Witches. The inhabitants of California are so accustomed to fancy dress that the approach of Macbeth, of Banquo, of Macduff and their retinues caused no surprise, for in Los Angeles it may be said that all the world's a stage and all the men and women merely movies.

Hugely though he seems to have enjoyed most aspects of California, and royally as he seems to have been treated there by everyone from Griffith down, Tree (whose theatrical knighthood was the first, though by no means the last, to impress Hollywood) was still uncertain about the new medium:

Acting to the lens requires a peculiar temperament and demands a much more 'natural' method than that of the stage ... to the newcomer it is also somewhat disconcerting to act a scene of carousal immediately after your death-scene ... although I had little difficulty acclimatizing myself to the new conditions, I confess I have not outlived my preference for the spoken drama.

Indeed so devoted was he to the spoken word that Sir Herbert insisted, despite the considerable cost in film footage, on speaking every word of

Macbeth to the silent camera. Constance Collier later took the view that Hollywood had failed to show 'due reverence' to Tree, citing the hours he would be kept waiting on the set before shooting began. Tree, more sensibly and rightly, assumed that this was normal film practice in an admittedly abnormal medium and took no offence.

Recalling his meetings with Chaplin, Tree later wrote of 'a young man of a serious and sensitive disposition, contrary to expectation, who has artistic ambitions of a kind not suggested by his public records, and who in private life is thoughtful as well as versatile and entertaining'. Chaplin, however, was to recall an evening of excruciating uneasiness when Constance Collier, who had promised to go out with them for dinner, failed to show up and the two men were left with only Tree's daughter to make conversation:

Poor Sir Herbert and Iris did their best, but soon she gave up and just sat back scanning the dining-room. If only the food would come, eating might relieve my awful tension. Father and daughter talked a little about the South of France, Rome and Salzburg – had I ever been there? Had I ever seen any of Max Reinhardt's productions? I shook my head apologetically. Tree now surveyed me. 'You know, you should travel.' I told him I had little time for that, then I came to: 'Look, Sir Herbert, my success has been so sudden that I have had little time to catch up with it. But as a boy of fourteen I saw you as Svengali, as Fagin, as Antony, as Falstaff, some of them many times, and ever since you have been my idol. I never thought of you as existing off-stage. You were a legend. And to be dining with you tonight in Los Angeles overwhelms me.' Tree was touched. 'Really!' he kept repeating. 'Really!' From that night on we became good friends.

John Emerson, who later married Anita Loos, was directing *Macbeth* for Griffith's production company and he too was somewhat overawed by Tree's theatrical pedigree: 'His adaptability and dramatic intelligence were of such a high order that a week after the picture started he was playing like a veteran.' By that time the cameraman, tiring of all the film wasted during the speeches, had set up a dummy camera to which Sir Herbert delivered the full text; while he was in mid-rant, a concealed camera would then take the comparatively few shots that were actually required for a silent film treatment.

This image of Tree in the Californian backwoods declaiming Shakespeare to an empty camera has a terrible kind of symbolism; he had not in fact discovered the key to filming Shakespeare and was the first to admit it, albeit by action rather than words. When the film was finally in the can, it was decided to celebrate with a studio screening. As Constance Collier recalled:

It is a very sensitive moment, the first time an artist sees himself on the screen, and it is a great honour to be asked into the dark room and shown the 'take' among the privileged few who have put up the money and backed the picture and the art directors and special critics. We filed into the little private theatre, thrilled and nervous, and the lights were turned down. It was a tense moment. Much was at stake. There was a hushed silence. I was sitting by Sir Herbert when the projecting machine began to click. There were the most important people connected with the picture in the room, and everybody was waiting in the greatest excitement to hear Sir Herbert's verdict. ... When the running was over there was a sigh of admiration and delight in the darkness, and whispered congratulations on the magnificence of the photography, acting etc. All were waiting eagerly for the word of Sir Herbert. Not a sound came. There was a pause. The lights were turned up. He was asleep.

Tree's somnolent verdict on his own *Macbeth* was echoed by audiences, who stayed away in droves. Critics were respectful, however: the *New York Times* called it 'a fine achievement' and *Moving Picture World* added that 'judiciously used close-ups of his wonderfully mobile features enable Sir Herbert to reveal the ever-increasing torture that eats into the soul of the usurper. The Lady Macbeth of Miss Collier is no less impressive.'

But if the film of *Macbeth* did badly at American box-offices, in London it did even worse. The plan was to give it a ten-week exclusive run at Tree's own His Majesty's, temporarily converted into a cinema expressly for the purpose; but audiences who had flocked there to see Tree 'live' in *Macbeth* showed little interest in a repeat performance on screen, and after only one week the film was somewhat shamefacedly withdrawn. Meanwhile the Griffith studio in California had to consider what to do with the rest of Tree's contract. Their original idea of an entire 'Tree in Shakespeare' film sequence ('not unlike Lamb's Tales', noted Sir Herbert) was rapidly abandoned but there was still the matter of the ten-month contract. Having been the first of Hollywood's guest stars, Tree was now to become the first of its contract casualties. He was asked to agree to a cancellation for reasons of 'mutual desirability'. Shocked and hurt, the great actor-manager declined; lawyers suggested he be offered a series of demeaning roles so that he would have to refuse and thereby destroy the contract. Instead, still perhaps curious to know more about the workings of Hollywood, Tree agreed, to general amazement, to play the very small role of 'a Senator' in a film by Rupert Hughes called *Old Folks at Home*. 'Ghastly,' wrote Tree to a friend back in England. 'I have to wear a toupée and elastic-sided boots.' Nevertheless he managed 'fairly well', said the *Motion Picture World*, but as soon as shooting ended Sir Herbert took the hint, tore up his contract and headed for the Los Angeles railway station. There to see him safely off and back into his own theatrical world was the lady who had also been there to greet him a few months earlier, Constance Collier:

I shall never forget Sir Herbert's exit from Hollywood. The cowboys adored him and they insisted on accompanying him to the station on their bucking horses, dressed in full regalia with pistols. Sir Herbert was essentially a man of peace, and he hated guns. He was an indoor man. As the train was starting, the cowboys encircled Sir Herbert and made their horses rear with their hoofs over his head; then with one accord they fired their pistols into the air as farewell. He was very honoured, but the alacrity with which he climbed into the train was remarkable. His face at the window had a look of supreme relief as the train began to draw out of the station and he waved us farewell.

Back in New York, Tree revived his *Henry VIII* and *The Merchant of Venice*, took them on a long American tour, returned to England and died there after a fall at a seaside cottage which he had borrowed from Constance Collier. It was just a year since he'd said goodbye to her at the station in Los Angeles; he was sixty-three, and he'd never made another film. As for his Lady Macbeth, Miss Collier went straight on to *Intolerance*.

But Tree did leave one final statement on the cinema behind him, in the form of a *New York Times* piece called *The Worthy Cinema*, published a few months before his death:

There seems to have been some astonishment in this country that I was sufficiently interested in the photo-drama to consider an appearance therein. I, in turn, am astonished at the astonishment. Can it be that you in America, where the photoplay has developed so amazingly and become so large a part of your recreational life, are behind us in recognizing its high artistic importance? The actor hitherto has lived but for his generation. The cinema has given him the enfranchisement of posterity. This is at once a spur and a warning to ambition. We can no longer live on our reputations, but on the other hand we can speak to millions where before we could reach only thousands.

Intriguingly, Tree seems in 1916 to have seen the coming of sound as only a matter of months away; in New York he had, he said, 'paid frequent visits to the studio of two enthusiastic young inventors' (unnamed, alas) 'who seem to have succeeded where others have failed in achieving the perfect synchronization of sight and sound in connection with the motion picture'. He was still nervous that this might mean the end of the theatre, but concluded in stirring terms:

Let every man reach the people of his generation if he can, and use whatever medium comes best to his hand. The authors of today are all beginning to use this new and fascinating medium of the screen for the output of their imaginations. It is bringing new thinkers into the arena and it has already created fresh exponents of artistic expression. Few who have seen *The Birth of a Nation* would deny the birth of a new art – and of a new artist ... even Shakespeare laments [in the prologue of *Henry V*] that he cannot give to the spectators in the wooden 'O' of the theatre the pride and pomp of history that filled his imagination. If he lived today he was just the sort of man who would try that very thing – with a cinematograph.

Sir Herbert Beerbohm Tree was not only the first knight of Hollywood, he was also that new town's most distinguished and thoughtful advance publicist.

5:
English Spoken Here

With the First World War raging in Europe, and America soon to enter it, the only British in California tended to be either those, like Sir Herbert, of a certain age, non-draftable women like Miss Collier, or faintly renegade types who did not proclaim their Englishness for evident reasons. Businessmen from Wardour Street still crossed the Atlantic as far as New York in search of American films for the home market, but few travelled on to California, and of the British already settled there few seem to have felt the urge to return. Certainly both Chaplin and Stan Laurel already considered themselves more American than English, nor were either of them exactly military types; the brothers William and David Horsley, who had gone out to America in 1911 to form the Nestor Film Co., were by 1915 supervising the construction of Universal City, but despite the formidable presence of Constance Collier the local papers were billing and interviewing Peggy Hyland as 'the first English actress ever brought to this country to act in moving picture plays', the distinction being, presumably, that Miss Collier had, as usual, brought herself.

Miss Hyland let it be known to *Photoplay* in July 1916 that she had run away from home armed with only £10 and a letter to Cyril Maude, had worked with him on stage in London and Birmingham, had made some early silents in London, including *Caste* (for which, said her publicity, Miss Hyland 'was supported by Sir John Hare'), and had now arrived in California for the filming of *Saints and Sinners*. Not a lot more is heard of her thereafter, at least not in America; by 1920 she was back in London, having set a useful precedent by overstating her British theatrical origins – Hare had not been seen in 'supporting' roles for about twenty years, but who in California was likely to know or care about that?

Curiously, it was often the British who showed more initial enthusiasm for Hollywood than native Americans. At the same time that Tree was writing home of the wonders of the new medium, Francis X. Bushman, who'd been sent out from New York by Metro to make one picture a month in 1914, was telling his friends back East of 'appalling fogs and a terrible climate. This is a semi-tropical country and Hollywoodsmen aren't used to working that much. The minute we turned our backs they were out in the sun or playing billiards. It'll never work.'

Chaplin, however, thought differently, not least because by 1916 he had signed with Mutual a contract worth $670,000 a year to be paid in weekly instalments of $10,000, plus a signing bonus of $150,000. Some indication of the hold that his bowler-hatted tramp figure now had on the United States can be gathered from press reports of a charity concert in New York on 20 February 1916, at which Chaplin agreed to conduct John Philip Sousa's band to raise money for old British and American actors. The audience, reported John McCabe, sat watching him in bored silence: 'Seemingly they found it difficult to connect the wiry little rogue on the screen with this well-mannered, handsome young man. Chaplin received polite applause, he bowed politely, took a polite curtain call, said a few polite words. It was all rather down. Then, realizing what the trouble was, Chaplin broke into the tramp's walk and sauntered about the stage twirling an invisible cane. The audience exploded. Now they saw *him*.'

Already, for Chaplin, the Hollywood image had overtaken the English reality, and within a week or two he was back at the aptly-named Lone Star Studio working with his own production unit.

Though, several months later, Chaplin was to be found in Washington with Mary Pickford and Douglas Fairbanks selling war bonds, he seems never to have identified himself with the war in Europe, except, of course, in the 1918 *Shoulder Arms*, which could be regarded as his very own war effort: made to entertain men who had, unlike him, had to go through the trenches (D. W. Griffith was among the many who told him it would be 'tasteless' to release the film before the Armistice, advice happily ignored by Chaplin), this was the little tramp in France and stood in satirical relation to the First World War much as *The Great Dictator* stood to the Second World War. Charlie dreams he can kick the Kaiser up the rear, succeeds in capturing thirteen German prisoners (as to how the capture was achieved, the subtitle reads simply, 'I surrounded them') and ultimately has to disguise himself as a tree trunk.

But there were other English actors working in California well before the end of the First World War, not least Cyril Maude, who at the age of fifty-three was doing a long American stage tour of a comedy called *Grumpy* when, early in 1915, he found himself in Los Angeles and was asked to stop over for an extra fortnight to make a film of *Peer Gynt*.

Maude, like Tree, had been brought up in the hard school of Victorian English provincial touring, and filming therefore presented no real problems to him either, though his diary does reveal a certain tetchiness with the ways of movie men:

Friday: Dressed in heavy leather trapper's clothes, I was told to get into an Indian canoe, paddle across the stream, and a man would shoot at me and splinter the paddle in my hand with a rifle-shot. (And this was *Peer Gynt*, yet.) I objected very strongly in Anglo-Saxon to doing this, but on the producer explaining to me that the man was a great expert, I consented to it. Jolly, wasn't it? The 'wild and woolly' with a vengeance! However, it came off all right, the paddle was duly splintered while I was paddling, and the shot spattered the water round me. Then I had to be photographed paddling across the water with my hands, while a great fat Indian swam out to the canoe with a knife in his teeth. We had a bloodthirsty battle in the water and then had to sink down right out of sight; after which he had to come up again dead, while I swam rapidly ashore. But the first Indian was short of breath and also, I fear, funky of my knife, having once before done this sort of scene and been stabbed quite badly by his over-excited enemy.

Saturday: I have just had to do a horrid scene with a pig, on which I was sitting astride with my witch-bride (Ibsen's stage directions having been liberally interpreted by Hollywood), who, poor dear, was in great fear of the pig, which was an enormously fat one and made the most hideous row imaginable, grunting and groaning and squeaking and kicking up no end of a fuss. I, too, was nervous about the pig biting or scratching me with its back legs. However, here I am back in my dressing-room, quite surprisingly safe and well.

Sunday: Taken off in a car to a picturesque place in the mountains where I did two or three scenes with an Indian maid and her tribe. Had a terrific struggle with the Indian chief and killed him; what a practised murderer I have become since visiting America! Then had to change and do a scene in the sea among the rocks near San Pedro. Very rough and very rocky. A sham log was put into the water and I had to cling to it. A fat cook had to come and cling to it too, for the shipwreck scene in Act 5. Whereupon I, in the brutal fashion prescribed by Mr Ibsen, beat off his hands, held him up by the hair and told him to say the Lord's Prayer. I eventually dropped him, after which the Devil came up from out of the water and I had a short scene with him too. He had the most horrible make-up.

Monday: Made up and did an extraordinary scene in a goblin's cave, surrounded by innumerable extras dressed as witches and horrors of every kind. They offered me snakes and toads to eat and blood to drink, but I had already had my lunch. Then I had to dress as the young Peer Gynt and do a scene in the water, swimming about while the figure of a deer was dragged across to look as if it were swimming. Very clever, but glad to get back to studio away from perils of land, water, snakes etc. Twelve hours' shooting done today. Not bad for an old'un.

An increasing number of actors were, like Maude, discovering that for a couple of weeks' shooting in California they could pick up often rather more than they were making for an entire six-month tour of American theatres; in addition, they could do it without complaint from the natives, which was more than could now be said of their American theatre work.

As early as January 1912 there had appeared in *The Green Book Album*, a Chicago theatrical publication, a long and anonymous article 'by an American actor' headlined 'The English Invasion' and complaining in no uncertain terms about the number of English actors who, brought out to New York for one single Broadway production, were often staying on to do others, thereby causing 'widespread unemployment' among equally capable American actors. That was, of course, the beginning of an inter-union dispute which was to rage across the Atlantic for the next three-quarters of a century. It was noted, for instance, with some fury that not only had Constance Collier arrived on Broadway in a role 'for which many American leading ladies would have been admirably suited' (in *Samson*) but that she also insisted on being accompanied on stage and off by her husband, Julian l'Estrange, 'thereby causing further American unemployment along Broadway'.

In Hollywood there were no such problems; indeed California had long been a haven for the impecunious English as well as the 'remittance men', black sheep of noble families whose allowances continued to be sent to them so long as they promised to stay far away from the stately homes of their fathers. California was reckoned to be far enough, and the tradition had been early established: one of the Marquess of Queensberry's 'mad bad line' had run to seed spectacularly there long before the Wilde trials of 1895, and during the opening up of the American West one American reported:

At the turn of the century I was cooking for four remittance men near Kindersley. .... I tell you they were quite a crew. They had been Oxford and Cambridge men and, let me tell you, we lived high. Peaches and cream for breakfast. We never wanted for nothing, and when one fellow's cheque ran out then the next fellow's would come in. One of them, Chris Murr, decided he'd like to go back to the old country for Christmas but before the end of January he was back in the shack. 'What happened?' we asked. 'Well,' he says, 'I'll tell you. We're sitting at breakfast one morning and I turned my head to say something to my sister just at the time the maid put a cup of coffee between us and my head hit the coffee and spilled all over her. So I yelled out, "Jesus Christ," and my mother fainted and my father jumped out of his chair and ordered me out of the house and when I came back to get my things they told me never to return and I got an increase in my remittance.' Those folks never had to earn a living; they didn't farm, they didn't do a thing but drink and ride their horses and eat my good food, but they were fine fellows.

Actors in California had to work rather harder for their money, but the mood of a magical land in the sun far away from the British family and other commitments, a land where you could be somebody altogether other than yourself, a land of escape and rebirth where the community only appeared to have been there a few weeks before your own arrival, this all lasted well into the early 1920s.

Yet it is important to remember that at this stage the British were not being welcomed to California, as they were to Broadway, because of any particular thespian talent; silent films had no need of a cultured accent, and native Americans were already rather better and more experienced at falling off horses than their more cautious and often elderly British visitors. Those who did make it out to Los Angeles from London, with such occasionally distinguished exceptions as Tree, were there to try their luck as they had so often tried it on tour in the past. The difference was essentially a chance to work in the open sunshine instead of a dusty theatre, and the freedom from their usual box-office worries, since films even then took a matter of weeks to release, by which time most of the actors had long since moved on to other jobs in other cities and were long past caring about audiences or reviews for their anyway often uncredited appearances. They had taken the money and, in the best traditions of strolling players, run.

Not everyone took easily to the view that the British could find work in American films, however: the pioneer film-maker Harry Furniss, writing in 1914 the first serious critical study of the new medium (*Our Lady Cinema*), had grave doubts:

From the standpoint of an artist with a fairly extensive experience of moving pictures, I have no hesitation in committing myself to the emphatic statement that to transplant cinematograph stories, or to satisfactorily produce them with the assistance of an alien company of actors in a country foreign to their nature, is quite beyond the bounds of possibility. ... A large number of American films press English tales into service and they simply bristle with incongruities; I have just witnessed an elaborate film of *David Copperfield* in which old Mr Micawber was portrayed by a young man with a profusion of ambrosial locks. To add to the gallery of absurdities, Uriah Heep was represented as a solid man of business and

David himself as a thick-set individual with sidewhiskers, while the immortal Sam Weller was a vacant-eyed idiot. ... Simply by using the tunic of an English policeman or the helmet of an English fireman you do not arrive, in California, at the making of an English film. These things can only be done at home.

Mr Furniss goes on to relate that he can always spot an American on the screen 'by the unfortunate cut of his hair, which even grows in an altogether un-British manner', though he does not relate whether this also applies to female American stars. His objections do, however, indicate something of the chauvinism that was then rife in the British cinema. American films were already doing well at British box-offices, and therefore had become a threat to the home product, such as it then was. Those British who actually worked for American studios in New York or California were in one sense, therefore, working for the enemy.

There was already a characteristic difference between the British who were filming in California and those who were filming in New York. As a generalization, those who were in California treated the new industry with a mixture of scepticism and delight; filming, for them, was a brief holiday in the sun with pay before a return to the touring theatre, while the New York people took it rather more seriously as an adjunct to, not an escape from, Broadway. They also tended to be a more inventive lot. Barbara Tennant, for instance, was a young English dancer and actress who'd started out as a child in pantomimes at the London Coliseum soon after the turn of the century. Later, finding work hard to come by in London, she'd gone to Canada to work with a touring Shakespeare troupe and from there made her way down to New York in 1912, where she began to get work in silent films. Regretting, however, the absence of any opportunity to use her Shakespeare training, she suggested to her producers that she should accompany some of her own films from cinema to cinema around New York, giving brief recitations on stage between screenings. This she did so successfully that she was in turn taken up by the Charles Frohman company and given leading work in Broadway dramas of the period, one of the first examples of a stage career emerging from, rather than leading to, one in films.

Another early English recruit to American films was Herbert Prior, who, after a brief and unsuccessful London stage career, joined the Edison Players in New York. 'I consider the time which I have already spent with them,' Prior told the *Moving Picture World* in January 1914, 'to have been the most desirable and instructive period of my life. I spent two winters filming in Cuba, covered the Canadian Pacific Railroad route through the Rocky Mountains, visited Colorado and Maine and now we are filming for the winter in Florida. I saw more and learned more of the beauty of nature in those trips than I have in all the other years of my life.' A list of Prior's screen credits between 1910 and 1914 gives some indication of the range of work then available to an Edison Player of reasonable looks and acting ability: titles included *The Doctor*, *The Battle of Trafalgar*, *His First Valentine*, *Why Girls Leave Home*, *Janet of the Dunes*, *Saved By The Enemy*, *The Pied Piper of Hamelin* and *A Night at the Inn*; additionally, as an author, Prior had already written for Edison the screenplays of *Bill's Career as Butler*, *A Pious Undertaking*, *The Desperate Condition of Mr Boggs* and *Othello in Jonesville*.

Perhaps the first indication that stage-trained British actors were going to have a specific usefulness to American film-makers came in 1913 when a player in Beerbohm Tree's London company, R. Henderson Bland (later billed as Robert Henderson), was approached by an American producer from the Kalem company:

He asked me if I could be ready in a matter of days to go to Palestine to play the Saviour in *From the Manger to the Cross*. I assented, took my leave of Tree, and travelled rapidly to the Holy Land. I felt, of course, that as an Englishman coming into an American company to play the leading role I was in a delicate position. As soon as I arrived in Jerusalem I was dressed by the director, Mr Olcott, in the costume of Jesus Christ and then he sent for all the other members of the company. They filed into the room, and looked at me very closely without saying a word. Then they went to Mr Olcott and told him that he had made a very wise choice and that they would stand by me even though I was not American. In passing through crowds in Jerusalem I was always protected from the natives, who would try to get near and touch the garments I wore, and every effort was made during the shooting to prevent my being disturbed in any way, so that I could keep in the spirit of the wonderful character I was to portray. I have seen so many pictures spoiled by overacting that I had to be extremely careful.

Mr Henderson was the first, but not alas the last, actor to find that after playing the Almighty the rest of his career proved somewhat anticlimactic. Nevertheless he usefully established the British actor in American films as a reliable type for the playing of roles requiring a certain aloof dignity which was not then the stock-in-trade of many Americans, least of all those mainly required in California to fall off horses with arrows taped to their shirts or execute elaborate pratfalls for Mack Sennett.

One actor, who was to enjoy a vastly longer transatlantic career in American films than Henderson, had by 1915 also made his first silent picture. Aged fifty and already the veteran of countless American stage tours as well as a first-class cricket season in South Africa, C. Aubrey Smith had been persuaded to join the Frohman Amusement Corporation 'with studios in two abandoned churches, one on Tenth Avenue in New York and the other in Flushing, Long Island. I must say they served our purposes very well; in those days actors were not held in high regard and the fact that we were working in churches somehow boosted our morale.' Smith made a total of four silents (*Builder of Bridges*, *John Glayde's Honour*, *Jafferay* and *The Witching Hour*) through the summer of 1915, before making a brief inspection tour of Hollywood, announcing that 'the photoplay can never touch the art of the spoken drama', and returning to the latter in England. He was not to film again in America until 1930.

6:
To Sin with Elinor Glyn

Even though Aubrey Smith, the archetypal Hollywood English gentleman actor of the 1930s and 1940s, had made such a brief and unproductive initial visit to California, with the ending of the First World War a number of others began to think of it in more permanent terms. Officers and gentlemen who also happened to be actors had returned from the front to find the London theatre drastically different from the one they had left behind in 1914: a generation of younger actors had taken it over, as had a sequence of plays far removed in tone and style from the heroically dashing melodramas of the pre-war years. Drawing-room dramatists from Ibsen and Shaw to the young Coward and Somerset Maugham demanded a more subtle and complex kind of actor than many of the old guard had been trained to be, with the result that a few of the latter began to filter out to California, where, according to the evidence of cinema screens all over Britain, the old clear-cut out-front dramatic virtues of good versus evil were still being enacted.

Accordingly, by the end of 1919, actors like Percy Marmont and Nigel Barrie (billed on 1920 movie posters for *The Better Wife* as 'Lieutenant Nigel Barrie RFC') were setting up homes in California, as were the brothers Wyndham and Guy Standing, the latter much helped in his Hollywood career by an hereditary baronetcy, which added distinct tone even in a world where mothers were already christening their sons Duke and King.

British actors in Hollywood were by now nothing new; some indeed had been there almost a decade. What was new was the idea of British writers in Hollywood, and that came in the early summer of 1920 to Jesse L. Lasky, first Vice-President of the Famous Players-Lasky Corporation. He it was who had in 1913 with Cecil B. de Mille made *The Squaw Man*, thereby effectively marking Hollywood as the American film capital; now, seven years later, Lasky's company had merged with

Adolph Zukor's, which had already launched an ambitious series of filmed dramas known as 'famous players in famous plays'.

It did not take anybody long, even in California, to notice that a great many of these 'famous plays' (if not yet many of the 'famous players') emanated from England; Shakespeare and Dickens were already among the most frequently filmed authors, and just as Broadway had for the past fifty years drawn much of its strength from the London theatre, so for the next thirty would Hollywood. It was Lasky who first set off, in June 1920, by train and the transatlantic liner SS *Celtic*, in search of British authors. His plan was to import them to California, though not necessarily for very long: his company was about to build a London studio, and his notion was that those authors who did not care for the New World could return to work in England, having been suitably versed in the techniques of writing for the new screen.

The *New York Times* of 18 July 1920, under the headline 'English To Study Here', reported him as follows:

Practically all the best-known playwrights and authors of England are about to turn their talents into the field of the movies and many are coming to America within the next six months to learn screen drama writing, says Mr Lasky, who has been to Europe chiefly to make arrangements with British authors to write scenarios. ... Judging from his own account of his success, almost no English author of note has escaped! For instance, G. Bernard Shaw, he said, was co-operating with the new form of picture narrative, while arrangements have been made with Sir James M. Barrie for him to come to America in the fall to direct the screen version of *Peter Pan*.

The *New York Times* was, of course, right to sound that faint note of disbelief. Shaw, in fact, never succumbed to the temptations of Hollywood ('all they talk about is art, whereas all I want to hear about is money' was the essence of his reply to Goldwyn's frequent begging cables), though he did eventually give in on home territory to Gabriel Pascal. Barrie, however, proved more susceptible, and did indeed prepare a draft screenplay of *Peter Pan* with a view to casting Charlie Chaplin in the title role; Barrie had already begun to doubt the wisdom of always having a girl for Peter, and had once tried to persuade his greatest Captain Hook, Gerald du Maurier, to take on the role. Now he went all out for Chaplin, writing him a long and extremely literary screenplay full of wondrous descriptions of what the Never-Never Land should look like; though the film was never made, these descriptions were reused some sixty years later to form part of the narrator's speech in the Royal

Shakespeare Company's revived and redrafted *Peter Pan* on stage at the Barbican in 1982–3.

But Barrie had *Mary Rose* in production that summer of 1920 and declined, as did Shaw, to make the trek to California. Lasky remained undaunted; he had, as the *New York Times* report continued, 'made arrangements with many others, including H.G.Wells, who is to adapt some of his stories for the movies. Arnold Bennett may come to America this winter to write for the screen; Edward Knoblock is due in September to write scenarios. Robert Hitchens, E. Phillips Oppenheim, Compton Mackenzie, R.C.Carton and Max Pemberton are all to write a set of moving picture stories. Also Henry Arthur Jones is to come here to study screen technique and write directly for the movies.'

As so often in the subsequent history of Hollywood, the advance publicity was rather better than the immediate outcome; remarkably few of that authorial cast list made it to California in 1920 and some never made it at all. But most did sell screen rights in their better-known plays or novels, and Lasky's buying trip resulted in the capture of at least one undoubted literary lioness, Elinor Glyn. A widow then fifty-five, the best-selling author of a sensationally risqué novel called *Three Weeks*, Mrs Glyn had more recently been known as a war correspondent for the American tabloid press, but when she received the summons from Lasky it was, she assumed, to convert *Three Weeks* into a screenplay. Boarding the *Mauretania* at Southampton that autumn, she noted in her diary: 'It was a considerable adventure for me, a lone widow no longer young, to venture forth into this strange, utterly different world of Western America, and to attempt to master the intricacies of a new and highly technical craft, but it was just such an adventure as I have always loved and I set off quite undaunted by the troubles and difficulties which I was told would beset me on arrival.'

She was encouraged, perhaps, by a Lasky contract which promised her $10,000 dollars for the picture plus all travelling and living expenses plus the guarantee of a renewal if the film worked out well. Her first surprise, on reaching the Hollywood Hotel ('a homely place with clean bright rooms, obliging waitresses and quite good food kept by a funny sporting old lady of over eighty who ran it extremely well'), was to discover that Lasky did not want a screenplay of *Three Weeks* at all. What he wanted was something altogether new, and preferably tailored to the talents of Gloria Swanson.

Mrs Glyn was not much impressed by her first glimpse of Hollywood, and even less by the discovery that she was merely being used by Lasky as literary window-dressing:

No one wanted my advice or assistance, nor did they intend to take it. All they required was the use of my name to act as a shield against the critics. Every person connected with the production studios, although few had travelled as far as New York, and many were all but illiterate, was absolutely convinced that he or she knew much better how to depict the manners and customs of whatever society or country they were attempting to show on the screen than any denizen of that country or society, and they were not prepared to amend any detail to meet criticisms.

When I arrived, spittoons were still being placed in rows down the centre of a set which was supposed to be the Baronial hall of an old English Castle, while an actress taking the part of an early eighteenth-century French marquise was encouraged to wear her hair in the exaggerated 'golliwog' style then prevalent in Hollywood.

But Glyn was a survivor, and her Hollywood writing career was to last right through to 1929, largely because, as Sam Goldwyn once noted, 'her name is synonymous with the discovery of sex appeal in the cinema'. The chances are, though, that the discovery would also have been made without her. The first Glyn script, *The Great Moment*, concerned Nadine, 'daughter of a reserved English diplomat and the Russian gypsy he married in a moment of ecstatic passion'. Nadine is therefore kept prisoner in the diplomat's English country house lest she should turn out as wild as her now deceased mother; an American gold miner rescues her and together they traverse the Nevada desert, where the unfortunate Nadine is bitten by a rattlesnake. Thinking to save her life, the gold miner pours a bottle of whisky down her throat, which revives her gypsy blood to such an extent that she makes love to him. Appalled, the miner sends her into the arms of an orgy-giving millionaire named Hopper and only at the last fade-out does he take her back to his ancestral Virginia home.

For this, her first original screenplay (*Three Weeks* had meanwhile been temporarily lost in a welter of inter-studio disputes about who owned the screen rights), Mrs Glyn thought justifiably that she had come up with a winner; the script of *The Great Moment* had everything from unmarried love to rattlesnakes, and she was thus appalled when the director Sam Wood announced that it lacked suspense and would have to be treated as knockabout farce. Swanson agreed, and Glyn's temper was not made any better by the news that Rudolph Valentino, whom she had also been promised, was held up on another film and would therefore be replaced by the somewhat less sexy (or starry) Milton Sills.

Several weeks of shooting went by while Mrs Glyn sulked in the Hollywood Hotel; then one morning she ventured down to the studio to find Wood in anguished conference with Swanson and Sills. Having shot most of the story in a frantic semi-farcical convention, they now couldn't find an ending that would work. 'Perhaps', she murmured icily, 'I might be allowed to suggest one. I am, after all, still supposed to be the author.' By chance she was overheard by Cecil B. de Mille, then one of Lasky's most powerful producers, and in the view of her son Anthony 'that one remark did her film career more good than anything else. It amused de Mille, and with his support and influence behind her she was in a far stronger position to battle on for the ideals and objectives which had brought her to California.'

Glyn's position was also much strengthened when *The Great Moment* was released and, despite its confusion of styles and plot, proved a considerable box-office winner. Swanson was signed for a second Glyn screenplay, *Beyond the Rocks*, and this time Valentino was available though Glyn was appalled to find that male American screen stars all appeared to be 'woolly lambs' with no notion of how to play romantic or passionate love scenes. 'Do you know,' she told a friend years later in amazement, 'Valentino had never even thought of kissing the palm, rather than the back, of a woman's hand until I made him do it?'

In retrospect, the Glyn phenomenon was admirably explained by Richard Griffith and Arthur Mayer:

Until the advent in Hollywood of Elinor Glyn, writers had played only a small part in picture production but she, like other British authors before and since, was smart enough to see that the citizens of the United States of America were still secretly awed by titles (she liked to be called 'Madame' Glyn) and loved to picture the lives led by European nobility as a combination of luxury and depravity. For an industry invariably described as still in its infancy, she was just what the doctor ordered. No sooner had she arrived in Hollywood than she proceeded to take charge of both its professional and its social activities. She instituted the strange custom of afternoon tea as a badge of gentility, intimidated movie hostesses by her criticisms of their manners, and gave innumerable interviews to the fan magazines on the ever-popular topic 'What's Wrong with Hollywood?' Magnanimously, she offered lessons in deportment to the local belles, and actually coached Gloria Swanson in the proper thing to do, something that took Miss Swanson several years to live down. ... The authoress also insisted on supervising every detail of the films made from her books, each of which was offered as 'An Elinor Glyn Production'. Her dictatorship grew so irksome that the studios were forced in self-defence into a tacit conspiracy. If Metro and Paramount both contemplated productions of her works, they were likely to begin filming them simultaneously, forcing Madame to distribute her time between them. Her vogue lasted through the Twenties, but by the time the full force of the Depression struck, Madame Glyn found herself expounding to an unheeding audience. ... In the atmosphere of the Thirties, Ruritania seemed long ago and far away, and no one appeared to care with Madame Glyn whether Lady Alyce had or had not dishonoured the family name by marrying a common gamekeeper. It was not only that *Lady Chatterley's Lover* had put a new evaluation on gamekeepers, with or without marriage. It was also that, now, Lady Alyce, the gamekeeper and those who had once thought no price too high for true love were exclusively concerned with the price of bread.

But to sin with Elinor Glyn on a studio tiger-skin was for a while regarded as the height of Hollywood success, and she herself became such a celebrity that she would make personal appearances as herself in other people's films (notably King Vidor's *Show People*) as well as giving demonstrations of how her more passionate love scenes ought to be played and photographed. She banished aspidistras from stately drawing-rooms, insisted on reasonable period accuracy for the English homes in which many of her scripts were set, and claimed credit for the discovery of John Gilbert, Clara Bow and Gary Cooper. But, most importantly, she learned how to make herself a star: cinema managers were soon being advised by studios to 'boom the author' whenever one of her films was due for release.

Yet Glyn was an intriguingly complex and cynical lady: her greatest contribution to Hollywood may well have been giving Clara Bow the scripts that made her the 'It' girl, but she remained a remarkably puritanical observer of the celluloid city. Noting that the celebrated Pickford-Fairbanks divorce was yet one more example of 'the California curse', she added: 'Early symptoms of this disease, which break out almost on arrival in Hollywood, are a sense of exaggerated self-importance and self-centredness which naturally alienates all old friends. Next comes a great desire for and belief in the importance of money above all else, a loss of the normal sense of humour and proportion, and finally in extreme cases the abandonment of all previous standards of moral value.'

To keep herself immune from the California curse, Glyn insisted on spending at least one month a year back in England and on retaining by her bedside at the Hollywood Hotel a complete set of Plato in what her son called 'a dogged and rather touching effort to try and retain her sense of values in that crazy looking-glass world'.

Glyn's first and best friend in California was predictably Chaplin, with whom she would spend long English evenings discussing the higher lunacies of their American employers and hosts; it was Glyn who first introduced Chaplin to Marion Davies, and all three were frequent guests of William Randolph Hearst at San Simeon early in the Hearst–Davies affair. There, being British, both Chaplin and Glyn lent a useful air of the country house party to Hearst's social requirements; but there was not always a great deal of love lost between them. Glyn did not much care for Chaplin's then wife, Lita Grey, and Chaplin found Glyn more than a little dotty:

She was ardently imbued with the occult. I remember one afternoon Mary Pickford complained of fatigue and sleeplessness. We were in Mary's bedroom. 'Show me the North,' commanded Elinor. Then she placed her finger gently on Mary's brow and repeated, 'Now she's fast asleep.' Douglas and I crept over and looked at Mary, whose eyelids were fluttering. Mary told us later that she had to endure the pretence of sleeping for more than an hour, because Elinor stayed in the room and watched her. Elinor had the reputation of being sensational, but no one was more staid. Her amorous conceptions for the movies were always girlish and naïve – ladies brushing their eyelashes against the cheeks of their beloveds and languishing on tiger-rugs.

Yet it is some comment on her Hollywood tenacity, or at the very least her determination to get the money out of there, that Glyn lasted more than seven years while the other notable British author taken out on that first trip by Jesse Lasky barely lasted seven days. He was William Somerset Maugham, then forty-six and re-established after the First World War as a best-selling novelist with *Of Human Bondage* and *The Moon and Sixpence* as well as a string of West End dramatic hits which made him even more attractive to a Hollywood then desperate for writers of 'the drama'. Lasky and Sam Goldwyn invited him out to California, also in the autumn of 1920, despite their recent disaster with another world-famous playwright, Maurice Maeterlinck, who had just delivered for several thousand dollars a wildly unsuitable screenplay about a small boy discovering fairies at the bottom of his wood.

Maugham arrived with his young secretary, Gerald Haxton, to be greeted by Chaplin and Doug Fairbanks and Mary Pickford, the latter still only in the throes of building Pickfair but already at the head of any Hollywood receiving line for foreign notables. Chaplin recalled Maugham outlining to all four of them over dinner the Sadie Thompson story that became *Rain*, and few novelists were in later years to do better out of Hollywood screen rights than this one, who, even on his first fleeting visit, managed to sell Lasky the *Rain* synopsis for $15,000.

Maugham, however, could not wait to move on with Haxton to more intriguing travels in the South Seas, noting of Hollywood in a letter home that 'there are directors here who desire to be artistic. It is pathetic to compare the seriousness of their aim with the absurdity of their attainment. ... I believe that in the long run it will be found futile to adapt stories for the screen from novels or from plays, and that any advance in this form of entertainment which may eventually lead to something artistic lies in the story written directly for projection on the white screen.'

Maugham also sensed in Chaplin a profound and melancholy isolation from England; the one time the novelist found the comedian happy was when they happened to be walking through a very rundown section of Los Angeles and Chaplin, seeming suddenly to recall something of his London childhood, began improvising a dialogue between two housewives in the slums of Lambeth. For himself, Maugham was content to spend most of his long life as far away as possible from Hollywood, consenting only by long distance and for large cheques to the filming of any of his stories.

Others were less fastidious: the dramatist Edward Knoblock, whose London stage career had been no less successful than Maugham's in the early years of the century (including as it had *Milestones* and *Kismet*), moved to California under the same Lasky encouragement late in 1920 and almost immediately developed the notorious local pneumonia (caused by hot days and cold nights) which was later to kill two other British writers out there, James Fagan and Edgar Wallace. But Knoblock survived to survey the scene:

Hollywood in 1920, although having a population of many thousands, still possessed the atmosphere of a sub-tropical village. The houses were hardly any of them over two storeys high, palms were growing in the avenues and pepper-trees overhung the side streets. Every now and then an open lot still displayed rows of orange trees – the remains of some large farm before the land had been cut up into blocks. Opposite one of these stood the studio of the Famous Players-Lasky Company. The original shed, barely thirty feet by twenty, in which the Company had started was incorporated in the rest of the rows of wooden buildings, which were painted an amiable white and grey. The large stages within were open at the ends, for the silent film still held the screen. Our words were left to the printed titles, which at times were overwhelming in their blatancy. Directors had not yet learnt the value of restraint, which was finally taught them less by those of us authors they engaged to superintend that part of the film than by the sarcasms poured on their pomposity by the New York press.

All technical equipments were excellent but what was lacking was any knowledge of the real world beyond a fantastic land of theatrical romance. Reality was always sacrificed for pictorial effect, and plausibility was thrown to the winds if a sequence could produce a thrill.

Yet Eddie Knoblock stayed with Lasky for nearly a year, during which time he was deputed to take Maugham to Dreamland, a second-rate Los Angeles dance hall which was one of the few places where good whisky (at $30 a bottle) could be obtained during Prohibition; customers at the next table, rather to Maugham's and Knoblock's amazement, were found in desperation to be drinking distilled Shellac.

During his brief stay, Maugham introduced Knoblock to Douglas Fairbanks Sr, who, always a push-over for a genuine English accent, immediately hired him away from Lasky to write a screenplay of *The Three Musketeers* in which Fairbanks wished to play d'Artagnan. After three months' work on it, Knoblock was (in already traditional Hollywood fashion) replaced by another studio writer. 'It is', he wrote sadly, 'the old story which happens to every author who is engaged to work in Hollywood. He is paid a large sum for going there, his name is used as "publicity", he is praised up to the skies in the papers, and then is gradually and safely suppressed by the powers that reign supreme in the studio. Later on, when I had learnt my lesson, one author after another used to drop into my office with the same tale of woe and I always used to say, "Are you here to produce a work of art or to make money? If it's the former, get out !"'

As early as 1921, then, British writers were already dividing into two distinct camps: those who, like Maugham, took one look at Hollywood and fled with their integrity more or less intact, and those, like Glyn and Knoblock, who stayed, resigned themselves to a certain loss of dignity and independence, yet managed to do some worthwhile work within an already rigid studio system, to which they were undoubtedly of considerable value. It was Knoblock, for instance, who first brought the then unknown Adolphe Menjou and Barbara LaMarr to the attention of Fairbanks, and he who led Fairbanks to the idea of filming one of his greatest screen successes, *Robin Hood*, though admittedly Knoblock had originally been talking about the possibilities of *Ivanhoe* instead.

But even Knoblock, happy though he was to stay with Fairbanks and earn some solid Hollywood cash at a time when his career as a London dramatist was faltering and he had just bought an over-expensive English country house, began after a while to feel that he was being 'kept' by Fairbanks not so much as a screenwriter but rather as a socially acceptable celebrity-companion with a good accent to impress callers at Pickfair. Just as wealthy New Yorkers would employ English butlers or secretaries, so wealthy Californians began to look on the English writers in their midst as advisers or adult nannies, guides to a world of social protocol which their sudden movie wealth had thrown them into unprepared.

Others put this arrangement on a still more commercial level: *Photoplay* for July 1922 reported the arrival in Hollywood of 'John Holmes Howell, a former footman to His Grace the Duke of Connaught who is now' (the footman, not His Grace) 'a great help to directors when filming the right thing in British society drama'. Howell, who also claimed to have danced with both Queen Victoria and Queen Mary during servants' balls at Balmoral, had arrived in California hoping to make his fortune as a film star but was content to make instead a tidy living on the Extras' bench advising on the precise hue of tweed jacket to be worn by a king at a Hunt Ball. Meanwhile Elinor Glyn (billed by now as 'one of the greatest writers of our time and a sister to Lady Duff Gordon', though alas without reference to the rumour that Lady Duff Gordon's husband had dressed in several of his wife's nightdresses in order to answer the 'women and children first to the lifeboats' command during the sinking of the *Titanic*) was writing a column for *Photoplay* largely concerned with the inadequate hair- and dress-sense of many Hollywood stars. Glyn's new dictum was that 'a woman should look straight as a dart, supple as a snake and proud as a tiger lily', and few of the new breed of Hollywood actresses seemed to be living up to it; she also noted with some alarm that far too many were married ('here in America it is easier because of the facility of subsequent divorce'), whereas in Paris, 'the home of truly great art', marriage was observed by her to be far less frequent among the talented.

However daft, irritable, gullible, or just plain avaricious the British in California early in the 1920s might have seemed to the more perspicacious natives, there could be no doubt that they gave an air of quality, refinement and, above all, reliability to an industry and a community still in chaotic birth-pangs. They also sounded in command of a language which, though still not in use on the actual screen, was widely if not exclusively regarded as useful on the studio floor. When Knoblock wrote a film called *Rosita* for Mary Pickford (during his years in residence at Pickfair) it was decided that Ernst Lubitsch should be brought over from Germany to direct. One morning on the set, recalled Knoblock, 'He rushed up to me shouting, "Vere iss dem dajer mid vass he iss geshtickt?" and it took some time before I realized he was asking about the whereabouts of a dagger with which the hero was to be stabbed. Another time, when Lubitsch and I had a difference about the interpretation of a scene, he lost his temper and started rushing off the set, but turned to face me and by way of an annihilating farewell exclaimed, "How do you do".'

Moreover, Englishness was then synonymous with utter respectability; with George V on the throne, and the papers still full of photogenic warriors-turned-actors, scandal was regarded as a largely American affair. Even the practitioner of black magic Aleister Crowley, passing through Hollywood early in the 1920s, wrote smugly of the natives as 'a cinema crowd of cocaine-crazed sexual lunatics', and the Fatty Arbuckle scandal of September 1921, when Virginia Rappe died in mysterious circumstances after an all-night party in San Francisco during which Arbuckle was alleged on doubtful evidence to have raped her, had caused a headlong flight towards the kind of 'respectability' that the English were supposed to symbolize. At least for another four months. Until, in fact, the night of 1 February 1922, when someone killed William Desmond Taylor.

7:
Indecent Exposure

Though his name seems now to have disappeared from all but the most ancient movie reference books, William Desmond Taylor was the first English director of note to work in Hollywood and rose in a brief time to a position of considerable eminence in the industry, partly on natural talent but partly also because he appeared to be the very model of English respectability and authority; indeed at the time of the Arbuckle scandal he'd just been elected President of the new Motion Picture Directors' Association. It transpired, however, that there was rather more to William Desmond Taylor than met the eye, starting with the fact (only discovered after his murder) that he wasn't really William Desmond Taylor at all. He was in fact an Anglo-Irishman called William Deane Tanner who, after a Clifton College education and a brief career as an officer in the British army, had gone to New York to try his luck as a theatre director; there he had married and had a daughter, but by 1908 was still without adequate work and decided therefore to abandon his family, change his name and start a new life out west.

This meant California, and California soon meant films; by 1920 Taylor had directed some huge box-office successes, including *The Diamond from the Sky*, and was reckoned to be largely responsible for the adult stardom of both Mabel Normand and Mary Miles Minter. This was where his troubles began. Though Eddie Knoblock, who had once shared a house with him while both were working for Lasky, found him 'quiet, reserved and extremely sympathetic', it turned out that he also led an extremely active and versatile sex life.

By January 1922 Taylor was the senior director at Famous Players-Lasky, which was now a Paramount subsidiary; the second Arbuckle trial was dragging towards its close with the month, and Paramount (whose brightest star Fatty the 'Prince of Whales' had been) were already in a high state of corporate nerves when, on 2 February, Taylor's black manservant went into his Westlake apartment and found him on the floor of his study with two .38 bullets in his heart. The manservant woke a neighbour, the film star Edna Purviance, who in turn rang Mabel Normand; she called Zukor at Paramount and, hours before the Los Angeles police were even told of the death, Taylor's flat was full of people retrieving potentially damaging evidence. Zukor sent a man round to clear out any whisky bottles, then still illegal under Prohibition; Mary Miles Minter sent her mother round to retrieve some dangerous letters written to Taylor; other studio executives were deputed to clear the flat of any of the drugs Taylor was known to have possessed, and so, when the police arrived, they found little more than a huge fire blazing in the grate.

Subsequent investigation of the flat did, however, also reveal several pornographic snapshots of the director in compromising poses with several of the leading film stars of his time, both male and female, as well as a batch of love letters from Mabel Normand tucked down a riding boot. The mystery deepened still further at Taylor's Hollywood funeral when his protégée, Mary Miles Minter, then twenty and rather less than half his age, approached the bier and kissed his corpse full on the lips before announcing to an understandably amazed press that he had managed to whisper to her, 'I shall always love you, Mary,' before final expiry.

Better was still to come: first the discovery of yet more love letters, this time to Taylor from Mary Miles Minter, and then the news that his faithful manservant liked to knit woollen scarves and take his master to exotic men-only clubs in downtown Los Angeles. Meantime there was also the little matter of the missing butler.

During Knoblock's earlier stay with Taylor, there had been a man called Sands who took care of them and the house; Taylor went back to England for a short holiday, during which time Sands requested a week off, a request granted by Knoblock. When Taylor returned to the house from England, it transpired that Sands had taken not only a holiday but also his master's chequebook and $5,000 and disappeared into Mexico.

Now, police investigation into Taylor's death revealed something else: Sands had been not only Taylor's butler but also his brother, a young lad apparently on the run from English law whom Taylor had taken into his house and disguised by bleaching his hair. He never showed up again after taking his leave of Knoblock, but the police did manage to patch together some other remarkable details about Taylor's private life. At the time of his murder, he had been having simultaneous affairs with Mabel Normand and Mary Miles Minter (both of whom were proved to have visited him on the night of his death) as well as with Mary's mother. Moreover there were strong reports that the recent suicide of a Paramount Studio scriptwriter, Zelda Crosby, was due to the fact that she had been abandoned by Taylor.

Other evidence uncovered by the police included an entire closet filled with ladies' underwear, some of it initialled MMM, but much of it of a larger size and said to have been worn by Mr Taylor during his visits to the more exotic downtown nightclubs. In fact the only element now missing from the Taylor case was a drugs charge and this, too, came along in a matter of days with the suggestion that he had been killed by a cocaine dealer while trying to get Mabel Normand off her tragic addiction.

Within hours of the opening of the inquest, it was clear that it was going to involve the whole of Hollywood in a scandal far nastier than the relatively containable Arbuckle affair. What it was not going to do was provide much of a solution to who did in fact kill the English director. The careers of both Mabel Normand and Mary Miles Minter were killed by the publicity, but there was never any real evidence that either of them had pulled the trigger; suicide was a physical impossibility, the drug connection was at best distant, a lot of the immediate evidence had been burned in the panic fire, and the only – and perennially intriguing – testimony came from another neighbour, Mrs Faith Cole MacLean, who on the witness stand said that she had heard two women depart at different times from Taylor's home that night, followed by 'some sort of explosion', followed by the departure of a third figure 'dressed like a man but, you know, funny looking in a heavy coat with a muffler around the chin and a cap pulled down over the eyes. But it walked like a woman with quick little steps and broad hips and short legs.'

Assuming this could have been neither Mabel Normand nor Mary Miles Minter, that left only one other possible woman then closely linked to Taylor. For at least one Hollywood gossip, the legendary Adela Rogers St John, there was never any doubt that the finger pointed firmly at Mary Miles Minter's mother, a lady who had been allowed to slip quietly away to Europe before the inquest opened.

'Everybody', said Mrs St John in a 1979 television interview, 'knew who shot Taylor. There was never any doubt in anybody's mind. We were in the wild and woolly west, and California had some unwritten laws. One was that a mother had a perfect right to shoot a man who had debauched her little girl.' Especially, perhaps, if he also happened to be her own lover as well.

Miss Minter, still very much alive in the late 1970s, firmly refuted this suggestion of her mother's guilt and, while refusing to be publicly interviewed, privately called into question a great deal of the St John evidence.

So there the mystery rests, while a still greater one remains: why Hollywood has never filmed one of its own best and most intriguing scenarios. We may never know who killed William Desmond Taylor; what we do know is that his exotic murder did considerable damage to the notion of the expatriate British as the moral guardians of Hollywood, and that within a month of his dramatic funeral, as a means of buying off any further police investigation, the Hollywood studio chiefs, led by Zukor and Lasky, had agreed to the hiring from Washington of Will Hays as the man who would 'clean up' the young film industry both on screen and off.

'But what will happen now?' asked someone of Elinor Glyn. 'What will happen now', replied Miss Glyn, who had learnt a thing or two about the ways of the new studio moguls, 'is whatever will bring in the most money.'

8:
Hays Fever

Although Charlie Chaplin was to become involved in several increasingly seedy marital and paternity lawsuits over the next thirty years, it was not until the Carole Landis suicide on 4 July 1948 (apparently provoked by her unrequited love for Rex Harrison) that the British Hollywood community again found themselves involved in real scandal, and even that could scarcely be considered comparable to the tortuous ramifications of the William Desmond Taylor affair. In the meantime, those Britons making their way in ever greater numbers out to California were intent on being identified on screen as well as off as 'class', a breed of men (and now, occasionally, women too) who could be relied upon to add tone and distinction and a sense of continuity and elegance to an ever more frantic celluloid community.

This desperate search for dignity amid the arc lights by the British in California was given a considerable boost when, in November 1922, Lord and Lady Louis Mountbatten chose to make Hollywood a stop on their honeymoon tour of America. The *New York Times* (under the headline MOUNTBATTENS FIND HOLLYWOOD VIRTUOUS) reported that 'they have found no wickedness there, and say that altogether it was a delightful place. Douglas Fairbanks lent them his house during the four days that they were in the Film City, and Charlie Chaplin was their escort in the absence of Fairbanks, who has been in New York on business for several weeks. Lord Mountbatten explained that he was especially interested in Hollywood because one of his private hobbies was making movies in a small way. He has a large library of films already, and manages to get from this country as well as Europe copies of all the important films that appear.'

The report neglected to add that the Mountbattens and Chaplin had shot a short silent comedy-thriller in honour of their wedding, one which was only to surface fifty years later during a television series about the life of the Queen's uncle by marriage.

But true Hollywood royalty was to be found only in the environs of Pickfair. Not until forty years later, when the English actor Peter Lawford managed to marry into the Kennedy clan, was there such a direct feeling of celluloid nobility as that inspired by Fairbanks and his son Doug junior. Both American by birth, they managed to convince many filmgoers around the world that they were, in fact, more British than the British, so that when Doug junior ended up with an honorary British knighthood for services to the King and country it seemed only right and proper, a fitting climax to a life and career of extreme Anglophilia.

There was still not much mileage to be had out of a British accent on the silent screen, but around the studios it undoubtedly began to sound somehow impressive and reassuring, especially at a time when local producers were beginning to suffer their first real crisis of confidence. The coming of 'Hays Fever', the first example (a quarter-century before McCarthy) of Hollywood blacklisting, in which more than a hundred actors and directors were in 1923 labelled 'unsafe' for a studio contract because of their private sexual or social habits, had brought with it a general insecurity in which the newly established studio moguls fled back to a kind of safety that they themselves were barely capable of understanding.

Many of these men – Zukor, Loew, Goldwyn, the Selznicks and Carl Laemmle (who, said Ogden Nash, had a very large faemmle, all employed by his own studios) – were themselves middle-European refugees who had fled to America to escape political or economic repression. Now they found themselves and their all-important new bank balances again under threat, this time from an inchoate but vociferous native American middle class demanding that Hollywood should get itself off the drink and drugs and stand for something vaguely to do with the great outdoors and the healthy life. Hays was to Hollywood what Prohibition was to the American alcohol trade: an unfortunate imposition which had to be worked around without too much loss of business. But in this new, cynical and hypocritical climate 'respectability' was all, and that in turn meant a new demand for 'legit' actors, men from the New York or better still the London stage who could look like bank managers or avuncular doctors or elder statesmen, the father figures that Hays demanded as part of the new puritanism.

This 'classical' breed of actor had another distinct advantage in that they were respected and praised by an increasingly powerful New York-based critical press who until now had regarded Hollywood acting as a subject for nothing but mockery in the new film columns. New York was still the power base which supplied the film industry with most of its money, and the feeling there too was that Hollywood had somehow to 'grow up'; it was no longer a gold rush border town where all laws could be invented and broken on the spot. There was big money to be made there, and accordingly the locals had to start answering to East Coast and European codes of behaviour. This, again, was good news for the British.

There was also the little matter of 'the profile'. With the exotic romances of Elinor Glyn had come a demand for hot-blooded Latin- or Arab-looking male heroes with aquiline features, screen faces altogether different from the butch cowboy stars of the early Hollywood years. Valentino was now the number one box-office draw for the women of middle America, who already constituted the cinema's most sizeable and loyal audience; between the beginning of 1919 and the end of 1921 he'd made twenty-one feature films, among them *Passion's Playground*, *Eyes of Youth*, *The Homebreaker*, *Once To Every Woman* and the two in 1921 that made him a superstar, *Four Horsemen of the Apocalypse* and *The Sheik*.

In other studios the search was on for Valentino clones – men like Ramon Novarro, who happened to be Mexican (Valentino was Italian) but could also conjure up images of the exotic East. Though, or perhaps even because, both men had strong homosexual tendencies their brand of romance somehow became acceptable for a while to the Hays Code; it was definably foreign, unAmerican, and though they were forever to be found on screen carrying off wholesome American girls like Gloria Swanson to fates worse than death in the desert, they posed no immediate local threat to the American Way of Life.

England at this time was unable to provide a suitable profile for export (the romantic stardom of men like Leslie Howard and David Niven was still a decade or more away) but Wales managed one; Ivor Novello was discovered by no less a director than D.W.Griffith, who by chance was responsible for the early screen careers of the two men who were to dominate the British musical theatre between the wars.

As early as 1917, while filming in Britain with the Gish sisters and their mother a patriotic First World War epic called *Hearts of the World*, Griffith had employed a then seventeen-year-old Noël Coward to push a wheelbarrow through the streets of a Worcestershire village. The filming, for which Noël was paid £1 a day, left little mark on him beyond a distinctly unpleasant memory of getting up at five every morning and

making his face up bright yellow for the camera's primeval requirements, and Coward did not make another film for seventeen years.

Five years later, however, D. W. Griffith had rather more success with
the other great musical genius of the British theatre: Ivor Novello.
Already in his early thirties, Novello had made his name at the end of the
First World War as the composer of *Keep The Home Fires Burning*. But
he was also an actor and in 1920 had begun to play starring roles in such
British silents as *The Call of the Blood* (by Robert Hitchens, later to give
Basil Rathbone and Aubrey Smith a considerable Hollywood-British
success with *Garden of Allah*), *Carnival* and *The Bohemian Girl*, in which
he played opposite Gladys Cooper, with whom he was widely announced
to be in real life deeply in love, a somewhat implausible publicity venture
in view of Novello's deep devotion to his own sex.

But the publicity, and the film, for which he was billed as 'the British
Valentino', brought him to the attention of Griffith, who happened to be in
London for the opening there of *Orphans of the Storm*. They met at the
Savoy Hotel, where Griffith told Ivor he bore a marked resemblance to
Richard Barthelmess and that there might therefore be work for him in
Hollywood. A few months later Novello received a contract guaranteeing
him $700 a week for a total of seven pictures, between each of which he
was to be allowed a three-month return to the London stage. Early in
1923 he therefore arrived in New York to a tremendous Griffith-
engineered welcome; though his surname was still causing some confusion (one paper introduced him as Ivor Norvelli, in Boston he was
described as 'the handsome Swedish actor' and in Philadelphia he was
said to be 'the handsome Russian actor and composer'), the week of his
arrival also saw the opening in a Broadway cinema of *The Bohemian Girl*.
The novelist Paul Gallico, then a young film critic on the *New York News*,
reckoned his chances were good: 'Mr Novello is as attractive as they
make 'em, and Mr Griffith is some picker. Novello looks a little like
Conway Tearle, a little like Ramon Novarro and a little like Richard
Barthelmess. He is natural and has no annoying mannerisms. A couple of
years under good direction should see him the great idol of the movie
fans.' Similarly the *New York Telegraph* thought him 'a Greek God who is
both handsome and intelligent' and the *Tribune* though his profile 'the
most gorgeous to have been seen on the screen since that of Francis X.
Bushman'.

So far, so good; early in 1923 it looked as though Britain was, almost a
decade after Chaplin and Stan Laurel, to supply Hollywood with a third

great star and this one for the first time not a comic but a romantic. Things, however, did not work out quite as well as had been anticipated. Novello's first picture under his Griffith contract was to be *The White Rose*, made not in Hollywood at all but on location in Miami. His co-stars were Mae Marsh and Carole Dempster, and Novello was cast as a priggish young trainee priest who leaves his real love (Dempster) for a roguish waitress nicknamed Teasie (Marsh). 'And the youth plucked a white rose', read the synopsis of the plot, 'and pinned it on her bosom. Their lips met, and on such a night, as the stars faded before the dawn, she hurried home to her sorrow and he arose *a man of sin.*'

Amazingly enough, given that synopsis, the film collected some reasonably good reviews on both sides of the Atlantic and Novello emerged from most of them very well indeed. But through no fault of his own other than unfortunate timing, Ivor had joined Griffith at the precise moment when the director's career was getting into considerable difficulties: he was now in both script and money trouble, with the result that after *The White Rose* he proposed to sub-let Novello to any other studio willing to come up with some money for his seven-picture contract.

This Novello declined to accept, and by the end of the year New York papers were full of a lawsuit in which Ivor was suing Griffith for $11,000 of back pay. In the meantime, without visiting Hollywood, Novello had returned to the London theatre, which was always to be his power base; and though he was to enjoy considerable success in later British silents, notably his own script *The Rat, Bonnie Prince Charlie* (again with Gladys Cooper) and Hitchcock's first thriller, *The Lodger,* he was only ever to make one other American film, the unsuccessful 1931 *Once a Lady,* though he did spend several months of that year in Hollywood as a writer.

Though Novello never made it as a star in Hollywood, he did at least manage to remain one for thirty years in his own country; several others of his generation abandoned promising London stage careers for a Hollywood life which often started better than it continued. Dorothy Mackaill, for instance, was the daughter of a man who ran a dancing school in Hull; she began to get work as a chorus dancer in London revues early in 1918, progressed to Paris as a nightclub dancer and began to make Pathé silent comedies. From there she went to America in 1920, became one of Florenz Ziegfeld's showgirls, and by 1922 was playing the leading female role in a Barthelmess swashbuckler called *The Fighting Blade.* She stayed in Hollywood, filming up to the outbreak of the Second

World War, most notably as the girl from whose clutches Clark Gable escapes to Carole Lombard in *No Man of Her Own* (1932). But though she had a breezy comic style, managed easily the transition from silents to talkies, had a Warner contract and starred in *The Office Wife*, which was the first American comedy to set up the wife against the secretary, Dorothy Mackaill was already at the end of her career by her thirtieth birthday, at which time she settled happily for marriage to a wealthy New York socialite, just as many of her showgirl contemporaries in London in the 1920s had married into a more local aristocracy. She had, however, been one of the first to discover that by the mid-1920s it was not enough in California simply to have come out from England as a prospector for film gold. Local talent was already too deeply entrenched for that.

Moreover there were now discernible differences between the British and the American cinema, and the distribution systems of the two countries were causing considerable transatlantic hostility, so that going to California, which only a year or two earlier had seemed an act of commendable courage much akin to pioneering in Australia, now began to bring accusations of disloyalty to the home industry. The problem then, as ever afterwards, was that vastly more American films were getting British screen time than the reverse, and the British film industry therefore felt that it was having to fend off unfair competition from a much wealthier and better-equipped moviemaking business in California.

Feelings were not much soothed, nor matters helped, by an interview given to *The Bioscope* in January 1925 by the American mogul Joseph Schenck, then on a visit to Britain for the purpose of acquiring various cinemas: 'British producers', he told a London press conference when asked to explain American film supremacy, 'have never troubled to produce good pictures. They simply produce pictures and shove them into cinemas without even wondering if they might be good enough for America as well. Nobody here seems to bother about anything very much. In Britain you have no personalities to put on the screen. The stage actors and actresses you insist on using are no good for the screen at all, it is a totally different technique which nobody here has bothered to learn because the cinema is still despised over here. Your special effects are no good, and you do not spend nearly enough money on your films.'

Sam Goldwyn, also visiting Britain that month, took a similarly dismissive line but added perceptively that Britain's real wealth was, as always, in its heritage – that line of authors from Shakespeare to Dickens whose writing was already providing Hollywood with much of its script material.

In Hollywood itself, Douglas Fairbanks Sr, now undisputed king of the silents and reigning at Pickfair with his consort Mary Pickford, was also turning his mind to Britain's apparent failure to live up to America in the film business: 'It is true', he told a reporter in August 1925, 'that the Californian sun helps us in our studio work, but no consideration of climate ought to prevent the British from producing good films. Some of the most successful films in recent years have come from Berlin, where climatic conditions are similar and have been overcome by artificial studio lighting. Hollywood has gone ahead alone because here we are a film colony. Everyone here is engaged in the same industry: we think, dream and live pictures and for that reason we get good results. Nowhere in England have you such a concentrated film settlement, and without it you cannot do first-class work. In England there is still the supremacy of the theatre; here the motion-picture screen is regarded as dramatic enough. You cannot imagine how far we shall one day go with it. I suppose that today Chaplin is our greatest screen genius. What does he achieve? He shows one inadequate man struggling against all the forces of nature. That particular thing he does very well: it is the best thing we can do today. But I believe we can get much further than that. I believe that the conception of all life is contained in the concept of motion pictures. One day the film may go beyond human action and show the meaning of life itself.'

This concept, bizarre though it must seem with hindsight, of Hollywood as the holy temple of the arts and of all human knowledge was echoed in the increasingly religious fervour with which films were now distributed and received. Shooting schedules and running times were growing longer, and once a major film had been finished it was conveyed with considerable ceremony to what was then Grauman's Egyptian Palace, where dim, orange-tinted lights set high in the ceiling cast a suitable aura of reverence over what was about to be unveiled. This, to English visitors and residents alike, was a cause of considerable astonishment; one reporter noted irately in *Picturegoer* that 'Grauman's ticket prices are now comparable to those of a leading West End theatre, and they have even started to have separate performance times instead of a continuous all-day showing'.

Films were definitely getting above themselves, as of course were film stars; except that these reservations remained exclusively British. To the

Hollywood community, as Fairbanks had said, films were all; to the European visitor, they remained a faintly second-class art form, and that nationalistic distinction was to hold good well into the 1940s.

Nevertheless a number of British actors were by now quietly and firmly establishing themselves in Hollywood; none of them had yet had the press attention that surrounded Ivor Novello, but in 1925 there were four who had all played leading roles in, admittedly minor, pictures. In order of arrival in Hollywood they were Percy Marmont (who been in New York filming for Vitagraph since 1913 and reached Hollywood a couple of years later), H. B. Warner (1917), and Clive Brook and Reginald Denny, who first reached Hollywood in 1919 and were both still occasionally to be found filming there in the mid-1960s.

These were, of course, by no means the only four British actors in Hollywood early in the 1920s, but they were the first quartet to make it clear that there, rather than on the Broadway stage or back in England, lay the best part of their professional future. They were the first of the declared residents, after Chaplin and Laurel, and they were soon joined by two other young men from London who were to become more famous than any of them: Ronald Colman and Boris Karloff.

9:
Officers and Gentlemen

Ronald Charles Colman, born in Richmond, Surrey, on 9 February 1891, was perhaps the archetypal Hollywood Englishman: from 1921 to 1957, the year before his death, he made a total of forty-eight films in a run uninterrupted by any professional return to his native land. He was Beau Geste and Raffles and Bulldog Drummond and the Prisoner of Zenda; he was, in David Shipman's view, 'the dream lover – calm, dignified, trustworthy. Although he was a lithe figure in adventure stories, his glamour – which was genuine – came from his respectability; he was an aristocratic figure without being aloof ... he was not always an inspired actor, but he was never bad or dull.'

In his own quiet way, he dominated the Hollywood British community for three decades; but how, I once asked Douglas Fairbanks Jr, who in 1936 was Rupert of Hentzau to Colman's Prisoner of Zenda:

I think because he led the perfect colonial life. The longer he stayed in California, the more English he got; but he never wanted to go home. He always said that he'd been unhappy there, both professionally and privately, and that the press had never forgiven him for settling abroad. He led a very private life, would never lift a finger to publicize any of his films, did the work and went home to tea at five o'clock, played canasta with a small group of friends and kept himself to himself up in the hills. The great difference between Ronnie and Basil Rathbone was that Ronnie knew it was enough to *be* English where Basil, pushed by his wife Ouida, felt that you had to keep reminding people of your nationality by raising flags and playing polo and all that sort of thing. Colman had a tremendous inner sense of security; he didn't worry much about the films that failed or gloat over the ones that were hits. He just went quietly on to the next, whatever it was.

Colman was what the rest of the Hollywood English of his generation and type wanted to be and somehow never quite became; most had to settle for the relatively minor stardom of a Brook or a Rathbone, actors often used in support of dominant female stars, or as 'best friends' to the hero, or as 'heavies'. Unless, of course, they had some other speciality. Chaplin having mastered the comic, and Colman the romantic, it was left to Karloff to corner the horrific, and then only in 1930, after ten years of such undistinguished Hollywood silent work that one leading English movie magazine thought *The Criminal Code*, made in that year, was his first Hollywood film. In fact it was his fifty-first.

But most of this first generation of the Hollywood British had been old enough to fight in the First World War; Colman had indeed had his ankle fractured by a German shell at Messines in 1914 and been invalided out after a decoration for valour. That experience, one also shared by such later additions to the Hollywood British community as Nigel Bruce and Aubrey Smith, seemed to form a bond of military brotherhood. Under the faintly acid headline 'Their Country 'Tis Of Thee', an American film magazine of 1927 noted: 'When one has fought for one's flag and shed blood for it, one does not relinquish it easily. Perhaps that is why so few of our British stars in California have yet become American citizens. But they have a good word for us all the same: "I must admit that I can't consider myself a foreigner here," says Ronald Colman in his nice British voice. "No Englishman should consider himself a foreigner in the United States. To me, Hollywood is as much my home as London. In fact I expect to stay here much of the time even after I leave pictures."' (There lingered at the back of Colman's mind, as was the case with so many of his compatriots in California, the faintly guilty feeling that they were really supposed to be stage actors.) And, continued this early magazine survey of the exiles, 'Clive Brook, another ex-officer of King George, never ceases to marvel at the wonders of America: "The schools, the roads built through the wildernesses for automobiles, the luxuries working men are able here to know, the modern conveniences [one doubts that he meant lavatories] in even the smallest village, the overwhelming number of independent women and the equally overwhelming number of divorces. America has brought me mental and physical comfort: mental because I can do the work here, physical because I have leisure to be with my family, to enjoy a home, a good motor, and a beach cottage."'

The magazine then went on to try to find some British actors resident in Hollywood who had actually renounced their original passports and taken up American citizenship; they found only two, Ernest Torrence and George K. Arthur, neither of whom could ever be said to have achieved in Hollywood the kind of success enjoyed by Brook and Colman.

Was it possible, as some had perhaps already realized, that part of the equipment required by the Hollywood English, long before they even had the chance to use their voices on screen, was a valid British passport?

But not all depended on the Californian côterie life; one of the many advantages of the silent screen was that the Hollywood British could also appear American when required to do so: Percy Marmont got one of his earliest silents, *You Can't Get Away With It*, in 1921 'because the director said he liked my work and could make me look American, so he took me down into Los Angeles to a tailor he knew and ordered me five or six suits cut in the American line. We had these things made up and the first day I appeared on the set he looked at me and said, "Just an Englishman in an American suit." I loved Hollywood in those days. We had our own bunch of friends, by no means all of them English – William Powell, Warner Baxter, Warner Oland, Jack Holt and Tim McCoy, we all used each other's houses at the weekends and had a wonderful time. But only at the weekends; in the week one just could not be social. If there was a party then, and you were on a film, you unostentatiously left at about nine o'clock because you wanted to go to bed. You had to be in make-up by six the next morning, so you simply did not burn the midnight oil.'

Despite the publicity and the occasional scandal, from which the British were usually careful to keep their distance, the life then was a comparatively cloistered one, in which the beginning of one film followed the ending of the last by no more than a few days. Unsurprisingly, therefore, the Hollywood community was regarded with considerable amazement by the occasional British travelling player in Los Angeles on theatre rather than film business; most simply played the stage date and carried on touring, torn between envy at the salaries that their old London stage partners were now commanding and delight that they did not have to stay more than a transient week or two in the moist heat of a city where bedtime appeared to be nine o'clock.

The first mass arrival in Los Angeles of the stage British occurred in April 1926, when Gertrude Lawrence, Beatrice Lillie and Jack Buchanan opened the El Capitan Theater in Hollywood with the post-Broadway tour of *Charlot's 1926 Revue*. The first problem, recalled Miss Lawrence, was her sense of dress: 'At last in the sun, I began to go about the place with bare legs, stockingless, which I found both comfortable and economical; and as soon as it was announced in the local press that Gertrude Lawrence was going about bare-legged, the papers began to interview other actresses to get their opinion of the fad I had started.' Marilyn Miller, when interviewed, expressed ladylike disapproval of the innovation and announced that she had brought back from Paris two hundred pairs of silk stockings which she had every intention of wearing around the studios. Carmel Snow, fashion editor of *Harper's Bazaar*, was quoted exclaiming in horror, 'The idea is disgusting and will never catch on. It will just never be done by nice people.'

The first night of the Charlot revue in Hollywood was recalled by Bea Lillie:

We started by singing 'God Save The King' loudly and to the amazement of the American orchestra, who thought they were playing 'My Country 'Tis Of Thee'. In one of the boxes sat Charlie Chaplin and his wife of the day, Lita Grey. In the front row sat Pola Negri, like a white orchid, whispering sweet nothings into the gallant ear of Rudolph Valentino. ... On the last night, half the audience seemed to be leaving during our last number, which was set in Scotland. Then, to our amazement, onto the stage behind us marched Valentino in a Scots bonnet, Chaplin wearing his dinner jacket tied around his middle like an improvised kilt, the Marx Brothers in false beards, Barthelmess in one of his wife's dresses and John Gilbert carrying for no apparent reason a very long ladder over his shoulder.

The next morning the rest of the Charlot troupe began the train journey back to New York and then home, but Bea Lillie was signed by MGM to make a caper called *Exit Smiling* with Mary Pickford's brother Jack. She took a dim view of the local talent ('Jack Gilbert and Greta Garbo were forever making eyes at each other, Jack really believing the studio press releases that dubbed him "the Great Lover" and Garbo characterized by a desperate kind of solemnity which I tried to puncture by sending Jack one anonymous red rose every morning for a month') and didn't even much care for La Casa Grande, the large house on the San Simeon estate where Marion Davies was already living in often lonely splendour with William Randolph Hearst.

'The first time I was invited', recalled Bea later, 'I was a touch afraid of being informally introduced to a few of the lions, leopards, wildcats and polar bears that roamed the place; what shook me more, however, was the sight of one castle, Italian, used, complete, lying around the lawns packed in numbered crates.'

The Hearst-Marion Davies affair was a constant fascination to the Hollywood British, perhaps because it corresponded more closely than most Californian habits to the London tradition of wealthy elderly stage-door johnnies picking up chorus girls and setting them down in large baronial castles surrounded by acres of private territory. One night, Chaplin and Bea Lillie were at a Hollywood party and found themselves looking out at the dazzling lights of Los Angeles spread out below them. 'I suppose any minute now', said Bea, 'they will all come together and spell out MARION DAVIES.'

Hearst was originally a considerable Anglophile (though later he, like Joe Kennedy, was to be among the most outspoken and fervent opponents of his country's entry into the war on Britain's side) and his great dream at this time was to have Bernard Shaw visit San Simeon; the dream was eventually realized during Shaw's one and only American trip in April 1933. For now, Shaw replied, 'I have never heard of Marion Davies and would not go to see her if she were all the 11,000 virgins of St Ursula rolled into one.'

If there was one thing which characterized the Hollywood British, it was their apparent inability or unwillingness to develop much beyond the performances they were giving on first arrival in California. At a time of considerable type-casting, they were either too intelligent or too lazy or simply too limited as actors to give American co-stars or directors any real surprises. Certainly it is possible to trace in their performances an increasing confidence and camera-relaxation as the size of their roles and bank balances grew; but there were few real changes. Twenty or thirty years after first arrival, it is possible to find the British giving much the same performances on screen as the ones that won them their first studio contracts.

There was, however, one notable and unique exception to this rule, and he was Reginald Denny. Though remembered now as the all-purpose, tight-lipped, ramrod-backed second or third lead, an actor perhaps most typically cast by Hitchcock in the 1939 *Rebecca* as Frank Crawley, Olivier's hugely discreet estate manager at Manderley, there was a time in the 1920s when Denny was (after only Chaplin) the second-highest-paid silent comedian in the world.

Born Reginald Leigh Daymore in 1891, Denny had started out at the Royal Court Theatre in London as a child actor in 1899; he ran away from school at sixteen, worked his passage to New York and opened on Broadway as one of eight chorus boys in *A Quaker Girl*. He then toured America and England until 1917, often with comic-opera companies, and after that became a pilot in the Royal Flying Corps. When the war ended he returned to New York to find that his wife had deserted him for another actor and had subsequently been taken into a sanatorium; with a baby daughter to support, he went into small Broadway parts until a stage actors' strike forced him to find work in the films then still being made out at Fort Lee in New Jersey.

It was there, almost accidentally, that Denny began to develop a style of knockabout comedy which was to lead him out to California, where throughout the 1920s he made a sequence of slapstick successes like *Oh Doctor* and *California Straight Ahead*, films he often wrote and co-directed himself in an unrestrained style vastly different from the work he was to do later. The coming of sound in 1927 revealed, however, his impeccably English accent, one which seemed ill-suited to custard pies and pratfalls, and it was then that Denny had to start slowly re-building an altogether different and somewhat less starry or profitable career.

Yet for the rest of the Hollywood British, always excepting Chaplin, who was as ever a lonely law unto himself, it was just the opposite: the coming of sound, instead of putting an end to careers, launched and boosted and sustained literally hundreds. From the release of *The Jazz Singer* in October 1927, it became slowly but abundantly clear that the British colony in California now possessed something of remarkable commercial and artistic worth: a clearly intelligible speaking voice, often stage-trained, readily understandable to the American audiences who still made up over ninety percent of the studios' cash takings.

True, there were to be the occasional complaints from the mid-west about tight-lipped, fast-speaking and heavily nasal intonations, but at the very least the Hollywood British and their American hosts now shared a common tongue, which was more than could be said about the other visiting or resident Hollywood actors from Scandinavia or the European mainland.

Though, with very few exceptions, the British in California were only ever interested in acting or writing for the movies, leaving all financial and technical studio dealings to locals or middle-European exiles, they had in the silent days always had to compete against equally good-looking actors and actresses, notably from France, Italy and Sweden. Now, with the coming of sound, the British had a clear lead and, apart from Denny (who was distinctly silent on the subject), it was really only Chaplin who viewed the new Vitaphone development with anything less than out-and-out delight.

Chaplin sensed, long before the film historians, that a lot more than silence was going to end with the silents: a whole way of making films, a whole sense of humour, indeed a whole vision of the world was to vanish with the coming of a more cumbersome talking reality.

In March 1928, along with his old United Artists partners Fairbanks and Pickford, and John Barrymore (who must have been the most at home, given his already over-the-top booming theatricality) Chaplin did a *Big Broadcast* on American radio from Miss Pickford's bungalow at the studio. Though Charlie, or so he said later, 'nearly died of fright', the broadcast was in fact a public relations exercise designed to prove to a now curious and waiting America that her favourite film stars did indeed have voices and could use them coherently.

But for Chaplin there was a special problem: he alone of the great stars of the silent era had created one single and totally universal character – The Tramp. If that Tramp now had to talk, in what conceivable accent should it be? Ought it to be Chaplin's own faint traces of South London Cockney overlaid with twenty years of Californian? Rather than face the problem immediately (it was indeed to be another seven years before Chaplin was heard on screen, and then only for the nonsense song in *Modern Times*) he decided that attack was the best form of defence against the talkies and gave a correspondingly scathing interview to *Motion Picture* magazine in March 1929:

Talkies are ruining the oldest art in the world – the art of pantomime. They are ruining the great beauty of silence. They are defeating the meaning of the screen, the appeal that has created the star system, the fan system, the vast popularity of the whole – the appeal of beauty. It's beauty that matters in pictures – nothing else. The screen is pictorial. Pictures. Lovely looking girls, handsome young men in adequate scenes. What if the girls can't act? Of course they can't. They never have. But what of it? Who has cared? Who has known the difference? Certainly I prefer to see, say, Dolores Costello [then Mrs John Barrymore] in a thin tale than some aged actress of the stage doing dialogue with revolting close-ups.

It was left to Al Jolson, who had as much to gain from the talkies as Chaplin then thought he had to lose, to see Chaplin off in an interview given two months later:

I was at a party the other night, and from 8.30 until around 5 a.m. Charlie never stopped talking and singing. ... If he wants to keep what he calls 'the great beauty of silence' let him go lock himself in a room, become a nun's brother or something. ... Charlie goes on the record as loathing talkies. Well, I'm just the opposite and I think he'd better get to like 'em or he'll find out the public don't like him. What he's really got is a gentleman complex. He's afraid he talks too nice to fit in with the characterization he has built up on the screen.

10:
Wallace in Wonderland

So whether Chaplin liked it or not, and he patently didn't, the talkies had come to stay and for most British actors they were very good news indeed. Victor McLaglen, for instance, had arrived in California in 1924, three years before *The Jazz Singer*, able only to find work after considerable difficulty:

I knew the Pacific coast of old [he wrote in his 1934 autobiography], having toured it as a boxer, but I had never previously been as far down it as Los Angeles. My first impression on stepping out of the train was one of acute disappointment. Actors back on Shaftesbury Avenue spoke of Hollywood with bated breath, mentioning it as an El Dorado where the streets were paved with gold and the tables covered with long-term contracts. To my travel-tired eye, as I viewed it for the first time, it seemed remarkably like any other suburb of any other Pacific city. I presented a curious spectacle as I stood on that platform. I had, I admit, been anxious to create a good impression. In consequence I was well dressed, in the English style, which must have looked museum-like to the natives. My kid gloves, my spats and my walking cane divulged the fact that I was English; the natives stopped and stared at me as though I were a freak show. There was about twenty dollars in my pocket, representing about four pounds in English money, and that jaunty feeling in the heart that comes when a man finds himself on the threshold of a new life.

Though McLaglen had at least the promise of a studio contract also in his pocket, his first meeting with the head of publicity at Vitagraph was not exactly encouraging: 'It may be nothing much,' said the pressman, 'but very few of you English fellows do well out here; reticence and absurd self-consciousness tell against them in a land where everyone has a pat on the back for the next man.'

Accordingly, McLaglen resolved to be desperately cheerful and friendly to all, a posture he managed to continue even when his promised first film was postponed and he found himself living with several rats in a small flat overlooking a sewage farm. But after some undistinguished silents McLaglen was one of the first to grab the character opportunities that the talkies provided, and by 1930 was on $1,000 a week starring opposite Dietrich in *Dishonored*.

Others who had done rather better than McLaglen in the silent 1920s were to find the transition to the talking 1930s more difficult to achieve. Elinor Glyn, for instance, having enjoyed a period of unique and unrivalled fame as the most distinguished literary figure in Hollywood (a claim which rested largely on her publication in *Cosmopolitan* magazine of a story about a hero possessed of the elusive 'It' quality of sex appeal; Paramount read it, asked her to change the character's sex for Clara Bow, and the rest was a kind of screen history), found that with the mixture of scandals and sudden unfashionability which ruined Miss Bow's career, her own work was no longer in much demand out west either, and she accordingly retreated to a happy New York life in a penthouse atop the Ritz Tower.

Before she left California, however, Miss Glyn did see the arrival of one more remarkable troupe of visiting English theatrical celebrities; this time it was the tour of Max Reinhardt's lavish production of *The Miracle*, led by Lady Diana Cooper, which reached Los Angeles early in 1927, as Lady Diana's diary indicates:

24 January: We went to call on Marion Davies at the MGM studios. Surprising. A place like a dockyard or lunatic asylum, with 'abandon hope' gates only opened for bosses and holders of red-tape permits that need to be signed repeatedly. Marion Davies's dressing-room is built in the middle of the sets and is as big as a church, in W.R.Hearst's unfailing Spanish-Gothic taste.

31 January: The first night [of *The Miracle* in Los Angeles] was cruelly alarming and altogether rude and miserable, and the house was packed with screen celebrities. In my unblinking gaze [as the statuesque Madonna] I saw Pickford, Fairbanks, Norma Shearer, Marion Davies, W.R.Hearst, Emil Jannings and Elinor Glyn. To my surprise no one did anything in honour of Reinhardt or any of us – no party, no flowers, no telegrams, no visits to congratulate. Hollywood is unlike any other American city. It would be impossible for, say, the Fairbanks or Guitrys or Stanislavsky to have a first night in London and not be fêted by the profession at the Savoy or at a private house, wouldn't it? I'm outraged. ... I hate this town, hate it. I believe that they despise us for being 'legitimate' stage.

1 February: In the new *King of Kings* picture, Schildkraut tells me, the betrayal of Christ is explained as due to a wave of jealousy for Mary Magdalen! No comment. They don't mind their 'p's' here. A newspaper said Miss Constance Talmadge had got a separation from her 'Scottish souse Mr Ali Mackintosh'. Iris

[Tree] and I went together to see Elinor Glyn. She had a cluster of beautiful young men in attendance.

Another writer who left Hollywood to return to New York and London, in the face of the dozens who were now hurrying in the opposite direction (for the coming of sound had also meant the coming of dialogue, and for this as often as not the studio moguls were now summoning writers with a West End or Broadway track record), was Edward Knoblock. By the late 1920s he had decided to return to the theatre, but some indication of how things had changed in the few years since he had left it for Hollywood was given to him by his travelling companion on the return voyage, Charles Chaplin:

The crowd at Waterloo [wrote Knoblock] was a thing not to be believed. Charlie himself was completely bewildered. It must have seemed to him like a fantastic dream. Not so many years before he had left London as an unknown down-at-heel music-hall artist earning at the very most five pounds a week. And here was a seething mob cheering and trying to force its way through the police cordon before he stepped into his car. It was really very frightening. He kept turning to me and shouting through the din, 'Stick to me! For God's sake, stick to me!' I was carrying a bundle of my overcoats in a strap. I did my best to follow him. But as I tried to jump into the car after him, a policeman who took me for some enthusiastic madman dragged me off the step, slammed the door of the car and shouted to the chauffeur, 'Drive on.' I was hurled back into the crowd and my overcoats taken from me. Somehow, I got home. I sent my servant later on to collect my luggage. My overcoats, which I had luckily labelled, were returned to me the next day with a curt note. 'Herewith the overcoats. I thought they were Charlie Chaplin's. I see they are only yours . . .' I couldn't help feeling sorry for Chaplin, when I thought of the overwhelming odds that success was holding out against him. I myself went to Worthing to recover from Hollywood.

Other British writers were, however, eager to sample the fame that so appalled Knoblock; comparatively few had been willing to take the risk in the silent days, and those who had did not always enjoy the good fortune of a Glyn or a Knoblock. The First World War poet Robert Nichols had, for instance, settled in Los Angeles as early as 1925, uninvited and simply because of a fascination with the film medium. 'Is film good to work in?' his friend Aldous Huxley asked him in an appalled 1926 letter. 'I say no, because you can't do it yourself. You depend on Jews with money or "art directors" or little bitches with curly hair and teeth, or young men who recommend skin food in the advertisements, or photographers.'

To some extent Huxley was right, of course: Nichols had made the mistake of arriving unannounced and so the best job he could get was inserting gags into silent screen titles for Douglas Fairbanks, whereas (as Edward Beddington-Behrens, the London banker who was one of the most acute observers of Hollywood in the 1920s, once explained) had Nichols arrived as a distinguished foreign visitor with letters of introduction from Bernard Shaw and Barrie, then all would have been well and the big producers would have rushed to give him a contract to prevent his being taken up by a rival studio.

That mistake was not made twice; when Ivor Novello went back to Hollywood in 1931 it was at the express invitation of MGM to convert his recent Broadway success *The Truth Game* into a screenplay. However, the experience was not a very happy one; 'in nine months', Novello told his biographer Peter Noble, 'I wrote no less than eight different screen drafts of *The Truth Game* and all that remained of my original play by the time I got to the last one was the title and the names of the characters and all of them were altered on the first day of production.'

The film eventually became a Robert Montgomery vehicle called *But The Flesh Is Weak*, and Novello stifled his pride at the loss both of his original dialogue and of the leading role; he stayed at the beach house of Edmund Goulding, one of the rare English directors to make a long-term career in Hollywood, which spanned the mid-1920s to the mid-1950s, and while there took on some other hack screenwriting assignments, one of which was, bizarrely enough, to polish up some Johnny Weissmuller dialogue (uncredited) for the first of the MGM Tarzan series. Seeing Novello's considerable and understandable depression at the way Metro were using him (or rather not using him), his old Broadway friend Ruth Chatterton got him the second lead in a romance she was then shooting at Paramount; but *Once A Lady* did not do much for Ivor in Hollywood and by the beginning of 1932 he was back in London, breathing sighs of relief at his second escape from a world he did not begin to understand or care for.

Nöel Coward, still Novello's only true rival in the British theatre, had come to much the same conclusion about Hollywood without ever troubling to work there; of a brief holiday stop-over in Hollywood for Christmas 1929 (despite a career of eleven films as an actor and as many again as writer or director, he never made one in California) he was to write later:

I felt as though I had been whirled through all the side-shows of some gigantic pleasure park at breakneck speed. My spiritual legs were wobbly and my impressions confused. Blue-ridged cardboard mountains, painted skies, elaborate grottoes peopled with several familiar figures; animated figures that moved their arms and legs, got up and sat down and spoke with remembered voices. The houses I had visited became indistinguishable in my mind from the built interiors I had seen in the studios. I couldn't remember clearly whether the walls of Jack Gilbert's dining-room had actually risen to a conventional ceiling, or whether they had been sawn off half-way up to make room for scaffolding and spluttering blue arc-lamps. I remembered an evening with Charlie Chaplin when at one point he played an accordion and at another a pipe-organ, and then suddenly became almost pathologically morose and discussed Sadism, Masochism, Shakespeare and the Infinite. I remembered a motor drive along flat, straight boulevards with Gloria Swanson during which we discussed, almost exclusively, dentistry. I remembered, chaotically, a series of dinner parties, lunch parties, cocktail parties and even breakfast parties. I remembered also playing a game of tennis with Charlie MacArthur somewhere at two in the morning with wire racquets in a blaze of artificial moonlight and watching him, immediately afterwards, plunge fully clothed into an illuminated swimming-pool. I remembered Laura Hope-Crews appearing unexpectedly from behind a fountain and whispering gently, 'Don't be frightened, dear – this – *this* – is Hollywood.' I had been received with the utmost kindness and hospitality, and I enjoyed every minute of it; it was only now, in quietness, that it seemed unreal and inconclusive, as though it hadn't happened at all.

For some writers, like Coward, Hollywood was a place to be cheerfully visited and then forgotten; for others, like Novello, it was a kind of spiritual and artistic death; for still others, like Edgar Wallace, it was something even more terminal. Wallace went out there for the first (and last) time in November 1931; he was then fifty-six and at the height of an extremely prolific and successful career which had included novels as popular as *The Four Just Men* and *Sanders of the River* as well as stage thrillers like *The Ringer* and *On The Spot*. Accompanied by a secretary and a valet, he had decided to go out to California partly at the request of the *Daily Mail*, who wanted three articles on Hollywood, but mainly to discuss with RKO the prospect of some lucrative film-scripting assignments, since Wallace was perennially short of money but had a considerable British reputation for being a rapid and versatile writer.

His diary for 5 December 1931 records:

I hired a car and drove to the studio; it is about five miles from my hotel, but we did it in about ten minutes. ... [David O.] Selznick is the big noise here; he is young, massive, well-educated and with tremendous vitality. ... I was then picked up by an awfully nice fellow who is at the head of the publicity department and he took me into the block where the executive writers are kept chained up and I was given a room, the key thereof and the telephone book, which helps me keep in touch with everybody in the block. ... They want me to do a horror picture for them. I think there is a big market for it, and they have 'lined me up' with all their stock artists and I am to use them just as I want: Erich von Stroheim, Anna May Wong and a few more of that kind.

By the middle of the month, however, the projected new screenplay had not got very far and Wallace was now worrying about Christmas decorations for his rented Beverly Hills home: 'It is the practice out here to decorate the trees in front of the houses – if possible, a fir tree – at Christmas. The chairman of our Chamber of Commerce, a Miss Mary Pickford, about whom you may have read, has ordained that we shall be illuminated by Friday 18 December, so today the electrician is coming. I am now also supposed to be writing a big picture for Constance Bennett. Selznick says if he can get two big pictures out of me in the four months I am paid to be here he will be damned lucky.' On Christmas Day, continues the diary, 'Merian Cooper [one of Selznick's RKO producers] called and we talked over a big animal play we are going to write or rather I am to write and he is to direct. I am to turn out a scenario for him. It will take six months to make. He's a terribly nice fellow and I get on well with him, as I do with David Selznick, who is a regular fellow.'

The 'big animal' play was in fact *King Kong*, and for it Wallace immediately shelved his other RKO projects and started banging out a screenplay: 'An announcement has been made in the local press that I am doing a super-horror story with Cooper, but the truth is that it is much more his story than mine. I am rather enthusiastic about it, but the story has got to be more or less written to provide certain spectacular effects. I shall get much more credit out of the picture than I deserve, if it is a success, but as I shall be blamed by the public if it's a failure that seems fair.'

Despite an extremely active social life, and the writing of daily thousand-word letters back to his wife in England, Wallace managed by the middle of January to complete the first draft of *King Kong* plus his *Daily Mail* articles, a couple of short stories for *Collier's* and the script of a new stage thriller, which he airmailed back to Gerald du Maurier in London as a follow-up to their triumphant *Ringer*.

Cooper and RKO were not, however, very happy with Wallace's treatment of *King Kong* (at that stage they didn't even care for the title and it was temporarily agreed that they should call it *The Beast*). As Cooper said later, 'Wallace was the fastest writer in the world, but he wrote for the ear, not the eye, so his picture stuff never came off. He hadn't the slightest idea how to write for the screen but I recognized the publicity value of his name, especially in England, so I agreed with him over dinner one night that he could write the book version of *King Kong* to be published under our joint names, and in return I would give him co-screen credit.'

In fact, Wallace's screenplay did encompass most of the special effects that Cooper wanted, and in the end was not so very far removed from what appeared on the screen under his joint byline. But whereas many English writers might have been depressed or made distraught by this traditional if unusually amicable falling-out between a writer and his producers (Cooper and Selznick), Wallace was made of sterner stuff. As an experienced Fleet Street journalist to whom the concept of failure was unknown, rewrites were familiar, and the weekly pay cheque the only one which truly mattered, Wallace now turned over *King Kong* to other hands and cheerfully returned to work on the two earlier projects he had been given by Selznick.

Like all journalists, Wallace was also fascinated by the moguls who ran the big studios: 'We were talking about how film companies change the titles of the books they buy, and Mayer gave me an instance of a book that had been bought called *Pigs*. When it was put over as a picture it was called *The Smile of a Cavalier* ... Hollywood abounds in stories about Sam Goldwyn. An actor went in to settle a contract. He said, "I'm asking fifteen hundred a week." "You're not asking fifteen hundred a week," said Goldwyn fiercely, "you're asking twelve, and I'm giving you a thousand." Today I am going to go back to the horror scenario and will also do an article for the *New York Times*.'

In the middle of January, much impressed by his speed and industry, Selznick at RKO renewed the studio option on Wallace's contract and set him to work on two or three other possible scenarios, apparently unperturbed by his failure with *King Kong*. Wallace was now in his element, finding London stage friends from Heather Thatcher to Laurence Olivier on every studio street-corner and even getting an Edgar Wallace Handicap run in his honour at the local racetrack. Both his daily diary and his letters home for the end of January 1932 exhibit an utter, almost childlike, delight with Hollywood; he plans to have his wife and children brought out to join him, starts giving celebrity lectures to the local Los Angeles citizens ('best audience turn-out since Will Hays') and is thrilled now to be recognized by his trademark cigarette-holder in the local bookstores. Some of the RKO contract players seem even to have read his novels, and the news from London is that du Maurier thinks they will have a hit with the new stage thriller, *The Green Pack*, despite the fact that in Wallace's transatlantic absence the cast at Wyndham's were having to do a good deal of work on the plot.

Then, on 4 February, comes a brief diary entry to the effect that Merian Cooper (with whom he was still working on some of the rewrites for *King Kong*) had developed a sore throat, and that these things seemed to be catching in the damp of a California winter. By 5 February Wallace has a cold, though he is well enough to go to lunch at the Embassy where he meets 'Marlene Dietrich with Sternberg and her little daughter'. On 6 February he gives a dinner party and the following day, complaining faintly of rheumatism, he decides that he will not after all be well enough to attend Ivor Novello's farewell party.

A few days later, Novello left California for good, taking with him a beloved dog, which had to be put in the guard's van for the long train journey to New York. At Chicago they changed trains, and Novello went along to the new guard's van to make sure the dog was being properly fed. There he found a black porter sitting on an enormous packing case; jovially Novello remarked that he hoped there was no one inside. 'Sure there is,' replied the porter, 'it's a film writer who died suddenly of pneumonia in Hollywood.' Novello turned over the label: it read 'EDGAR WALLACE'.

11:
Disraeli Wins an Oscar

Laurence Olivier, whom Wallace had met in California a few days before his death, was also out there for the first time. Now twenty-five, his already starry career had suffered a considerable setback when he abandoned the chance of starring in *Journey's End* after a Sunday-night tryout to go into an altogether disastrous stage version of *Beau Geste*. Noël Coward had rescued him from that, however, by giving him the only other male role in *Private Lives* and, together with Coward and Gertrude Lawrence and his first wife, Jill Esmond, Olivier had been playing that triumphant comedy on Broadway in 1931 when he was urged, not least by Coward himself, to go and seek his fortune in California.

Coward's notion was that Olivier and Jill Esmond could be to American films what his beloved Alfred Lunt and Lynn Fontanne were to the American theatre; and though Noël himself had not much cared for the Hollywood life, he reckoned that given a profile like Olivier's there was no reason why Larry should not enjoy for a few years the kind of sunny and wealthy existence then already being taken for granted by such lesser talents as Ronald Colman.

As the success of *Private Lives* on Broadway, where its three-month run was entirely sold out, came at the precise moment when Hollywood talent scouts were thronging New York in search of actors who could speak intelligibly in front of a camera, and as Olivier had already had minimal film experience in Europe with a quota quickie called *Too Many Crooks* and a German drama called *The Temporary Widow*, it did not take long for RKO to offer him a three-picture two-year contract. In fact the studio was rather more interested in Jill Esmond, in whom they saw the makings of a fine romantic lead; Olivier himself presented more of a problem, since in the words of one studio executive: 'He has no chance – he tries to look like Ronny Colman but his face is too strong and his looks are too rugged rather than weak and suave. When it comes to rugged actors, we don't need Englishmen. We've got plenty of Americans around to handle those parts.'

Nevertheless the RKO publicity machine ground into action for Olivier, and he was soon being photographed for the fan magazines in grimly determined baseball poses. His first film was, however, something of a disaster, as he himself later noted:

The cast included no less than Adolphe Menjou, Lili Damita and Erich von Stroheim, with me taking fourth place in equal billing [RKO were building up their small drop of new blood]. . . . This first engagement embodied for me all the most horrific aspects of Hollywood. An extravagantly dramatic romance by Maurice Dekobra had, inevitably, been completely rewritten but it was considered that the deal had been worth the money for the sake of the title – *The Sphinx Has Spoken*. Needless to say, by the end of the picture it was decided to change the title to *Friends and Lovers*. It may have been realized that Lili Damita was not exactly sphinx-like. The cast, apart from its eminence, was wretchedly ill-assorted. So my first Hollywood picture died the death of a dog.

Next, after a healthy pause, I was supposed to be leading man to Pola Negri in a talkie about Queen Draga, whom François I of Serbia elected to marry. Draga was shot and the King was thrown from a window; he managed to cling to the sill, pointed out to me in 1957, until his fingers, crushed by rifle butts, lost hold and he fell to the street below. This horrid occurrence brought monarchy to an end in Serbia.

Sad to say, I contracted yellow jaundice and had to give up this opportunity and go to hospital. In place of this, with yellow jaundice there came *The Yellow Ticket*, a decent old English melodrama renamed, for some odd reason of censorship, *The Yellow Passport*. . . . Lionel Barrymore was the heavy lead and it was really quite all right. After this came a truly promising picture, *Westward Passage*, with the pretty and highly respected Ann Harding. . . . My own part had splendid opportunities and I found myself feeling the stir of optimism, but it did not last; conditions were against any seed becoming fertile.

Those conditions included now the Depression, which was causing RKO productions to be shut down for lack of funds, and the arrival at that beleaguered studio of a young David O. Selznick, whose brief was to cut salaries by half and end contracts where possible. Olivier's seemed one of the most possible; it had run its initial three-picture course without covering the young English actor in any particular glory, and there was as yet no indication of the wuthering heights of screen stardom to which he would ascend before the decade was over. His wife, Jill, had been doing rather better at RKO, but even for her the long-promised chance to star in Clemence Dane's *Bill of Divorcement* was now being threatened by the whirlwind arrival at RKO on long-term contract of Katharine Hepburn.

David Selznick (whose agent brother Myron was to remain one of Olivier's most ardent Hollywood advocates and to be instrumental in getting him briefly cast opposite Garbo a year later as well as in getting his next wife, Vivien Leigh, cast for *Gone With The Wind* six years later still) took the then-current Hollywood view that Olivier, though undoubtedly a stage actor of extreme talent and promise, somehow lacked screen potential. The figures on his early films were already in, and little short of disastrous: *Friends and Lovers* had lost RKO $260,000 at the box-office while *Westward Passage* lost only $10,000 less. Olivier could thus be safely returned (complete with his more reluctant wife) to London.

'The reason', said one local Hollywood talent scout, 'that Olivier never became the great movie star many people thought he should have been was not due to his so-called contempt for film acting, his high-handed above-it-all attitude towards movies [which Olivier himself later admitted was how he felt about them up to his education by William Wyler on *Wuthering Heights*], nor was it because he did not want to be a star. It was because he has no screen personality ... he transforms himself magnificently on stage, but on screen all that comes through is his basic personality, which he himself has called "hollow". That hollowness may be just right for a stage actor, who uses his roles to fill himself in; but it is his hollowness that the camera captures.'

Thus Olivier failed (one suspects much to his own relief) to become one of the Hollywood British; ironically, however, it was during his first term of trial and error out there that another and much less talented English actor was laying down what became the guidelines for a whole generation of subsequent British theatrical exiles, and doing so rather surprisingly at a studio then famous mainly for low-budget gangster movies and the early Depression musicals of Busby Berkeley. But in 1929, Warner Brothers had come up against a problem; as the pioneers of talking pictures they wished rapidly to establish their lead in several different areas of the cinema. They already had social realism and the musical; what they wanted was something to give the studio a bit of class and tone. That, in the view of one of their directors, Alfred Green, meant history, and European history at that. It meant a Famous Life, and the life chosen was that of the British Prime Minister Benjamin Disraeli, largely because it had already worked well as a silent movie (to which Warners now had the rights) and allowed for a good diplomatic battle over the ownership of the Suez Canal.

Early British arrivals in California: LEFT the pioneer motion-picture cameraman Eadweard Muybridge in Yosemite, 1872; ABOVE Charles Chaplin (in lifebelt) and Stan Laurel (*left*) on their way to America in 1910; BELOW Sir Herbert Beerbohm Tree (*left*) as Macbeth with Constance Collier in a 1916 Hollywood silent produced by D. W. Griffith (*right*).

Hollywood, 1922: Chaplin LEFT with
Edwina Mountbatten, then on
honeymoon in America, and BELOW
breaking the news to her husband
that, despite their co-starring roles
in a home movie, Mountbatten will
never become a film star. Freddy
Neilsen (*right*) is in agreement.

To sin with Elinor Glyn: the first British novelist to turn her best-sellers into screen financial gems seen RIGHT with the stars of her *The Only Thing*; BELOW Aileen Pringle and Conrad Nagel in Glyn's 1924 shocker *Three Weeks*.

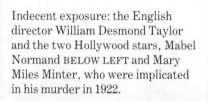

Indecent exposure: the English
director William Desmond Taylor
and the two Hollywood stars, Mabel
Normand BELOW LEFT and Mary
Miles Minter, who were implicated
in his murder in 1922.

Journey's End (1930): director James Whale (*centre above*), scenarist George Pearson (*left*) and cast including Colin Clive, David Manners and Anthony Bushell were all British, but the film was shot in Hollywood, where studio facilities were superior to anything yet available in Britain.

"How can I eat when Osborne's lying out there?"

ABOVE The first great star of the Hollywood British, George Arliss, in the 1929 *Disraeli* that won him one of the first Oscars. Anthony Bushell (*left*) and Joan Bennett were also featured.

BELOW By 1933, and Paramount's *Midnight Club*, the clans of British gentlemen character actors had begun to gather in the Hollywood Hills – among them Clive Brook (*centre*), Alan Mowbray and Sir Guy Standing.

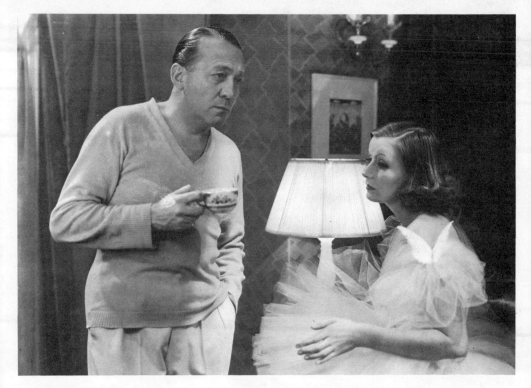

ABOVE One of the first British directors to settle in Hollywood, Edmund Goulding, directing Garbo in the 1932 all-star *Grand Hotel*. Tea was, apparently, already being taken on the set.

BELOW Coward's stage epic *Cavalcade* became, in 1933, one of the first great screen gatherings of the Hollywood British.

The Hollywood Cricket Club: ABOVE at home in Los Angeles, David Niven (*second from left, back row*), Nigel Bruce (*far left, front row*) and the club's founding captain, C. Aubrey Smith (*seated centre*); BELOW away in Vancouver, 1936, when the team included Frank Lawton (*middle row, third from right*), Errol Flynn and Nigel Bruce (*left of front row*), captained as usual by Sir Aubrey.

HOLLYWOOD C.C. AND VANCOUVER.

The problem lay in finding an actor for the title role: now that Disraeli could talk on the screen, he clearly had to be played by an Englishman of a certain age and distinction. The problem was that in 1929 such Englishmen simply did not exist in California; those that were now settled there were either the young romantics like Colman or men who had been filming so long in such a wide variety of silent screenplays that they had lost all claim to whatever original stage distinction they may once have possessed. Not since the departure of Sir Herbert Beerbohm Tree in 1916 had there been in California an English actor of the required stature for Disraeli. One, therefore, now had to be imported by Warners, and the obvious choice was the one who had already made the silent *Disraeli* a decade earlier.

George Arliss was now just over sixty; the son of a London publisher, he had started an undistinguished London career as an actor when in 1901 Mrs Patrick Campbell (later to follow him to California with rather less spectacular results) had taken him out to New York, where he remained for many years, first playing Disraeli on the Broadway stage in 1911. Early in the 1920s he had made a few unmemorable silents and then returned to the live theatre, where he was giving his Shylock when Hollywood sent for him to recreate his Disraeli.

Arliss now realized something very important: he was perhaps the first English actor since his great predecessor Tree to be going out to Hollywood with all the cards up his sleeve. Warners needed him for *Disraeli* a great deal more than he needed them, and instead of being just another young Olivier-like screen hopeful he was an elder statesman going out on his own terms to work on a script that was entirely his own preserve, since he had been playing the part on stage and screen already for the best part of twenty years.

Accordingly, Arliss was able to lay down a pattern of old colonel behaviour in 1929 which was to be eagerly imitated in the years ahead by the likes of Cedric Hardwicke and Aubrey Smith. In the first place, he realized that his strength lay in remaining as English and distant as possible from the chaos of a Hollywood studio; by regarding himself as visiting royalty bestowing some immense favour on Warners by allowing them to photograph him in one of his most celebrated roles, he rapidly persuaded the Warners personnel to regard him in that light too. But it was, as Douglas Fairbanks recalled for me, an immensely carefully stage-managed performance both off screen and on:

Arliss was really where the whole Hollywood English thing started; most people in Hollywood referred to him as Sir George, though there was never any real likelihood of a knighthood because his career just hadn't been that distinguished back home or even in New York. But the image was tremendous, and in those days the image was all that mattered. He arrived with his wife Florence Montgomery, who always also played his wife whenever he was being Disraeli, and he always came on the set followed by a valet, who was so faithful to him that whenever Arliss had a sore throat the valet also spoke in a whisper. Then, every day, precisely at four o'clock, no matter what was happening on the set or what scene he was in the middle of, Arliss would tear off his toupee and go home for tea. And this was in the days when we were working six, seven days a week and all the hours God made; but Arliss got away with murder because everyone thought of him as somebody special.

Had *Disraeli* not worked out at the box-office, that immense studio respect for Arliss would doubtless have vanished overnight; as it was, the film rapidly became an enormous artistic and commercial hit, with its star being billed on posters as 'Mr George Arliss', presumably to distinguish him from the usual untitled Hollywood riff-raff then turning up on screens all over the country. The performance won him *Photoplay*'s Gold Medal as well as *Movie Fan*'s nomination as 'The Finest Actor on the Screen'; a movie poll now showed Arliss second only to Chaplin in world screen popularity, well ahead of Garbo, Marie Dressler, Janet Gaynor and such lesser Hollywood English as Colman and Brook. Most important of all, *Disraeli* won Arliss a 1929 Oscar for Best Actor; he was the first British actor to get the statue, and only Laughton and Donat were to be similarly honoured before the Second World War.

By way of reward, Warners now guaranteed Arliss $10,000 a week (a salary only matched by that of Marion Davies) and put him into a succession of other stagey vehicles, many of which Arliss had already tried and tested in the live theatre or on the silent screen ten or fifteen years earlier. For about three years, he could do no wrong whatever he played, from Voltaire to Alexander Hamilton (in his own script); whenever Warners had somebody real and old to be incarnated on screen, then it was Arliss they cast. Occasionally he was allowed to burst forth from the history texts and create some fictional role, though in *The Green Goddess* (1930) it was again one he had been playing on stage for years, that of the evil Rajah: 'At sundown you are to die, not simply but with torture. Personally I regret the course, but what am I before the Gods?'

Arliss repaid Warners' loyalty in the studio as well as at the box-office; his strength was such that he usually had casting approval and in 1932, while warming over another of his silent roles for the microphones (as *The Man Who Played God*), it was he who found Bette Davis at an audition and gave her a start at the studio in a minor role. When Darryl Zanuck left Warners in 1933 he took Arliss with him, and though there were one or two successes still to come, notably *Cardinal Richelieu* and *The House of Rothschild*, his career thereafter went into a steep decline. Nevertheless, Arliss managed to leave Warners in a blaze of suitably historical glory as Voltaire: 'You can burn my body, but never my soul; that is in the keeping of the people of France.'

Richard Griffith later noted that 'Hollywood screen biography consisted chiefly of George Arliss tinkering with the course of history until the mid-1930s. Brought back to the screen by the talkies, he was hailed as a distinguished actor by nice old ladies and other such judges. According to Arliss, Disraeli, Voltaire, Richelieu and even Alexander Hamilton all looked exactly alike, except for details of costume, and all were crafty but benevolent old gentlemen who spent most of their time uniting unhappy young lovers.'

Not every archetypal Englishman was as happy in Hollywood at the beginning of the 1930s as George Arliss. For a start there was P. G. Wodehouse, who in 1929 had managed to land a contract from MGM for six months at $2,000 a week for the writing of screenplays. This was not due to start until the early summer of 1930, but Wodehouse saw no reason not to bite the hand before it had begun to feed him and accordingly published, in the *Saturday Evening Post* of 7 December 1929, a marvellously acid little piece called 'Slaves of Hollywood'; in this, after lamenting the silence of the Algonquin now that all the Broadway writers had gone west, he continued:

With the advent of the talkies, as might have been expected, radical changes have taken place in Hollywood. The manufacture of motion pictures has become an infinitely more complex affair. You know how it was in the old days – informal, casual. Just a lot of great big happy schoolboys getting together for a bit of fun. Ike would have a strip of celluloid, Spike a camera and Mike a friend or two who liked dressing up and having their photographs taken, and with these modest assets they would start the Finer and Supremer Films Corporation DeLuxe and clean up with orgy scenes and licentious clubmen.

For talkies you require much more than that. The old, simple era has passed. You can't just put on a toga, press a button and call the result 'The Grandeur That Was Rome' or 'In the Days of Nero'. An elaborate organization is needed. You have to surround yourself with specialists – one to put in the lisps, another to get the adenoid effects, a third to arrange the catarrh. And above all you must get hold of authors to supply the words. [But] Hollywood is no fit spot for an author. The whole atmosphere there is one of insidious deceit and subterfuge. In Hollywood, nothing is what it affects to be. What looks like a tree is really a slab of wood backed with barrels. What appears on the screen as the towering palace of Haroun-al-Rashid is actually a cardboard model occupying four feet by three of space. The languorous lagoon is a smelly tank with a stage hand named Ed wading about in it in a bathing suit.

Imagine the effect of all this on a sensitive-minded author. Taught at his mother's knee to love the truth, he now finds himself surrounded by people making fortunes by what can only be called chicanery. He begins to wonder whether mother had the right idea. After a month or two of this sort of thing, could you trust an author to count his golf shots correctly or to give his right circulation figures? Answer me that. Or rather don't. It is not necessary.

In the second place, if motion-picture magnates must have authors, they should not keep them in hutches. In every studio in Hollywood there are rows and rows of hutches, each containing an author on a long contract at a weekly salary. You see their anxious little faces peering through the bars. You hear them whining pite- ously to be taken for a walk. And does the heart bleed? You bet it bleeds. A visitor has to be very callous not to be touched by such a spectacle as this. After all, authors are people. They are entitled to life, liberty and the pursuit of happi- ness. It cannot be right to keep them on the chain. ... They tell me there are authors who have been on salary for years at Hollywood without ever having a line of their work used. All they do is attend story conferences. There are other authors on some lots whom nobody has seen for years. It is like the Bastille. They just sit in some hutch away in some corner somewhere and grow grey beards and languish. From time to time somebody renews their contract, and then they are forgotten again.

Nevertheless Wodehouse decided to take up his contract, presumably not least because it was to provide him with such a rich source of anecdote and amusement:

I have been away for a week [he wrote to his friend William Townend on 25 February 1931] at Hearst's ranch. ... It is on the top of a high hill, and just inside the entrance gates is a great pile of stones which, if you ever put them together, would form an old abbey which Hearst bought in France and shipped over and didn't know what to do with so left lying by the wayside. ... Meals are in an enormous room, and are served at a long table, with Hearst sitting in the middle on one side and Marion Davies in the middle on the other. The longer you are there, the further you get from the middle. I sat on Marion's right the first night, then found myself being edged further and further away till I got to the extreme end, when I thought it time to leave. Another day, and I should have been feeding on the floor.

Wodehouse was no less amazed by the working habits of the Hollywood society he had now joined. 'So far', he wrote to another London friend, Denis Mackail, 'I've had eight collaborators. The system is that A gets the original idea, B comes in to work with him on it, C makes the scenario, D does preliminary dialogue, and then they send for me to insert class and what not and then E and F, scenario writers, alter the plot and off we go again. I could have done all my part of it in a morning, but they took it for granted that I should need six weeks.'

Other writers from Britain had begun by now privately to express, like Wodehouse, their amazement at the amount of time and money being wasted around the Hollywood studios; it was, however, Wodehouse alone who, with that innocence which was later to get him into broadcasting from a German radio studio at the beginning of the war, managed to blow the gaffe in public. What happened, as Frances Donaldson reports in her definitive biography, was that on 7 June 1931 the *Los Angeles Times* published an interview with Wodehouse in which he said, among other things:

It dazes me. They [MGM] paid me $2,000 a week – and I cannot see what they engaged me for. They were extremely nice to me, but I feel as if I have cheated them. You see, I understood I was engaged to write stories for the screen. After all, I have twenty novels, a score of successful plays and countless magazine stories to my credit. Yet apparently they had the greatest difficulty in finding anything for me to do. Twice during the year they brought me completed scenarios of other people's stories and asked me to do some dialogue. Fifteen or sixteen people had tinkered with those stories. The dialogue was really quite adequate. All I did was to touch it up here and there. Then they set me to work on a story called 'Rosalie', which was to have some musical numbers. It was a pleasant little thing, and I put in three months on it. When it was finished, they thanked me politely and remarked that as musicals didn't seem to be going so well they guessed they would not use it. That about sums up what I was called upon to do for my $104,000. Isn't it amazing? Personally I received the most courteous treatment, but see what happened to my friend Roland Pertwee at Warner Brothers. He did a story for Marilyn Miller, and they slapped him on the back and said it was great. He returned to the studio the next morning, and was informed by the policeman on the gate that he could not be let in as he was fired. It's so unbelievable, isn't it?

Compared to the goings-on in Hollywood, those dreamed up by Wodehouse for his Blandings novels pale into total normality; but he was not thanked much for putting them on the public record, at least not by those inside the industry or still receiving its handsome weekly cheques. The *New York Herald Tribune*, on the other hand, thought he had performed a considerable service: 'Mr Wodehouse must be among the first to bring it all out into the open, to mention names and firms, and thus assure us of the truth of the astounding legends. He confirms the picture that has been steadily growing – the picture of Hollywood the golden, where "names" are bought to be scrapped, talents are retained to be left unused, hiring [of distinguished authors] is without rhyme and firing without reason. It is indeed amazing . . .'

Yet so seductive was it that within five years Wodehouse himself was back, hired by MGM and set to work yet again on the musical of *Rosalie* which still stubbornly refused to materialize, though this time he did at least get to work also for RKO on a film treatment for Fred Astaire of his old *Damsel in Distress* story. In October 1937 he left Hollywood for good, noting rather sadly: 'My record here is eighteen months with only small bits of pictures to show for it. I would be perfectly happy if I could just be left alone to write stories, as I hate picture work.'

When *A Damsel in Distress* finally opened, Wodehouse was credited with one-third of the non-musical writing; on *Rosalie* he was not credited at all.

12:
Journey's End in Tinsel Town

The lure of Hollywood, or at least of its cash, was still proving strong for others who had been dismissively treated on their first visits there; barely a year after Laurence Olivier had been so summarily despatched from RKO by David Selznick, the latter's brother Myron was on the transatlantic telephone to inform Olivier's London agent that there was something new in the offing.

In the intervening year Olivier had made *A Perfect Understanding* in London, co-starring with Gloria Swanson, and was enjoying a long and successful stage run with Gladys Cooper in a play called *The Rats of Norway* when the suggestion came up that he might like to return to California to co-star with Greta Garbo, no less, in *Queen Christina*. Subsequent cables indicated that this was a firm offer, though the director Rouben Mamoulian later maintained that everything was going to depend on 'whether or not Olivier, once in costume and make-up and in the actual studio, could hold his ground in experience and authority opposite Garbo', who was then, of course, at the very height of her considerable career.

Olivier duly raced back to California as soon as he could escape *The Rats of Norway* but, as he recalls in his autobiography,

realized in the first two weeks with ever-increasing apprehension that I was not by any means making the best of myself; something was stopping me. I was too nervous and scared of my leading lady. I knew I was lightweight for her and nowhere near her stature, and began to feel more and more certain that I was for the chop. I made up my mind that I must make a big effort to get along with her and find some way to get on friendlier terms. Before work had started one morning, I found her sitting on an old chest on the set. I went boldly up to her and said the three or four sentences that I had made up and practised: but no utterance came from her. I began to flounder and grab at anything that came into my head: some sayings of Will Rogers, of Noël – anybody – anything at all, until I came to a wretched end and stopped, pale and panting. After a breathless pause, she slid herself sideways off the chest saying, 'Oh vell, live'sh a pain, anyway.' I knew then that the end was not far off.

And sure enough, next morning, Olivier was sent for by the producer Walter Wanger, who paid him off in full and put him on a boat to Hawaii for a fortnight's vacation with Jill, having first taken the precaution of hiring Miss Garbo's usual co-star, John Gilbert, for the role of Don Antonio. Within another month, Olivier and his wife were back on Broadway rehearsing a new play.

Despite Hollywood's currently insatiable appetite for British writers and actors to give their new talkies a kind of authority and experience, not everyone approved of the two-way transatlantic traffic of the cinema. In February 1930 Sir Alfred Knox, Conservative, rose in the House of Commons to ask whether 'in order to protect the English language as spoken by the people of this country, the government will now take steps to limit the import of American talking films'. He got a dusty answer from the Board of Trade, but three months later a complaint was to be heard from the critic George Jean Nathan in New York of a similarly chauvinist nature.

Mr Nathan was not objecting to any possible corruption of the American language by the large number of English actors now being hired to speak in American films, but, rather more intelligently, to the quality of the actors themselves:

> There are, on the English stage, a number of actors and actresses highly skilled in their art and expert in speech and human in deportment. But for every such one there are a hundred who are caricatures not only of actors, but of human beings and of funnels of English speech, and it is these, unfortunately, who most often come to America ... it is these who, with their accordion-pleated trousers, bib-waistcoats and other such sartorial lampoons, with their affected gait and Bloomsbury version of *savoir faire*, make themselves and their profession ridiculous. They are not Englishmen, but burlesques of Englishmen; they are not actors, but burlesques of actors. There was a time when the inexperience and cheap snobbery of American audiences combined to work for an acceptance of such mountebanks as the real and rather correct thing. But that time is now past. I have seen a number of English actors on the London stage who know their jobs perfectly and who know how to speak their language beautifully. But we do not often see that kind over here. They stay at home and what we get in their stead are a pack of acting pretenders suitable only for the roles of English butlers in American farces.

Nathan was the first (and remained for several years the most vociferous) critic to pinpoint one of the essential problems about the Hollywood

British: they were, by and large, a second-rate lot. Either they were past their often not very great prime, or else they were the ones who had realized that the sudden and drastic improvement in local British acting standards which came about with the generation of Olivier, Richardson, Gielgud and Redgrave was likely to condemn them to minor roles on regional tours, to which they sensibly preferred a wealthier life in the Hollywood sun. The American film industry did not, in the 1930s or ever, decimate British theatrical strength; it merely used up some of its weaker elements.

But, as Cecil Beaton said about Hollywood in an article he wrote for American *Vogue* in 1930 after the first of his many visits there: 'Only seeing is believing ... it is impossible to exaggerate about Hollywood and impossible to burlesque, for it is the craziest place in the whole wide world and far beyond one's wildest flights of imagination in extravagance and extraordinariness.'

Beaton went on to recall a photographer solemnly being assigned by the studio to photograph Ronald Colman's book bill in an attempt to prove that he was 'a truly cultured and literary person'; Mae Murray lecturing on Universal Peace; Hollywood Boulevard being officially re-named Santa Claus Lane for the month of December; Aimée Semple McPherson giving a hundred willing victims 'baptism by total submersion' in a magenta-lit tank; a snack bar called 'The Pig 'n' Whistle Renaissance Restaurant'; Louella Parsons announcing that Bebe Daniels' voice was 'good enough for the Met'; and a monk in a cowl driving a large Cadillac while telling his rosary.

Beaton also had a sharp diarist's eye for the borderlines where the Hollywood dream was already starting to turn into a kind of nightmare; in December 1930, for instance, he is on a visit to the Paramount lot: 'There, suddenly, a rather horrible surprise – of all people I encountered Elsie Janis. A great revue star in London during the 1914 war, she was one of the hottest of my boyhood's enthusiasms ... now she is writing scenarios, looks spinsterish and schoolmistressy, and although she fights gallantly and keeps going, her pithy wit is blunted and she exudes everything that is démodé.'

Beaton finds Garbo, however, in distinctly better form: she arrives one afternoon, unexpectedly, while he is staying with the English director Eddie Goulding, who had just made her *Grand Hotel*:

For years now she had become quite an obsession with me. Her screen image haunted me. I collected her every published photograph and now, in a valiant though doomed attempt to take my own pictures of her, pestered MGM. ... Meanwhile, Miss Shearer was offered on a plate, or Miss Crawford. ... Then I looked out of the window. In the garden below my host and hostess were gossiping. With them was a visitor. Garbo was sitting cross-legged on a garden seat, smoking a cigarette held high in two definite fingers. ... I was overcome with stage fright when the introduction was made, but finding myself confronted by such an understanding smile, something so sympathetic and encouragingly helpful, I was able to continue to breathe ... the situation became even more piquant when the voice showered me with compliments: 'But you're so yorng? How do you stay so yorng? Are you like one of those people that never grow up? And you're so white.'

This first meeting ends with Beaton begging to be allowed to lunch at Garbo's studio the next day: '"No." Surely this cannot be the end? Shall we never meet again? Will we be able to communicate in some way? In desperation I seized hold of a feather duster with a long handle, a curious object that was lying by her side in the big, rather shabby motor car she was driving. "Can I keep this as a memento?" "No." "Then this is goodbye?" "Yes, I'm afraid so. *C'est la vie.*"'

Until the beginning of the 1930s, British contributions to American film-making had always been piecemeal; a single actor or actress or writer or director would arrive in Hollywood from London, sometimes with a contract and more often without, to do more or less whatever they were then told. Even if there had been some sort of discussion before their arrival (usually through a New York 'studio representative') about precisely what picture they were being brought out to make, it was more than likely that the entire plan would anyway have changed in the five days that it took them to get cross-country on the train.

Then came *Journey's End*, the R.C. Sherriff play about life in the trenches during the First World War; Sherriff, at the time a young and obscure insurance agent, had in fact written the play for his local Kingston Rowing Club as a change from their annual concert. They, however, turned it down, as later did countless professional London theatre managements, on the grounds that the play had no leading lady, no love interest, and was anyway about a war now ten years over that everybody wanted to forget.

Apart from Sherriff, the only other man who believed in the play was a young director named James Whale, later to give Hollywood its first film of *Frankenstein*. Whale sent *Journey's End* to Bernard Shaw, who also admired it and encouraged the London Stage Society to risk a single Sunday night performance of it, the one that starred Laurence Olivier. He, however, then went off into *Beau Geste*, and several more months went by before one London manager, Maurice Browne, cautiously agreed to risk a run at the Savoy.

The play lasted in London for six hundred performances, and then repeated its triumph on Broadway; the night after the American reviews appeared, Sherriff found at the theatre a cable from Carl Laemmle inviting him out to Hollywood to write the screenplay of Remarque's novel *All Quiet on the Western Front*, since he seemed so good at that barbed-wire territory.

Sherriff declined, on the grounds that he had already spent quite long enough in America while *Journey's End* was in rehearsal for Broadway and was keen now to get home to mother. He had meanwhile let his own screen rights go, in a muddle of modesty, benevolence and inefficiency, for £2,000 to Gainsborough (a further £13,000 was made out of them by the play's original London and New York producers). It might have been thought that an English studio at last had the property and a tried-and-tested cast with which to storm the American cinemas whose doors had for so long been closed to British films.

In the event, however, the producers Michael Balcon and George Pearson decided that if *Journey's End* were ever to have the chance of being shown as a film in America, then it would have to be made to American standards and in Hollywood; 'nothing', said a contemporary leader in the London *Evening Standard*, 'has been done yet in British studios to inspire the belief that work done there could readily be sold to America'. Balcon did, though, manage to do a deal with the Tiffany Studios whereby Gainsborough would retain absolute control of the production, sending over their own people to supervise it and make sure that the cast remained all-British. In return they were also guaranteed minimum American cinema bookings worth £50,000, the first time any British-originated film had broken into that lucrative market. Thus did the first film package arrive in California from London.

Pearson himself went out to Hollywood from London to oversee the production; the director was again to be James Whale, who, having staged *Journey's End* originally in both London and New York, had already been snapped up by Howard Hughes as an additional dialogue writer on the first 1914–18 war aviation spectacular, *Hell's Angels. Journey's End* was for him the beginning of a long and gothic Hollywood career which included the best of the Boris Karloff horrors and ended some years before a never satisfactorily explained drowning in his own swimming pool in 1957.

To play the lead, Colin Clive was released from the London stage production for a bare eight weeks, which meant that Whale had to shoot fast and theatrically, in a scene-by-scene convention which was later unfavourably compared to *All Quiet on the Western Front* and *The Big Parade*; *Journey's End* was the first of many British imports to be derided by some American filmgoers as nothing more than a 'photographed play', but in laying out the cast list (all bar Clive recruited from the local Hollywood English) George Pearson also managed to lay down the guidelines for dozens if not hundreds of later war films. He wrote later:

Each character had to symbolize a type and a class, instantly recognized and accepted –

Stanhope, a strong man afraid of being afraid, drinking to forget, and only the love of a woman keeping him from giving way to fear.

Osborne, schoolmaster and visionary, reading *Alice in Wonderland* while shells burst outside his dug-out, but when ordered to lead a raid that meant certain death, obeying with calm and a flow of trivial conversation.

Trotter, a Cockney risen from the ranks, who thinks more of the apricots for supper than of saving his life, talks only of his 'missus', his garden at home and the height of his hollyhocks.

Raleigh, straight from his public school, where he had been with Stanhope, whom he hero-worships, arriving to find his god a whisky-sodden churlish brute, but unaware of Stanhope's reason for resentment against him. Raleigh's sister was the girl whom Stanhope loved; it was fear that the boy might write to her of his drunken downfall that had embittered him.

Mason, Cockney servant, his only problem how to keep the taste of onions out of the tea. His one aim to make bully-beef look different.

Hibbert, cowardly, malingering, but eventually proving as brave as any when he conquers his cowardice and faces death.

As that tabulation by Pearson clearly proves, the gift of R.C.Sherriff (later himself to become a prolific and successful Hollywood screenwriter) to the cinema in 1930 was not just one hit play. It was the basis, allowing for regional and annual variations, for almost every army, navy and air force film of the next thirty years. In Britain the Stanhopes were later to be Jack Hawkins and Richard Todd while in America they were to be John Wayne and Rock Hudson, but the essence of the characters remained unaltered on either side of the Atlantic until, with the coming of the 1960s, the whole nature of the war film underwent drastic revision.

Pearson managed to assemble an intriguing Hollywood English cast, few of whom were to do well in films afterwards: Billy Bevan, who played Trotter, was a comedian who had spent ten years with Mack Sennett; Tony Bushell, who played Hibbert, became Olivier's co-producer on *Richard III*; David Manners, who played Raleigh, was a cousin to Lady Diana Cooper; and the man who played the Sergeant-Major, Tom Whiteley, had been the last passenger to escape the *Titanic* alive. By no means all of them were Pearson's first choices, but with *Hell's Angels* already shooting and other studios rushing into a batch of First World War films to keep up with Hughes, British officers and gentlemen in California were at a premium.

Once he had gathered his supporting cast and arranged for Colin Clive's brief visit, Pearson had a chance to look around him at the wonders of Hollywood. He had decided, in the time available, that it would be wisest and most faithful to Sherriff's original intentions if the play were not to be 'opened up' in any way, but shot almost entirely within the confines of a replica of the original stage set. He could not, however, get over the extravagance that appeared to be going on elsewhere:

I visited Cecil B. de Mille in the studios where he had just completed his ambitious film of the tragic Gospel story, *King of Kings*. The whole floor of one huge studio was covered with a plaster contour replica of the barren slopes that led to Calvary ... in another building he showed me a perfect model of some great city centre of our own day, such as Piccadilly or Broadway, complete with tiny human figures, vehicles and street lights. He had intended to use it for a sudden dissolve from the tragic climax of Calvary to this brief glimpse of the modern busy world ... he felt there was some subtle symbolism in that clash of epochs, some disquieting but chastening thought which in his uncertainty he abandoned.

With an eight-week shooting schedule and a modest budget, Pearson and Whale could afford no such luxuries, though Pearson did once manage to lunch at

a queer restaurant shaped like an enormous bowler hat and called The Brown Derby. Despite the Prohibition regulation there seemed to be no difficulty in obtaining alcoholic liquor, the only stipulation being that you placed your drink, if intoxicating, on an under shelf to your table; soft drinks had pride of place on the table top. One other most extraordinary sight amazed me when I spent an evening in Pasadena, that homeground of millionaires, for slowly approaching I saw a complete house resting on a vast wheeled under-carriage as wide as the road, moving towards me. It would eventually be lowered on to a prepared plot awaiting it. We live and learn.

The diminutive British stage comedian Lupino Lane was also then in Hollywood, just coming to the end of a lucrative career in silent two-reelers (somehow his voice never seemed to suit his personality on screen) before returning to a long and happy life around the British vaudeville circuit, leaving his niece Ida Lupino Lane to carry on the family tradition in pictures. He and Victor McLaglen would occasionally arrive in Pearson's hotel room with hampers of port to reassure him that, though thousands of miles from home, he was not without English friends to sustain him as the casting continued : 'British nationality was imperative. No matter the reputation of the actor, the slightest trace of an American accent ruled him out. We had a few sentences that held traps for the unwary, such as, "I can't see why I can't do it," and, "Is there a doctor in the house ?" It was remarkable how that fatal word "doctor" tripped them up ... we tested two hundred applicants to find the five we needed.'

Pearson also needed a writer to convey Sherriff's dialogue faithfully to the screen with the few changes essential for the camera; looking around, his eye fell on Moncure March, who had already done *Hell's Angels* but was still under contract to Howard Hughes. 'Met that fabulous oil magnate in his most unpretentious office,' recalled Pearson, 'and found him helpful and friendly but exceedingly shrewd. He lent us March on a gentleman's agreement.'

Colin Clive, meanwhile, had been briefly released from the Savoy Theatre run in London, hastened aboard the *Homeric* at Southampton and found he had just twenty minutes in New York to get from the dock to Grand Central Station, where the train was departing. He arrived in Los Angeles somewhat breathless, went straight to the studio and did a voice test which sounded to Pearson like 'an inarticulate grumble'. Experts from RCA were called in, microphones were replaced and all went well with the filming itself until they reached the moment in the script where Stanhope has to show a photograph of his sweetheart to Osborne. America would be scoured, said the studio, and the photograph of the most beautiful girl in all the nation thereby obtained regardless of cost. Pearson disagreed.

That face was for Osborne alone to see ; even if Venus herself could be obtained there would still be disappointment in the audience for many. We decided not to show the picture, but to leave it to the imagination. That evening the news had spread, as studio gossip does spread in Hollywood. I was dining in the Embassy restaurant, sitting between Lubitsch and Stroheim, when Lubitsch put an affectionate arm on my shoulder and in a guttural whisper said, 'Good boy ... I like your decision ... it was right.'

Restraint became an early password to British success in Hollywood, even if the most usual emotion of the visitors was deep confusion. Pearson again:

Christmas Day arrived. ... Hollywood was one mad whirlpool of merry-making, banners and balloons, woollen snowmen, a Father Christmas at every street corner, crowded saloons, constant health-drinking punctuated with carol singing, strangers shaking hands with strangers and persistent calls of 'Just one for the road'. My mind flew back to England, my wife and my children, and I longed to be back with them in a saner English Christmas. ... Colin and I had been invited to McLaglen's but in the darkness we lost our Hollywood bearings. ... A brilliantly lit building attracted us. ... A perfect butler opened the door. Colin, who had been a victim of the festivities, was in a deep sleep. The butler said he would fetch his master, an immaculately dressed gentleman of imposing appearance who seemed to be expecting our arrival. He said he was sorry for our sad mission, but that even death can be consoled by reverent obsequies; it was only then that we realized we had struck a Funeral Parlour.

13:
Hollywood Cavalcade

Having survived Christmas and the making of *Journey's End*, Pearson was about to return to London when he and Prime Minister Ramsay MacDonald's son (an architect much interested in the construction of cinemas and then something of a social catch around California because of his parentage) finally got the royal summons from Fairbanks to his own private saloon at the United Artists Studio. What they found there was a table, twenty feet in diameter, entirely covered with every known brand of alcohol from the Poles to the Equator; if by any chance the bottle you desired was too far across the table to reach for easily, then there was an automatic fishing-rod apparatus to haul it across to you. In an alcove there was also an elaborately equipped barber's parlour where you could get an instant shave, haircut or shampoo. Beyond that was a Turkish bath with several white-garbed attendants, where Fairbanks insisted on conducting Pearson, Sam Goldwyn and Joe Schenck for an earnest discussion of films and film-makers. 'I felt', said Pearson, 'that of all my strange experiences in the Hollywood wonderland this was the most incredible.'

He returned, as did Colin Clive, to a London press eager to hear of their pioneering experiences. 'By Jove,' Clive told *The Times*, 'people earn their money out there. Everywhere the English actor and the English voice is wanted, and there is an immense opportunity for us in the new "talkie" field' – a theory proved accurate some months later by a report in the September 1930 issue of a magazine called *Motion Picture Classic*. It was written by Cedric Belfrage, an English actor who after a brief and comparatively unsuccessful Hollywood film career had turned to journalism and was to make a vastly better living reporting on his fellow-countrymen in California.

According to his perhaps exaggerated estimate:

Englishmen are now on Hollywood payrolls to the tune of a round $4 million a year, and that doesn't include Canadian colonials like Mary Pickford. ... Such a mob of Englishmen could hardly be present in any community without having some effect. ... One of the more recent arrivals, Reginald Sharland, is actually trying to start a Hollywood cricket team: he has sent emissaries to England with instructions to bring back with them bats, balls, wickets, stumps, nets, pads, weed-killer and plenty of teacups.

And that fully three months before the arrival of Aubrey Smith.

English clothes were to be seen, reported Belfrage, and English accents heard on almost every Hollywood Boulevard corner:

But the new English spirit is probably most in evidence here at afternoon tennis parties. Grass tennis-courts are becoming increasingly popular. ... The tea habit has even been carried into the innermost shrines of celluloidia – the studios. ... The strange rite was introduced to Hollywood by the *Journey's End* Englishmen and soon other studios were taking to it. Sam Goldwyn now makes tea a regular thing.

Indeed, to the horror of the local press corps, tea was now being served at gatherings known as 'Press Teas', which had in the past for Prohibition reasons always been understood to be an invitation to something rather stronger.

Hollywood's attempts to go British were not being allowed to pass without a certain amount of mockery in the London press; commenting on Jean Harlow's 1930 performance as the supposedly British leading lady of *Hell's Angels*, the film critic of *The Times* noted, 'Though seemingly of North Oxford lineage, Miss Harlow has the costume of a torrid Californian and corresponding propensities; during the aerial climax the producers leave her on earth, and do not bother to revisit.'

But the studio net was by now dragging in all kinds of Englishmen if, thus far, surprisingly few women; some were ambitious young actors determined on a screen career, others were cast more in the Wodehouse mould – eccentrics who regarded a Hollywood invitation as something in the nature of a brief magical mystery tour, a kind of journey into space. One such was George Grossmith, the veteran musical-comedy star and co-author of *Diary of a Nobody*, who in October 1929 happened to be playing in New York and at a Broadway dinner party found himself seated next to the mogul Joseph Schenck; making polite conversation, Grossmith murmured that one day he really would quite like to have a look at California. Three days later he found himself in Schenck's private coach on *The Super Chief*, and a week later he was in Schenck's office at

United Artists. Both men then had to face the fact that Grossmith was now in California with nothing at all to do; he was given a room at the Roosevelt Hotel, which Schenck then owned and where to Grossmith's amazement he found both Fatty Arbuckle and Clara Bow in cabaret. After about three days of wandering around the United Artists lot as a 'privileged visitor', Grossmith drifted off into Los Angeles to deplore the current state of the live theatre there, since 'poorly attended plays only run here for a week or two and actors take part in them at very nominal salaries, hoping picture magnates might come along and single them out for "promotion" to the screen'.

As a live theatre man, Grossmith did not much approve of that, and was about to return to London when a small paragraph in the local paper happened to announce his Hollywood arrival:

After taking a solitary bus-ride to inspect the surrounding countryside I returned to my hotel to find batches of telephoned invitations waiting for me; no one either writes or acknowledges letters in Hollywood, it is all done by means of the telephone or telegram. But here was an invitation to dinner from Ronald Colman, welcomes from Clive Brook and John Barrymore, also an intimation that the great comedian Will Rogers, who is the unofficial Mayor of Los Angeles, would drive me round next morning in his motor.

Desperate as the British community already was for news of home, Grossmith became the celebrity of the month on the dinner-party circuit and was thus not altogether surprised to receive a summons to Paramount to take part in a filmed revue with Maurice Chevalier called *Paramount on Parade*. Grossmith was, however, no fool: 'On the set I met Gary Cooper, Clive Brook and many other of the galaxy of contract stars who were due to take part and I decided there and then that it would be extremely unwise of me, with problematical stage material, to vie with such a host of experience, so I decided to withdraw.'

A day or two later, just as he was once again heading for the New York train, he had a phone call from Twentieth Century-Fox. They were, he was told, then working on a musical called *The Dollar Princess* and someone had told them that, coming from the musical theatre, he might know something about it. Grossmith admitted that he had quite by chance written the London stage version of it twenty years earlier and therefore would be happy to advise, even happier when he discovered that the director was to be Eddie Goulding, to whom Grossmith had given a first job as a chorus boy at the Alhambra. The producer was to be a young Alexander Korda, then on his first Hollywood venture, and Grossmith was duly hired to come up with a screenplay. 'Forget your original script,' he was told, 'and come up with something new; don't bother about the sequence or the continuity, we have people here who do all that, just work out something snappy in short story form. We'd like it to be about flying, and the lead is to be a New York singing star called J. Harold Murray.'

Grossmith refrained from asking why then it still had to be called *The Dollar Princess*, since all plot and character lines were to be abandoned; he was learning fast. 'But I had just completed my script, all about the handsome singing private pilot to a wealthy heiress, when a terrible tragedy happened. Fox were doing another flying picture at the time with Warner Baxter, since pilots were very fashionable, and during the shooting the director and three cameramen were killed in a crash over Santa Monica Bay, so the order came down that there were to be no more flying pictures.'

Grossmith was packing for the third time when a further order came through from Korda that *The Dollar Princess* was now to be made as a Foreign Legion adventure; by this time Grossmith had been offered a six-month contract as a writer, and was soon busily concocting a tale about Moroccan gun-runners only without any songs, as Fox had by now decided they didn't want any more musicals either:

Before going any further [wrote Grossmith in a report home to *The Listener* in August 1931] I think I should give you some idea of what the Fox Studios look like. Fox have two sets of studios, the new studios up at Fox Hills, which cost six million pounds to build and look rather like an Earl's Court Exhibition, and the old studios, where my office was, on Western Avenue. On the one side of the Avenue there are four huge stages which look like Zeppelin hangars or a series of Paddington Stations, the carpenters' shops, repair shops, costume departments and school, where children and the younger dancing girls have to do many hours' work a day. At the other side of the Avenue are the executive buildings, the bungalow offices, the projection rooms, which are like miniature theatres, the make-up department, which resembles the laboratory of a modern hospital, the rehearsal rooms and Writers' Row. This last consists of a beautiful garden kept in perfect order by a Japanese gardener and surrounded by the bungalows of the scenario writers. On the doors of these bungalows one may read the names of some of the greatest authors, writers and dramatists of Europe and America. The garden is crossed by four little streets or paths, each with a signpost. On one of these posts is painted 'Broadway', on another 'Piccadilly', on the third 'Rue de la Paix' and on the fourth 'Unter den Linden'. Here the writers sit, day after day, when they are not in conference evolving their stories and treatment. The first thing a successful writer learns is to lose any self-conceit as to his abnormal abilities. When William Shakespeare, sitting in Bungalow No. 1, has sent in his story to the supervisor, the latter, if not immediately satisfied – a very, very rare occurrence – will pass it on to Ibsen in Bungalow No. 2 or Maeterlinck in Bungalow No. 6 for treatment, and if this be not satisfactory it may yet be submitted for further treatment to a budding Bernard Shaw at the other end of the grounds. When a final treatment is decided on, then the wisecracking department may be called on to distribute a few funny lines, and the composers who congregate in another part of the studio set to work in competition to supply one or two 'hit' numbers. Having no undue pride nor too much self-assurance, I managed to fit myself in with this scheme of things and spend some happy months under the Fox banner.

According to this elaborate process, Grossmith's original *Dollar Princess* musical comedy had now become a Casablanca drama called *Women Everywhere* and starring Fifi d'Orsay; Korda himself was by now directing, with Grossmith in a supporting role and, among the extras, 'one thousand Arabs and two waiters, one in real life a nephew of the Kaiser and the other a cousin of the Czar; there was also a costume designer who was an ex-German naval officer and had been in command of the *Emden* during the War. This is Hollywood.'

By now, to his amazement, Grossmith was something of a fixture at Fox:

Before we had finished shooting *Women Everywhere* I was sent for by a Mr Sol Wurtzel, who was the head of the Fox Studios. He informed me that an English stage actress, as he called her, named Beatrice Lillie had been engaged by their New York office to make a picture. She was arriving in six weeks' time and they had nothing ready for her. He had never seen the lady himself, but understood that her line was revue and thought I might be the right man to write something 'typically English' for her.

Here was my opportunity for a little British propaganda. For years the Americans had been flooding England with their pictures and had also been giving the British public, already a little depressed with home conditions, a sometimes exaggerated view of American prosperity. Now, I thought, we'll show them what London is like. We'll let them have a glimpse of the incomparable English countryside, the City on a busy morning, Bond Street in the afternoon, Epsom, Lord's, Brighton, Cowes and a fashionable nightclub.

Accordingly, Grossmith started to work out a thriller which would have Bea Lillie cast as the charlady to Edgar Wallace who comes across some clues and sets up as a private detective on her own and saves the

British nation from betrayal before marrying the Prime Minister. 'Proudly', recalled Grossmith, 'I took it to Mr Sol Wurtzel, whose verdict consisted of one sentence, a pet studio phrase of the time: "It don't mean a thing." Consequently my story was sent in to the bungalow of a Czechoslovakian journalist for further treatment.' The result of this apparently didn't mean a thing either, though Miss Lillie did eventually make a Fox film called *Service For Ladies* in which she played a detective.

Grossmith was cast in that, too, as a master of foxhounds, and spent several days on a ranch in ninety-degree heat recreating a complete English hunt with the help of an expert huntsman who had been brought in for the occasion from Leicestershire. By then, however, his Fox contract was drawing to a close and there was the chance of some 'real' work back on Broadway:

I began to feel quite sad, though, at the thought of leaving Hollywood. Nowhere in the world is there such a perfect climate. It rains hard for a week or two after Christmas and then there is not another spot until the end of the year; there is always a blazing sun and a pleasant breeze, and the nights are just cool enough to sleep under a blanket. In twenty minutes or so one can run down to Santa Monica beach and lie basking among the penguins or call on any of one's friends, nearly all of whom have marvellous swimming pools in the back garden. People drive along the roads in bathing costumes, and what roads – twenty or thirty or forty miles long, with room for a dozen vehicles abreast, and there is one car to every two-and-a-half people! So enormous is the real estate business in California that these roads are laid out, and smaller ones cut in the mountains, replete with lamp posts and flanked with marked-out plots, with the almost absolute certainty that in a month or two homes will be built there for the ever-increasing number of immigrants. I shall always look back with pleasure on the happy days I spent with Fox; though at first there was no one there who had ever heard of me, and I was regularly called either Goldspink or Goostooth, by the end I had become GG to all, and I don't suppose my humble rivalry ever disturbed Greta Garbo. Others were treated more luxuriously – for John McCormack the studio prepared a replica of an entire Irish cottage standing in its own little hedged garden in which native trees from Ireland had been transplanted – but few can have been happier, and an excellent lunch was always available in the studio canteen for as little as two shillings.

Other writers were also now beginning to make the journey from the West End of London to Hollywood, bringing or sending back reports much like those of the early visitors to Disneyland thirty years later and couched in a similar mixture of mockery and bemused delight; Frederick Lonsdale had now joined Wodehouse and Grossmith in the writers' block (a phrase that was often all too apt), while Jack Buchanan was making early Jeanette MacDonald musicals for Ernst Lubitsch; Leslie Howard and Basil Rathbone had joined Colman and Denny and McLaglen and Chaplin and Laurel among the highest-paid stars of the day, many of them now earning well over $1,000 a week on year-round contracts. Some mornings the unwary walker down Sunset Boulevard (there were, in those days, still one or two) must have thought he was on Shaftesbury Avenue instead. 'The trouble with America now', as Lonsdale told a California journalist unwary enough in 1928 to ask him how he was enjoying his first Hollywood writing assignment, 'is that it seems to be losing much of its distance.'

Lonsdale was, in fact, to be the despair of more than one Hollywood studio; after the success of the first 1929 film version of his *Last of Mrs Cheyney* (with Norma Shearer in a title role later to be played in Hollywood remakes by both Joan Crawford and Greer Garson) he agreed to return for $75,000 to work on a yet undecided project. Setting sail from Southampton aboard the *Mauretania*, he got off at the first stop, which happened to be Cherbourg. 'Consenting to go back to Hollywood was an act of cowardice,' he explained to reporters back in Southampton, 'my sudden decision to return home instead the bravest of my life. I was going to Hollywood to make money; I came home to find peace.' His daughter and biographer, however, took the view that he had merely been bored at the prospect of yet another Atlantic crossing.

In 1930 Lonsdale did go back, to write for Ronald Colman and Loretta Young an immensely successful comedy called *The Devil to Pay*, which was generally credited with being the most literate and witty in the few short years since the movies had found a voice. It was also the first to give London theatre managers any feeling that they ought perhaps to be nervous of competition from the new medium. While in California, Lonsdale also wrote a lesser screen comedy called *Lovers Courageous*, but once again returned rapidly to London: 'I could never live in a film city,' he explained, 'because there is no conversation.'

Others were apparently prepared to overlook that drawback, and already among the older and more established Hollywood British residents there was a faint feeling that there was altogether too much mockery going on. Many had now settled there permanently, and were eager that their fellow countrymen should not harm their local standing by either misbehaving in the nightclubs or arriving in numbers so great as to threaten their rarity value.

Long before Aubrey Smith, it was George Arliss who became the first spokesman for the more elderly Hollywood British; his screen roles as statesmen and other historical heroes seemed to cast him naturally for this role too, and as early as July 1931, while back in London on holiday, Arliss was already taking to the BBC airwaves to defend his new-found gold mine, and asking indignantly:

What is the meaning of all this raising of eyebrows and shrugging of shoulders when Hollywood is mentioned? What is the matter with Hollywood? Is it the place? Is it the people? Or is it the pictures? My contention is that if the picture business were really in the hands of ignoramuses, motion pictures would have ceased to exist long ago. It is useless to argue that all the brains are in Wall Street ... there are now 30,000 actors and actresses in Hollywood and every one of them is potential copy for the newspapers. To keep out of print you not only have to be respectable but lucky. And as for scripts, ten have to be turned out each week to meet the demand of the public ... the marvel is that the level of bad pictures is not lower than it is. .... I wish some honest person would come out to Hollywood and write about it; somebody who hasn't anything to sell, or who doesn't want to find a job for a daughter or niece. In short somebody who hasn't an axe to grind, so the public shall no longer be fed on imaginary evils but shall be told the truth about Hollywood.

It was left to the *New York Times*, in an editorial, to reply to Arliss:

Hollywood's morals and manners, its slipshod business methods, its lack of intelligence and taste have been so completely described by returned visitors that one New York playwright was able to make a fortune out of a Hollywood drama without ever having set foot in the place. The East is convinced of the truth of this picture. 'Is it reasonable to suppose that such a trade can be made and maintained by a lot of brainless idiots?' inquires Mr Arliss. New York is likely to respond with laughter and a loud 'Yes'. Mr Arliss wishes 'some honest person' would visit Hollywood and write about it. If such an individual ever does, he will have to consider the sedate inhabitants, but he can not safely overlook the flashing temperaments and unconventional morals – not if he wants a paying lot of readers.

So by the beginning of the 1930s, battle lines were already drawn between those Hollywood insiders craving respectability and those on the outside still determined to mock them on every possible occasion; where the British stood in this battle was usually well to the side. Most of them were too intelligent not to recognize a certain truth in many of the press complaints now coming almost daily from New York and London about the higher lunacies of movie-making; on the other hand, they saw no reason why they should be asked to join in rocking the boat in which many of them were now sitting very comfortably. 'Going home' was a concept known only to the short-stay contract people; men like Colman and Denny and Arliss had long since given up any thought or chance of an equivalent career back in England and were Americans in all but passport.

And the British still had a lot to offer Hollywood: having already supplied, with *Journey's End*, the basic character outlines for another hundred war movies, they now, with Coward's *Cavalcade* and *Clive of India*, began to realize the celluloid visions of Victorian London and Empire that were to form two more of the great American film genres from 1930 well into the Second World War.

Though written and originally directed as a stage epic at Drury Lane by a man who had already decided that Hollywood had nothing to offer him personally, it was obvious soon after the opening of *Cavalcade* in London in October 1931 that here was something the cinema would have to come to terms with sooner or later. Inspired by Nöel's glimpse of an old *Illustrated London News* photograph of a troopship sailing for the Boer War, *Cavalcade* was a grandiose show in three acts and twenty-two scenes that was to cost an unprecedented pre-war sum of £30,000 and to keep a cast and backstage crew of nearly four hundred people employed at Drury Lane for more than a year, playing to a total box-office take of around £300,000.

Its plot concerned the Marryot family and their below-stairs servants (characters who were indeed to be strongly echoed in a television series called *Upstairs, Downstairs* more than forty years later) living through the thirty years from January 1900; stage scenes were to include not only entire railway trains leaving for the First World War but the sinking of the *Titanic*, the sighting of the first cross-Channel aeroplane and the coming of the Jazz Age. Though some characters died premature deaths in action, and some ran privately to seed, these two families of masters and servants were to state something Coward felt very deeply about the nature of the British, their continuity of personality and their tight-lipped sense of decency and fair play. The Marryots were the quintessential English ladies and gentlemen, and their adventures through thirty years of eventful British home and colonial history must have seemed the answer to a Hollywood studio's dream.

Within very few weeks of the opening night, Fox (having rapidly bought the screen rights from Coward and his producer Charles Cochran, who had already decided that it would be economically impossible to do

Cavalcade in America except as a film) despatched one of their dialogue directors, George Hadden, to London. His mission was twofold. First, he was to sign up as many of the original cast as possible for the film (this proved possible for only three players, the rest having all signed year-long contracts at the Lane) and second, he was to arrange for a silent film of the stage production to be made from the back of the stalls so that Hollywood art directors would have some notion of what *Cavalcade* was supposed to look like.

As Nora Laing reported from Hollywood in November 1932, casting was not a problem:

From every dominion, crown colony and protectorate they come to the Fox Studios – South Africans, Australians, New Zealanders, even Egyptians and West and East Indians swarm outside the studio gates trying to crash in and land a part in this great English story. The fortunate few who have been granted an interview sit patiently in the casting office beneath lithographs of Queen Victoria, King Edward, the Prince Consort and Kitchener, all bought by Mr Hadden on his recent trip to London. ... In his office now the English accent is as pronounced as at an Eton and Harrow match. All types are represented: shy little Cornish girls, ex-servicemen with a Lancashire dialect, burly Yorkshire farmers, Cockneys with their shrill, sharp banter, distinguished old men with an atmosphere of Debrett surounding them, elderly spinsters from God knows where and a sprinkling of mothers with children. Many of these children have already lost their English accents; others left England before they had cut their first teeth and have never had an accent to shed; but all of them have been carefully coached to speak with a broad 'a' for this momentous occasion and entreated solemnly to bury their Americanisms. One mother nearly wept when her small son, in answer to the director's 'Well, my boy, feeling well this morning?', absently relapsed into the vernacular and responded cordially, 'You bet; fine and dandy.' Needless to add he failed to land a part.

Canadians who had left Toronto or Montreal before they were able to lisp and had long since been American citizens suddenly remembered their British heritage and arrived in droves, carrying crumpled, mildewed birth certificates. Even an Egyptian with a name that sounded like Achmed Abdullah claimed himself English by right of being a loyal subject of King George. And all had come because of the news that there would be 140 speaking parts and 15,000 extras in *Cavalcade*.

The star was to be one of the local Hollywood English, Clive Brook, who had already proved himself a stalwart of the Empire on screen by playing Captain Durrance in the 1929 *Four Feathers* and the British officer who falls in stiff-upper-lipped love with Marlene Dietrich aboard the *Shanghai Express*. Alongside Herbert Marshall, and second only to Colman and Niven, Brook was to remain one of the pillars of the British community in the Hollywood 1930s and it was *Cavalcade* which gave him much of his credibility. Opposite him, the director Frank Lloyd (himself a Welshman born in Scotland) cast Diana Wynyard, one of the first of the Hollywood English leading ladies but, like so many of them during the 1930s, only out there to give that one performance, for the British Empire, even on film, was a male-dominated world where few women could make a decent living.

Though its original London first night had virtually coincided with Britain's departure from the Gold Standard and the coming of a National Government, because *Cavalcade* was retrospective it per-fectly summarized everything that Hollywood and America seemed to want to know about England: Trafalgar Square, St Paul's, the East End and the seaside holiday were all faithfully recreated, and, as the *Observer* noted of the film, 'though it avoids any really controversial issues, it is so close to the emotional memories of every British man and woman that it must sweep audiences off its feet wherever it is shown'. But *Cavalcade* was also about the death of the old England, with Queen Victoria, and the coming of the new, and in that transition lay its fascination for American audiences, who had only ever known the new; in Coward's final toast there lay something very close to the heart of any American with even the faintest of ties to the mother country:

Let's drink to the future of England. Let us couple the future of England with the past of England. The glories and victories and triumphs that are over, and the sorrows that are over too. Let's drink to our sons who made part of the pattern, and to our hearts that died with them. Let's drink to the spirit of gallantry and courage that made a strange heaven out of unbelievable hell, and let's drink to the hope that one day this country of ours, which we love so much, will find Dignity and Greatness and Peace again.

A toast, incidentally, still so central to the belief in a Great Britain that it was quoted at some length (though not attributed to Coward) by Mrs Thatcher in a television address the night before her election as Prime Minister in 1979.

Here, as in *Journey's End*, one or two critics were to point to an almost defiant 'staginess', a refusal to cover up or open out the play's original theatrical framework; but that, too, was part of the stock-in-trade of the Hollywood British: not for them the camera tricks of a new and all-too-mechanized world.

A decade later, *Cavalcade* was to be seen as a direct forerunner of *Mrs Miniver*; for now, it introduced Frank Lawton to American audiences in one of the doomed-but-clean-limbed roles that he was to make his own, and it temporarily solved much of the expatriate unemployment around Los Angeles. No expense was spared on the production: a budget of £200,000 was allocated (ten times what Fox had paid Coward and Cochran for the rights) and it was proudly announced that to do the 'screenplay' (largely a matter of cutting up Coward's dialogue into shot sequences) Reginald Berkeley was being brought over specially from London. Mr Berkeley, it was quickly added, was not only a successful London playwright and Liberal MP 'but also winner of the Military Cross during the War'. Miss Wynyard used her Hollywood time most brilliantly, managing also to land the role of the Grand Duchess in the three-Barrymore *Rasputin*, which was in production at a rival studio; the vaudeville comedian Dick Henderson, who was also in California at the time, got his young son Dickie well cast as one of the children in *Cavalcade*.

The result was not only a film which managed to satisfy even English demands for period accuracy (something no other Hollywood-made film had yet achieved) but also one which was to win Frank Lloyd an Oscar in 1933 for best director as well as itself another for best film. No other English subject was to be similarly Oscared until *Mrs Miniver* in 1942, though the 1950s and 1960s were to bring no less than six more Oscars to 'best films' of British origin. Sad to relate, however, critical and Academy enthusiasm was not enough; along with *The Informer*, it was one of those rare Oscar-winners to do badly at the box-office. Asked to explain this, de Mille said succinctly, 'The public does not want literate pictures.'

14:
Campbell in the Soup

For every British actor who succeeded in Hollywood, there were probably a dozen who failed abysmally. Some returned rapidly to the reps and regional tours of the English theatre that they should never have left; others settled for the sunshine and became extras or chauffeurs or barmen, able always to command a few dollars or at least a free bourbon on the strength of some good anecdotes and a still-unusual accent.

Few, however, failed quite as spectacularly in Hollywood as Mrs Patrick Campbell. The legendary creator of Eliza Doolittle in Shaw's *Pygmalion* was sixty-five when, in 1930, she decided to revive her flagging career with a visit to California. By this time she was already, in Alexander Woollcott's celebrated phrase, 'like a sinking ship firing on all rescuers'; she had been totally cut from the British screen version of Michael Arlen's *Green Hat*, but was determined that her perennial financial problems could be solved were she to set up as a *grande dame* on film. The problem was that, although she had a large and loyal band of followers, ranging from Bernard Shaw to John Gielgud, few of them were in California to explain to others the greatness and the eccentricity of this hugely theatrical lady.

Those few who did know her from Broadway, such as Cedric Hardwicke, maintained a kind of irritable respect:

> Of all the women on the MGM lot, the temporary dowager queen was Mrs Campbell, who arrived to make a picture during my days there. The crew and cast were instructed to be most respectful and considerate towards this indomitable veteran, whose manner grew more regal as her memory faltered. .... At the close of one day's shooting, Mrs Pat was no closer to remembering her words than at eight o'clock that morning. She had wearied of it all, too. 'What's the time, dear?' she asked brightly. 'Five o'clock.' 'No, in London, dear.' 'It's eight hours ahead there. That would make it one in the morning.' 'As late as that?' said Mrs Pat, registering dismay. 'No wonder I'm so tired.'

But at least Hardwicke knew who she was and what she had stood for in the history of the British and American theatre; others in Hollywood, less involved with live drama, thought her at best a mad and at worst a very rude old lady, an impression that Mrs Campbell took some pains to foster. Meeting a handsome young movie star at a party, she told him that he was good-looking enough to go into pictures. 'But', spluttered the young star, 'my name, Mrs Campbell, is Joseph Schildkraut.' 'Never mind about that, dear,' came the reply, 'you can always change it.'

When Irving Thalberg, thinking like so many others to do her a bit of good, put her into *Riptide* with an all-star cast including his wife Norma Shearer and Herbert Marshall, he was rewarded by hearing Mrs Pat say in a stentorian voice on the set: 'Look at that Shearer person. Her eyes are so far apart you'd have to get a taxi between them.'

Living at the all too aptly named Sunset Tower, Mrs Campbell managed to do less than twelve weeks' work in sixteen Hollywood months, most of it scrappy and undistinguished; she did, however, also manage to cling on to her beloved dog, Moonbeam ('What's it called?' enquired one electrician from the studio gantry. Mrs Campbell looked up imperiously: 'Tittiebottles, of course. What's yours?') and to deliver the occasional stinging blow. 'You're such a pretty little thing,' she is reputed to have told Joan Crawford, 'why don't you go into motion pictures?'

As an object lesson in how to lose friends in Hollywood, Mrs Campbell's film career was a textbook case; after a while even she recognized that she had gone too far and, after giving one indignant interview to the *Los Angeles Times* ('I don't mind going home and saying I wasn't wanted in Hollywood, but I do mind going home and saying they didn't realize the quality and value of my work and gave me no real opportunity of showing it'), she retreated to a log cabin in the hills, there to work ineffectually on her memoirs and note that 'the lumberjacks around here are more wonderful than movie stars and a lot better looking'.

Sadly, even Josef von Sternberg managed to get little out of her beyond a close-up of what she now always described as 'my ruined face'; casting her as the pawnbroker in *Crime and Punishment* he was appalled to note that 'she has read neither the book nor the script'; when told what she would be playing, Mrs Campbell sharply informed the great German director, 'I cannot possibly become a tradesperson.' Mrs Campbell did, however, find a few admirers in Hollywood, notably

Lillian Hellman (then an MGM screenwriter), who once lent her $400 to buy a dress and was promised in return, but never received, 'several letters from Bernard Shaw'.

It was to Shaw that Mrs Campbell wrote, indignantly, of her Hollywood treatment: 'The studios say I am too celebrated for small parts, and too English to star – that Kalamazoo and Butte, Montana, and Seattle would not understand my English style and speech. Whenever I ring up my agents they answer "MGM is thinking of you but nothing suitable has come along".'

Shaw advised a return to the theatre and home, advice Mrs Campbell eventually took at the end of 1935. Sadly, her greatest contribution to Hollywood was one that she may well never have known about. In George Cukor's 1933 *Dinner at Eight*, the dowager played by Marie Dressler was closely modelled on Mrs Pat and had many of the best lines: 'I'll have my double chins in private,' she tells Lionel Barrymore when there are suggestions of a comeback, and when Jean Harlow as the mistress worries that 'machinery is going to take the place of every profession', the Campbell–Dressler character replies, 'Oh, my dear, that's something you need never worry about.'

Mrs Campbell had never much cared for America, least of all for the American devotion to babies; at one gathering of Californian mothers who were admiring some children, Mrs Campbell remarked on how much one of them reminded her of her own little darling back home. 'And how old is your own little darling?' asked one of the mothers. 'Sixty-two,' replied Mrs Campbell, and left.

Her failure to come to any sort of terms with California, or perhaps just MGM's failure to come to terms with her wonderfully stagey presence, coincided with a sudden cooling of interest in the English generally. While, in London, Michael Balcon was announcing elaborate plans for star-lending agreements whereby MGM contract artists would be loaned out to Gaumont-British when not required in California, in America itself there was a sudden end to the Anglophilia which had peaked around 1930. Three short years later Pickfair was already up for sale, the Fairbanks–Pickford marriage deeply cracked, and the memory long gone of halcyon late-1920s summers when the guest-list there had included the Mountbattens, the Sutherlands and for one spectacular weekend the future Duke of Kent, on leave from the navy, who was taught by Fairbanks how to dive like a stunt-man through sugar-pane windows. When the *New York Times* broke the story of his imminent divorce, Fairbanks was pictured on the golf course at Sunningdale with both Prince George and the future Edward VIII: one royal family had evidently recognized another.

But now, audible murmurs of discontent could be heard about Hollywood's apparent obsession with all things English; in April 1933 it was announced that Mr Garsson, a special Assistant Secretary of Labor, had been deputed by Washington to 'investigate' (a word that did not yet carry its awful McCarthy overtones) all foreign players in the film capital and see how many of them had visas and work permits that were in order. The problem did not, of course, solely relate to the British: 'Like schoolboys', wrote one indignant American journalist, 'we have listened at the feet of fabled foreigners while they told us how to run our own business. We harkened to the sacred pronunciamento of Bernard Shaw, who said with a Shavian sneer, "No American director should be permitted to make a moving picture until he has served apprenticeship to some of the German or Scandinavian masters of this trade." So we took Shaw's advice and imported a flock of Germans and Scandinavians and Russians.' Most of them, it now transpired, had entered America on six-month visitors' visas which they would periodically renew simply by crossing the border into Mexico, attending a race meeting at Agua Caliente, and then returning through the US border post for a new stamp. This, said Washington, now had to stop, though the Labor Secretary sent out west to clean up the illegal immigrants was quick to explain that he wasn't going out after the big names:

> We do not object to the bringing of a player like Maurice Chevalier here to do a part no one else could play; we also love George Arliss, who's in a class by himself and takes no work away from anyone; and we have room for a Ronald Colman or a Clive Brook. But we do object to hordes of players coming out here and settling, many of them illegally, and while claiming allegiance to another flag taking the work which is so badly needed by our own players.

Mr Garsson also noted that he had heard alarming rumours about 'certain native Americans who are now posing as foreign aristocrats in the hope of getting a better chance in pictures'; quite who these were he could not, alas, reveal but the heat was now definitely on. One magazine did a head-count of leading British players then in Hollywood and came up with Arliss, Chaplin, Brook, Wynyard, Lawton (the latter three all, of course, leading players in *Cavalcade*), Colman and Colin Clive, which did not seem an unduly huge number. Both Stan Laurel and Victor McLaglen were apparently by now regarded as all-American, and when Garsson needed a test-case to prove that he was in fact doing something to root out the foreigners, all he could come up with was an unfortunate Australian writer, John Farrow, who was picked up in a nightclub for not having a work permit and sent smartly back to Melbourne. Honour thus satisfied, Mr Garsson went back to Washington and things reverted to whatever in Hollywood then passed for normal. Mr Farrow, incidentally, returned to Hollywood three years later, became a prolific director, married Maureen O'Sullivan and fathered Mia.

Distinguished guests were being made extremely welcome, however, especially if they had no intention of either staying or working, and though Pickfair had gone up for sale there was still the Hearst castle at San Simeon, which was where Bernard Shaw and Winston Churchill both stayed during brief Hollywood visits in the early 1930s. Marion Davies kept careful notes of their behaviour in her guest book: Churchill she found 'a very good guest because he had so many things to do that he didn't become a nuisance at all; he liked his Scotch and his cigars, and they were what kept him alive'. Shaw she found altogether more trouble:

He had that caustic Irish wit which is very detestable and he kept saying that Hollywood would never last because it was all so phony. Also he never seemed to know who anyone was; when John Barrymore asked him for an autograph for his little son, Shaw refused, saying that the boy was far too young to appreciate it, and when Ann Harding told him that she had been in his *Androcles and the Lion* he said, 'Then it must have been a pirated version.' He was very rude to everybody at the studio, but up at San Simeon, when we got him to sit by the fire surrounded by a lot of pretty young girls, then he seemed much happier.

Others were making rather more of a home for themselves in the studios; *Photoplay* for April 1933 reported the progress of

a gentleman, Sir Gerald Grove Bart (meaning Baronet), whose sole business it is to dash about from one studio to another to correct mistakes on the set. He sees to it that an English hostess in the tropics never commits the unpardonable *faux pas* of asking the plantation overseer in for a cup of afternoon tea when what she really means is tiffin. ... Then there's a lady who does much the same thing. It's whispered she was once a Keeper of Queen Mary's Robes in London. Now she watches with a hawk's eye such details as the setting of a dinner table and the correct use of forks.

The Hollywood British off the set: ABOVE LEFT Ronald Colman; C. Aubrey Smith; BELOW LEFT
Leslie Howard with the polo player T. Bodley; and RIGHT a nine-year-old Elizabeth Taylor.

The Hollywood British on the set: ABOVE Leslie Howard and strongly British supporting cast in the 1936 *Romeo and Juliet*; BELOW David Niven as a 1939 *Raffles*, and Basil Rathbone as the admirable British colonial administrator in *The Sun Never Sets*, also 1939.

Party time: ABOVE George Bernard Shaw lunching with Marion Davies and friends including Louis B. Mayer, Clark Gable and George Hearst at her bungalow in 1933; BELOW a costume ball given in 1929 by Mrs Basil Rathbone. Among those present, Theda Bara, Jack Benny, Herbert Marshall and H. B. Walthall. Basil Rathbone is at centre, having presumably just seen the bill.

The Californian life of an English country gentleman: ABOVE Clive Brook at his desk, and BELOW Cary Grant at his piano.

CARY GRANT
in Paramount Pictures

Two of the greatest and most romantic screen achievements of the Hollywood British:
ABOVE Ronald Colman and Madeleine Carroll in the 1937 *Prisoner of Zenda*, and
BELOW Laurence Olivier and Merle Oberon in the 1939 *Wuthering Heights*.

ABOVE Alfred Hitchcock on the set of his first Hollywood film, *Rebecca*, which starred Laurence Olivier and Joan Fontaine, 1939.

BELOW Basil Rathbone and Nigel Bruce as the definitive Sherlock Holmes and Dr Watson in a wartime series of twelve Hollywood British mysteries.

English nannies and their charges in wartime Hollywood: Anna Lee (*standing centre*) is surrounded by the offspring of Herbert Marshall, Victor Saville, Robert Stevenson and John Loder.
BELOW *Forever and a Day*, made in 1943 by the British in Hollywood to aid war charities: (*left to right*) Ian Hunter, Montagu Love, guest star Buster Keaton, Cedric Hardwicke, Charles Laughton and Jessie Matthews.

ABOVE Sir John Gielgud in Tony Richardson's screen version of Evelyn Waugh's Hollywood satire *The Loved One*.

Perhaps the last great gathering of the Hollywood British: Jeremy Brett, Audrey Hepburn, Rex Harrison and Wilfrid Hyde White in the 1964 *My Fair Lady*.

Wondering how to explain the continuing popularity of British actors on the Hollywood screen, another magazine of the time went to interview a comparative newcomer to the ranks, Leslie Howard:

It all seems to me to go back to the fundamental difference between English and American actors. For instance, my friends in New York seemed to consider an acting chap not exactly a red-blooded he-man and certainly not a gentleman. In England, on the other hand, acting is an honourable profession. A gentleman's job as well as a man's job. The type of Englishman who takes up acting as his life's work is most often like the kind of American chap who goes in for banking or the law.

Perhaps because of his Hungarian parentage (he was English only by an accident of birthplace) Howard brought to the Hollywood gentlemen-acting colony an altogether new dimension; he was neither a distinguished old buffer like Arliss, nor a moustachioed romantic like Colman, nor a clean-limbed officer like Clive Brook, nor a character man like Claude Rains or Herbert Marshall, nor a villain like Basil Rathbone or Boris Karloff. Instead, Leslie Howard was visibly a poet and a dreamer, perfectly typecast in his first Warner Brothers film *Outward Bound* (1930) as a man already beyond the grave and belonging therefore to some other world.

Despite that initial success, Howard was to remain so apparently ineffectual in Hollywood that, when summoned a year or so later to San Simeon to rehearse in her private theatre with Marion Davies for their forthcoming *Five and Ten*, both she and the director Bob Leonard had to ask the butler to point out Leslie to them when he was already standing in the, admittedly gigantic, hall. 'He had to stand on a little platform for the love scenes,' recalled Miss Davies, 'and he had a wife who was very fat and fortyish and used to treat him like a little boy and stop him going in our pool in case he caught a cold. I think he found her rather a handicap at parties.'

In fact, Howard was deeply bored by the grandeur of San Simeon ('I am sure', he told his wife, 'there are many dukes in England who have never seen such awe and respect as that with which Mr Hearst and Miss Davies are treated by their gigantic staff') and was himself a creature of considerable intelligence and wit who took refuge from the higher lunacies of the film world behind an absent-minded donnish façade: 'Even stage actors get rather odd out here,' he told his daughter after an evening spent with John Barrymore and his new wife Dolores

Costello in a house full of tame parakeets and monkeys. 'How can John stand having all those monkeys clambering over him when he's got Dolores to do that?'

Howard took the view that no performer who was not either a romantic young girl or a vain half-wit could conceivably derive any pleasure from performing to microphones and cameras instead of to real people, and whenever possible he would return to the New York or London stage; but as the Hollywood money grew increasingly hard to resist through the 1930s, Howard took refuge in writing for *The New Yorker* and *Vanity Fair* a series of increasingly acid 'trivial fond records'. One of these, in fact, pre-dated his first Hollywood film; written for *The New Yorker* in 1927 and entitled *Holy Hollywood*, it was a reaction to the publicity then surrounding the first of Cecil B. de Mille's many biblical epics:

Mr de Mille, we read in the public prints, has delivered an edict to the effect that all actors employed by him must lead moral lives and that all future con-tracts with him will contain a guarantee by the actor to live a pure and holy life. Imagine the cumulative effect of this in a few years' time. The movie actor of the future will pause before the commission of any act which might be construed as improper in any way, and will consult with his conscience or his lawyer as to whether such an act might constitute a breach of contract. Gradually the desire to do wrong will depart from him through natural atrophy, and he will really become a holy person of whom any nice girl could say reverently, 'He's a movie actor, Mother,' just as she said in the old days, 'He's a minister, Mamma.' There will be no more of those wild Hollywood parties. The ghastly spectre of Breach of Con-tract will have turned them into prayer meetings. Divorce will become unknown, the horror of infidelity will be banished forever, and the sanctity of the moving-picture home will prove a model for all good families. Even marriage, among the stricter members of the sect, may be shunned in favour of a life of celibacy. Thus will the new religion arise to which the whole weary world will look – its high priests the great stars and directors, its acolytes chosen from the lesser fry of supers, continuity writers and cameramen. Hollywood will be its Mecca and Holy City. The Papal authority will be vested in one great leader, possibly Mr de Mille himself, and a number of Archbishops will be created from such prominent members as Harold Lloyd, W.S. Hart, John Gilbert, Harry Langdon, Douglas Fairbanks, Chester Conklin and others, while Messrs Lasky, Zukor, Goldwyn, Fox and Schenck will be made honorary Bishops. It is more difficult to foresee what part will be played by the ladies in this new Cinema Faith. It may possibly be decided that since women are usually the cause of all the trouble, they may only be lay worshippers until they really reach a state of grace. But should they be formed into a Sisterhood of Mercy, it seems certain that Miss Mary Pickford will be at their head, while as Abbesses we may be sure of the devout presence of the Misses Gloria Swanson, Norma and Constance Talmadge, Norma Shearer, Alice Joyce, Mabel Normand and many others. The churches of the new faith will, of course, be the picture studios themselves, and the ritual the actual filming of the great masterpieces. Thousands of pilgrims will flock to the de Mille studios, and watch in reverent silence the stirring ceremony of Mr de Mille in his papal robes directing some great scriptural story while the sanctified actors go through their religious roles to an organ accompaniment of sacred music.

It might say something for the generosity of Hollywood that Mr Howard was welcomed so warmly in the studios there three years later, but then again the chances of Cecil B. de Mille or even his publicity men having ever read *The New Yorker* were probably remote.

By 1935, the English actors who had been resident in Hollywood for almost a decade were at last joined by one or two actresses; following the success of Diana Wynyard in *Cavalcade*, Lilian Harvey (the English actress who had made such a success in the German cinema with *Congress Dances*) and Heather Angel (billed initially as 'the English girl with the name no one can forget') had both gone out under contract, as had Evelyn Laye, though for one picture only. By and large British musical stars had considerably more trouble in Hollywood than their dramatic counterparts: Jessie Matthews, after a decade of making the most successful British film musicals of all time, was only once to work in Hollywood and then not as a singer; Coward and Novello stayed well away, and even Buchanan did not go back after the early 1930s until *The Bandwagon* in 1953.

The British were being used more selectively by the big studios, either to recreate vehicles from the London or New York stage or for roles which no local American actor or actress could conceivably play. Kiplingesque adventures of the old Empire were always good news for the Hollywood British, as were country-house thrillers and historical epics; westerns, musicals and downmarket crime dramas were generally left to native talent. Nevertheless there was still a lot of work to be had; in May 1933 MGM announced that it had added two new English actresses to its contract strength (Elizabeth Allan and the future Mrs Ronald Colman, Benita Hume), while Fox countered with three (Miriam Jordan, Una O'Connor and Merle Tottenham, the last two both survivors of *Cavalcade* on stage and screen).

The demand for gentlemen players was also as strong as ever, which meant that when the play *Cynara* passed through Los Angeles on two successive tours in the early 1930s its two stars, Guy Standing and Philip Merivale, were asked to stay on and film. Merivale later married my grandmother Gladys Cooper and became, with her, a stalwart of the Hollywood English through the war years; Sir Guy Standing, the title hereditary rather than theatrically endowed, went on to an all too brief film career (he was the father of Kay Hammond and grandfather of John Standing), playing such ancient colonels as escaped the grasp of Sir Aubrey Smith, until his life suddenly came to a sad end when he was bitten by a rattle-snake in the Hollywood hills in 1937.

Asked at this time whether too many foreigners (and especially Germans and English) were not being allowed to flood into the film capital, the President of the Motion Picture Academy answered judiciously:

The slogan 'Buy American' was never supposed to apply to actors. We furnish movies to all the world. If we take to shunning foreign players, the rest of the world would be justified in shunning our films. Our screen badly needs its imported talent. We might as well face the facts. Americans, with a few notable exceptions, lack European glamour and class. The screen needs that, and foreign players supply it; but the supporting cast is predominantly American. The technicians are American. The studio personnel is American. The theatre employees are American. Would you jeopardize the livelihood of many thousands of your fellow-countrymen in order to vent your spite upon a handful of foreigners? Think this over before you start talking about 'Americans first' in motion pictures.

15:
We Play for an Empire

If Hollywood was still generally happy with its quota of British residents, there were increasing signs of discontent at home. A number of British film producers, Michael Balcon most vociferous amongst them, had always been unhappy with the American stranglehold on English-language film production. Far too much money and talent appeared to be available to American producers, with the result that British cinemas were all too often full of their wares, creating a vicious circle in which not enough of the local product was getting to the screen to make money to pay for more. It is an argument that has raged for as long as Britain and America have been making films, but in 1933 it reached the first of many crescendos with the rebirth yet again of the British film industry, this time largely as a result of Alexander Korda's creation of London Films.

Korda had himself spent a brief and deeply unhappy period in Hollywood at the end of the 1920s, when his first wife Maria had been under contract to First National: he could bear neither the endless sunshine nor the brusque effrontery of studio life. 'Here', he once complained, 'the stupidest producer on the lot can give orders to a director like me, and everybody's nephew is a producer. I should have come here as a producer myself or, better yet, as a nephew.'

Korda's loathing of Hollywood was such that he began to understand the regular Santa Monica suicides-by-drowning: 'Happy? Who could ever be happy in this bloody paradise?' When he finally escaped from California and his marriage, there were those who saw in his setting up as Britain's only true movie mogul a kind of revenge for the years of Hollywood neglect. 'It was one of my father's greatest achievements', his son once said, 'to have made people forget that he was ever in America.'

He therefore took considerable delight in tempting back to England several of the Hollywood English, and in starting to tie up local British talent under the kind of contracts (hitherto virtually unknown in London) which made it impossible for them to answer the call of the American studios. This happened to coincide with a brief mid-1930s Hollywood slump, and nervous articles soon began to appear in the American press:

Right at this moment [wrote an editor of *Movie Classic* in June 1933] Hollywood is poised atop a powder house that may explode at any moment ... and if the explosion does take place, the American motion picture industry will be blown into such a chaotic state that the Depression will seem like boom times. I refer to the catastrophe that would occur if, for any of several possible and logical reasons, British actors and actresses should suddenly desert Hollywood and return to Great Britain ... boats would be filled with British players bound for England, and within a brief period of time John Bull would be in a position to challenge Uncle Sam for motion picture supremacy. There are at present about two hundred British actors and actresses in Hollywood, and at least a score are of front-rank importance. Great Britain might suddenly recall all loyal citizens to her own studios, and if such a summons were put on a patriotic basis there is every likelihood that most, if not all, would respond. Many live like exiles, longing to return even if, like Colman and McLaglen and Karloff, they have now been here fully ten years. Other British actors in Hollywood have been very, very clannish, though not unfriendly; but reports of their dinner parties in the society pages indicate that they invite nine of their own people to perhaps one American, and that usually a stage actor from New York like Fredric March. The British play, work and study among themselves; English games, such as rugby and cricket, are becoming common sights on vacant fields. Restaurants that once omitted tea from menus now list that beverage before coffee; if the British haven't 'gone Hollywood' then Hollywood has certainly 'gone British'. Monocles and canes, which only a few months ago were the exclusive privileges of George Arliss, may often now be seen on drugstore soda clerks, while the stony-faced unemotionalism of the English stage has made itself apparent on the screen: Leslie Howard's underplayed love scenes appeal to American women more than the most burning American sex acrobatics. Few of the once-popular he-man lovers are headliners today, while the leading ladies whose eyebrows used to form question-marks have given way to actresses who can gaze upon the burning of Rome with no more than a twitch of the upper lip.

The problem, as one studio executive explained it to George Cukor (that most Anglophile of American directors), was that he had 'a lot of tuxedo scripts but no damn tuxedo actors except the English'. The French were all right for musicals (Maurice Chevalier) and exotic romance could be dealt with by the Scandinavians, while the Germans still made good villains, but for a really classy dinner party on screen you had to have the English.

Not that they were showing much sign of wishing to leave: whatever the home industry had to offer in the way of the occasionally lucrative single picture, it was never anything to match a studio contract. True, some of the women with husbands and families at home in England, and some of the men unwilling to give up the stage for more than a few weeks at a time, made sure that Hollywood never became more than a hotel address. But for the rest, it was now a permanent residence; and some of those intending a long stay were careful to trade on rather more than just their Englishness.

In this context, perhaps the most successful in cash and critical terms of all the Hollywood English, from the 1930s well into the 1960s, was the one who took most care never to be associated with the cricket-playing fraternity. Archibald Alexander Leach, born in Bristol on 18 January 1904, had started out as a call-boy in the theatre there, gone to Broadway as 'an acrobatic dancer' at the age of sixteen, and stayed; by 1932 he had been offered a long-term contract at Paramount (early reviews reckoned him 'efficient') so long as he changed his name. 'Who', asked B.P. Schulberg, 'wants to see a leech?' Paramount suggested Cary Lockwood; Leach suggested Cary Grant and that was more or less that, though it was Cukor, friend to so many of the visiting and resident British, who gave him his first real screen success opposite Katharine Hepburn (a kind of 'honorary member' of the Hollywood British) in his 1935 *Sylvia Scarlett*.

As Richard Schickel has noted, Grant's particular brand of debonair charm was unique: 'The drama in a Cary Grant movie always lies in seeing if the star can be made to lose his wry, elegant and habitual aplomb; the joke lies in the fact that no matter what assaults and indignities the writer and director visit upon his apparently ageless person, he never does.' But what made Grant so different from the rest of the Hollywood English was that he alone at that time was a totally celluloid creation; though he had a theatre background, it was minor and uninfluential. Unlike Howard, Colman, Marshall or Brook, he entirely lacked theatricality, and his early success did not depend on the recreation of roles he'd already made famous in the theatre. In that sense Grant was actually the founder of a new generation of Hollywood Britons, one which would stretch forward through George Brent and Ray Milland to Michael Caine; they were to be an oddly stateless lot, owing allegiance to individual directors rather than to any formal dramatic training, and they were survivors because the cameras, recognizing original film artists rather than resting stage players, loved them with an especial devotion. They were also the first actors out there not to have spent their formative years on long theatrical tours, and therefore the first not to think of Hollywood, however subconsciously, as yet one more date to be played on the road home to real London acclaim.

Early in 1934 there was to be another shock for those already becoming nervous about the British stranglehold on Hollywood: an English star again won the 'Best Actor' Oscar and won it, unlike Arliss, for a picture made abroad with no American involvement, indeed a picture made as a deliberate challenge to everything that Hollywood had hitherto regarded as its own exclusive property. To make matters still more galling, the winner was a man whom Paramount had once owned and then allowed to slip from their contract clutches because they found him 'unexciting'.

If Alexander Korda had set out, as he very probably did, to wound Hollywood pride in as many areas as possible, he could hardly have done better than *The Private Life of Henry VIII*. A lavish costume drama, of a kind the British cinema had long since decided itself incapable of affording, it guaranteed its four principal players (Charles Laughton and his wife, Elsa Lanchester, Merle Oberon and Robert Donat) long and lucrative screen careers on both sides of the Atlantic; it also launched Binnie Barnes on forty years of wisecracking, smart lady roles. Taking his attack straight into the enemy camp, Korda opened his *Henry VIII* at the Radio City Music Hall in New York before an English release and, even before it won Laughton his Oscar, the way was clear for him to return to Hollywood in triumph a year later as the incestuous old father in *The Barretts of Wimpole Street*, though he ducked out of playing Micawber in *David Copperfield* by convincing MGM that only W. C. Fields could do it justice.

But the Laughtons never really forgave Hollywood for its initial lack of interest in them ('Charles was a nobody and I was the wife of a nobody,' recalled Elsa Lanchester of their first visits there), and they too steered well clear of the local British resident community when they eventually did settle there just before the war, in a house whose architectural style Laughton was to describe as 'late marzipan'.

His success had, however, added a new dimension to what was now understood by 'Hollywood English': the team was becoming considerably more diffuse and diverse, encompassing as it did talents as wide-ranging as those of Grant and Laughton, and it was no longer quite enough to be a handsome young juvenile lead of the kind that, barely a decade earlier, had been most in demand. True, they too were still coming out on almost every boat, but of those who arrived in 1933 neither Hugh Williams (later

to return to the theatre with some elegant light comedies of his own) nor
Henry Wilcoxon (who played King Richard in *The Crusades*, a prime
example of the Hollywood history epic, and ended up as Cecil B. de Mille's
co-producer on *The Ten Commandments*) were able to enjoy the
immediate success of another Howard or Colman, whom, in type, they
most resembled.

The character men were now coming into their own: Boris Karloff with
a line of gothic horror (*Frankenstein, The Mummy* and *The Ghoul* had all
been released by 1934) and Basil Rathbone with a line of smooth villains
were both in constant contract work. 'Even the great Garbo', reported
one Hollywood gossip column of the time, 'admits to a preference for
English men and has twice sought Leslie Howard's services only to be
twice refused. Garbo respects the Britons because they do not engage in
"personalities" or become enamoured of fellow-players as some
Americans have done when playing with her, and she has a yen for these
men from Mayfair. In fact she has picked Herbert Marshall as her new
leading man for *The Painted Veil*.'

Maugham, like the British Empire, was to provide almost constant
Hollywood employment for the English: between 1932 and 1934 there
were to be films made of his *Our Betters* (with Alan Mowbray and Hugh
Sinclair), *Rain, The Painted Veil,* and *Of Human Bondage* (with Leslie
Howard, Bette Davis, Reginald Owen and Reginald Denny), and all but
the first were to be remade at least once in the next twenty-five years,
thereby very often giving further employment to a second generation of
London exiles.

Though Maugham still insisted on staying far away from California,
leaving local hacks to adapt his novels for the screen, the big studios were
still intent on capturing 'famous authors' whenever possible to add dignity and tone to what they still seem secretly to have regarded as a
somewhat shabby industry. Anglophiles like Cukor and Selznick were
forever trying to tempt literary lions out from Bloomsbury into the
Californian sun, and in 1935 they scored their greatest coup: 'I have',
wrote Selznick in a memo to Nicholas Schenck at the MGM offices in New
York, 'succeeded in bringing to this country (author) Hugh Walpole.'
Though Schenck doubtless needed to be reminded by that parenthesis
precisely what Walpole did for a living, there were precious few others
who did. Walpole was then fifty-one and at the height of his fame as a
writer, one moreover who had already made American lecture tours
and expressed an interest in working in Hollywood. On that same British

buying trip Selznick also found a ten-year-old child called Frederick Llewellyn, whom he much wanted for *David Copperfield*, the project for which Walpole was also engaged as screenwriter. Llewellyn's parents refused, however, to let him cross the Atlantic and it was left to a resourceful aunt to haul him onto a ship, change his name to Freddie Bartholomew and turn up with him a month later in Selznick's Hollywood office.

Though Laughton withdrew from *Copperfield* after three days' shooting ('he looked', said one observer, 'as though he was about to molest the child') and Micawber then went on his advice to Fields, the cast list still managed to be one of the first great gatherings of the Hollywood British for one single film : apart from Bartholomew there was Roland Young as Uriah Heep, Frank Lawton as the adult Copperfield, Elizabeth Allan as Mrs Copperfield, Jean Cadell as Mrs Micawber, Basil Rathbone and Violet Kemble-Cooper as the Murdstones and Maureen O'Sullivan as Dora. Walpole was engaged at £200 a week to supply suitably Dickensian dialogue : 'Very interesting but most exasperating,' he wrote home ; 'I work from 10 to 6 without ceasing and the seventh redrafting is no better than the first ; the whole of the second half of the script was pulled to pieces and there were hysterical requests for me to make something interesting out of Agnes.'

He did, however, take keenly to the Hollywood social life, reporting Katharine Hepburn to be 'divine' and much enjoying a stay at the home of Ann Harding, where he found it 'lovely to sit out in the moonlight at midnight and watch these beautiful creatures with practically nothing on play tennis under artificial light'. He also noted somewhat sadly that 'no one here cares a hang about the relative merits of English writers', but seems to have derived great pleasure from playing the small role of the Vicar of Blunderstone in the *Copperfield* film, Equity rules being in those days lax enough occasionally to allow the author to turn up in one of his own screenplays.

Walpole got a co-author credit for the screenplay of *Copperfield* (with Selznick's regular writer Howard Estabrook), but his next Hollywood project was considerably less happy : the conversion (with Lenore Coffee) of his own novel *Vanessa* was such a screen fiasco that it did considerable harm to Helen Hayes's film career for several years. From there he went on to work for MGM on screenplays of *Kim* and *The Prince and the Pauper*, but by now a certain disillusionment was creeping into Walpole's letters home : 'There is more actual positive reality in one square inch of the beach at Scarborough. ... This is partly the unreality of pictures, which simply get more unreal rather than less. It seems to me that they have gone back rather than forward since last year. ... No wars, no politics, no deaths make any effect here. We are all on a raft together in the middle of the cinema sea and nothing is real here but the salaries.'

That Christmas, H.G.Wells also arrived in Hollywood on a brief selling trip: Chaplin gave a dinner party for the two best-selling British authors of the day at which, Walpole recalled, 'Wells chucked me amiably under the chin and seemed very well and delighted with the pretty women'; after that the two men accompanied Paulette Goddard on the ritual visit to the Randolph Hearst estate: 'Magnificent tapestries,' thought Walpole, 'and everywhere marble statues, sham Italian gilt, and a deserted library where the books absolutely wept for neglect ... water buffalo and zebra look in at your bedroom window.'

When Walpole finally left Hollywood early in 1935 (having refused MGM's offer of yet another rewrite job, this one on *Captains Courageous*, which had already been through three different authors' typewriters) he reckoned to have made well over £10,000 in a little less than a year; he was unembittered by the experience, had gone through none of the creative agonies that were later to beset the likes of F.Scott Fitzgerald under the studio system, but remained well aware of the problems: 'This place is making me lazier and lazier. It isn't a good sort of laziness in which you recuperate, but a bad sort in which your character becomes weaker and weaker and you care less and less whether you do anything properly or not. ... I'm beginning to think of *money* more than at any time in my life before. ... This isn't life at all – it is shadow upon shadow upon shadow.'

A contemporary of Walpole's in Hollywood at this time was the journalist R.J.Minney, who, having done a book and a play about Clive of India, was invited by Darryl Zanuck to turn them into a film at the start of what was to become for Minney a long and prolific career as a writer and producer of British screenplays. He too was dazzled by his first encounter with the California sun:

Hollywood looks raw and unfinished – as though it were hurriedly run up, which of course it was. Some of it is as repulsive as a sore – the barren wastes by the roadside that serve as parking places for motor cars, the litter of cheap and awful bungalows with walls no stouter than cardboard, the glaring advertisement signs that befoul the mountains, the hideous petrol pumps, the freak architecture of the restaurants ... yet in the glorious sunshine I saw, for all its crudities, a picture-postcard town with mountains at hand as well as the sea. ... A pervading air of holiday is not confined to Sundays but persists through the week. Girls go to work in beach pyjamas, men in slacks and open shirts. ... I should think the crowning horror of Hollywood is that of which they are so proud – the Chinese Theatre. It was built by a showman called Sid Grauman and is a rapturous blend of temple and brothel, set in what appears to be a cemetery where on what look like tombstones you may see the hand and foot prints of the stars. ... Mr Grauman himself goes about only with his mother and is invisible without her. They dine alone together at one of the Brown Derbys and all Hollywood pays homage at their table. ... Greta Garbo's home is like a monastery in Algeria, very small – the size of a Golders Green semi-detached villa and all white, with tiny windows that were obscured by green shutters. That shows she was probably in when we drove past.

Minney, one of the more acid observers of the Hollywood British, was then admitted to the studios where they were to shoot his *Clive of India* :

I was taken to a little whitewashed room with a table, a telephone and a chair to sleep in. A girl, very blonde, brought in twenty-four pencils, some India rubber, writing paper and an inkwell. A workman nailed my name above the door. He used only one small nail, so that at the first argument it could be removed. ... After lunch I was summoned to the presence of the mighty Zanuck. Without further ado he began talking about Clive. 'I have seen the play and I have read your book. Now for the picture. We'll have to put him over big. The people in Nebraska – or anywhere else in the States for that matter – don't know who he is. They don't know the difference between Clive of India and cloves of India. There will have to be titles. Lots of titles. The public must be told that all this really happened, that there really was a man called Clive and that he lived in – well, whenever it was. I'll get sixty elephants, and we'll have a hell of a charge for the Battle of Plassey.' ... Every time he passed me he gave a jab with his hand to my kneecap, the ankle of my crossed leg or my shoulderblade. The vitality of the little man impressed me. ... Back in my own office, with two lots of Eddie Cantor voices and one Bing Crosby song belting through the walls from nearby projection rooms, a man intervened. 'Mr Minney ?' He handed me my contract. The clauses danced before my eyes, but one of them steadied itself and glared at me relentlessly. It informed me that the contract was liable to instant cancellation if I should happen to go out of my mind. Apparently such a consequence is natural in Hollywood. My wonder was how they would then be able to distinguish me from the rest. But perhaps it was a sort of trade union precaution to prevent there being more than a limited number of lunatics in employment ? The man shrugged his shoulders and pointed to the dotted line. I signed it.

Minney was to find no escape from his new career as a film writer, even when he left the studios :

I was waylaid in the street. 'Would you need a clever young child to put in your picture ?' 'I have a performing dog ; won't it be no use for *Clive of India* ?' At the hotel, the valet suddenly became very obliging. It appeared that his father was a very good character actor. A bespectacled old woman assisting at the counter in the drug store informed me that she was herself anxious to play mother parts. 'I can make 'em cry, sir, I can make you cry.' A bald, angry man in the elevator insisted that his son was a clever scenic artist and would be an asset to my picture. It was embarrassing and pathetic.

Even among the British colony, which welcomed him with open arms, Minney discovered that things weren't all they appeared to be: 'Boris Karlov [sic] came up and talked to me. Anyone less like a monster it would be difficult to conceive. But he isn't even Russian: his name is Pratt and he's an Englishman. One of his brothers, Sir John Pratt, is in the Foreign Office and another is a magistrate in Bombay who has sent Gandhi up for trial.'

Having (with Walpole's help) persuaded Ronald Colman to shave off his celebrated moustache in the interests of period accuracy, Minney stayed to see *Clive of India* safely onto the studio floor, where it became one of the touchstone pictures of British rule in California. 'We play for an Empire,' says Colman before the Battle of Plassey, thereby neatly encapsulating in five words the two things most Americans knew about the British – a love of cricket and of territory. Later the dialogue aspires to the almost mystical: 'India is a sacred trust. I must keep faith'; and though the London *Times* reckoned it 'a dignified and impressive historical drama which misses genuine distinction by a comfortable margin' there's no doubt that *Clive* set the pattern for a whole genre of Empire epics. Made as often as not by distinctly unEnglish middle-European Jews who'd also chosen Californian exile, they were frequently and rightly derided by British film critics; but as the American columnist Russell Baker recently noted, their importance to Americans was considerable:

Many of us still have a large emotional investment in the Empire we saw built in those Saturday matinees. They made us all imperialists in the same vague sense that Westerns made us all racists. Who, after all, could possibly cheer for Eduardo Ciannelli's pit of cobras when Gunga Din – 'you're a better man than I am, Sam Jaffe' – was willing to die to save India for the Queen, God save her? The standard British Empire film, in fact, was little more than the Western in South Kensington accents. Even Gary Cooper at one point changed from chaps to jodhpurs long enough to head 'em off at Khyber Pass. Instead of turkey feathers, the bad guys usually wore turbans. The regiment marched to bagpipes instead of bugles, but this did not prevent it from arriving invariably in the nick of time.

And in 1935, New York cinemas reverberated to the sound of those bagpipes: while Ronald Colman was Clive at the Rivoli, across town at the Paramount Sir Guy Standing, C. Aubrey Smith and Franchot Tone (in fact American, but allowed to 'play English' due to an extremely Sandhurst chin) were relating *The Lives of a Bengal Lancer*. The Union Jack may have been coming down in other parts of the world, but over America it still flew outside cinemas and studios alike.

16:
Hons and Rebels

Just as they had in India a century earlier, the British in California divided themselves into at least two teams: the respectables and the renegades. Heading the former, in life as on screen, were such distinguished figures as those of Sir Aubrey Smith and Ronald Colman, while the latter included such disreputable mirror-images as Sir Guy Standing and John Loder. Standing was, at the age of sixty-five, widely believed to be living with a then nineteen-year-old Betty Grable, while Loder went even further towards offending local susceptibilities. A witty, adventurous man who went from Eton to Sandhurst, he seemed at first sight to belong among the most traditional of the officer class: his background was after all not much different from that of Aubrey Smith (Charterhouse and Cambridge), David Niven (Stowe and Sandhurst), Basil Rathbone (Repton) or Clive Brook (Dulwich). But like George Sanders, who had already been put through some of the best schools in England, including both Bedales and Brighton College, Loder was a rebel who found nothing in California remotely as interesting as his own chequered past, one which had already taken in the 1916 Easter Rising in Dublin, where his father was the British Army commander, and the Battle of the Somme. After a couple of early and undistinguished silents (including a Jack Holt western for which, the director told him, 'we have three expressions: Love, Hate and Determination, all done with a jutted jaw; Fear we don't use any more') Loder was detailed to work with Rin Tin Tin, already ageing and extremely bad-tempered. He was, however, taken up socially by Fairbanks, and was delighted to find himself seated at dinner one night at Pickfair next to the visiting Duke of Sutherland, who turned to Mary Pickford and asked if she could possibly tell him the time, as his valet had forgotten to wind his watch.

Loder himself was rapidly dropped from his Paramount contract (as he once lamented: 'Why is it that I'm not able/To get the roles they give Clark Gable?/They always say you have no name/But when you have one, come again./By that time I'll be old and stiff/A kind of poor man's Aubrey Smith') and consoled himself by starting an affair with Marion Davies, which they carried on at San Simeon under Hearst's increasingly suspicious gaze. The English community were not pleased: not only was it a kind of *lèse-majesté* and, as Sir Aubrey would doubtless have said, extremely bad form for a visitor, but it was also reckoned to be extremely dangerous. One of Miss Davies's previous lovers had been the director Tom Ince, who disappeared overboard in 1924 while on Hearst's yacht and was never seen again, though Louella Parsons, who witnessed the fall, was reputed to have got her life's contract with the Hearst press in return for her silence. Friends now believed that Loder was likely to join Ince in some watery grave, and urged a rapid return to London. Instead, Loder stayed in Hollywood, survived to marry Hedy Lamarr, but like Sanders failed to achieve anything in front of the camera that was remotely as intriguing as the life he led behind it.

Sanders was, in fact, a later Hollywood arrival; the son of the best balalaika player in all St Petersburg, he left Bedales 'with a sense of utter worthlessness and the conviction that I was too stupid to cope with life; little that happened in the next thirty-five years made me feel justified in altering that conviction'. After brief spells in Manchester textiles and Argentinian cigarette-manufacturing he was thrown out of Argentina for duelling, and got into BBC radio as an actor; he understudied Coward in *Conversation Piece*, went with it to America and graduated to Hollywood in 1936, where for nearly forty years he was to do what David Shipman has called 'a roaring trade in one-upmanship; Claude Rains was more dapper, Basil Rathbone more villainous, Clifton Webb more supercilious, Vincent Price more arrogant, but for an elegant assumption of superiority over the other cast members, George won hands down'. Sadly, his career, which included such occasional work of distinction as *Rebecca* and *All About Eve*, also featured a vast amount of B-picture rubbish, not least *The Falcon* series (which he happily handed over to his brother, Tom Conway) and *The Saint*, and then deteriorated so fast during the 1950s and 1960s, through marriages to Zsa-Zsa Gabor, her daughter, Magda, and Ronald Colman's widow, Benita Hume, that early in the 1970s he was ready to take his own life 'through utter boredom'. 'The thing about me', said Sanders once, 'is that I am not one of those people who would rather act than eat; quite the reverse. Larry Olivier was born with the desire to act. I was not. My own desire as a boy was to retire. That ambition has never changed.'

Sanders was thus to remain an outsider even among the English colony in Hollywood, which tended to be as narrow-minded as any embassy compound and to retain a deep distrust for apparent Englishmen who either changed their names or had suffered non-British birthplaces. This was still the time when Aubrey Smith, asked by Joyce Carey what it had been like to work with the great and mysterious Garbo in *Queen Christina*, could reply simply, 'She's a ripping gel'; but there was now a grudging acceptance of Hollywood as a place where one could be seen without deep shame, and that had come very fast. As recently as 1930 the playwright and poet John Drinkwater had been severely mocked, not least by *Punch* and Hugh Walpole, for agreeing to write a biography of one of the studio pioneers, Carl Laemmle; so shaken was Drinkwater by this that two entire chapters of the subsequent book were spent defending the choice of subject and arguing that a film producer, just conceivably, could merit a Life. Within four years Walpole himself was to be taking Laemmle's gold in California, and Evelyn Laye was to be writing home in amazement about a dinner party at which 'twenty-one waiters marched into the room each bearing on his head a huge block of decorated ice cream fashioned into a letter of the alphabet, so that when the waiters were ranged round the walls you could read out in great ice-cream lettering the words WILLIAM RANDOLPH HEARST'.

Such goings-on, though distinctly unBritish, had begun to exert a definite fascination on those brought up in the more rarefied and less rewarded worlds of the West End or Bloomsbury.

Sanders also contributed some tantalizing, brief comments on his Hollywood British contemporaries, and the gap between their screen and real characters: 'Cary Grant, witty, sophisticated and debonair on screen, in life a prey to theosophical charlatans, socially insecure and inclined to isolation'; Joan Fontaine, 'whose impeccable bearing on screen is in fine contrast to a private life of considerable vitality and colour'; Basil Rathbone, 'master of the curled lip and patronizing glance, but in life warm, cozy and a pushover for a laugh'; Charles Laughton, 'an unprincipled sadist on the screen and stage but in life is interested in the gentle arts, painting, porcelain, people and poetry'.

What Sanders was suggesting, of course, in between those careful phrases (written for publication in 1960) was that Laughton was homosexual, a considerable problem in a Hollywood then still suffering from Hays Fever; Laughton did not take kindly to his compatriots (especially loathing the equally homosexual James Whale, who would talk about 'running Hollywood gold through his hair') but took an even greater dislike to Cecil B. de Mille during their making of *The Sign of the Cross* (1932), especially when de Mille began querying Laughton's determination to have himself followed around the set (he was playing Nero at the time) by a young and near-naked male slave. Mr de Mille had cornered the market in Biblical epics by screening large numbers of young and near-naked female slaves, but this was altogether something else and the resident British, with the exception of Sanders, took the view that Laughton had become a somewhat dangerous and over-flamboyant ambassador; they avoided him and Laughton avoided their cricket pitches, leaving Elsa Lanchester (later a bride of Frankenstein as well as of Charles) to make her own friends where she could.

In this she was not missing much, at least if Sanders's views are to be believed:

No Hollywood house was ever worth visiting [he once noted] unless you made a point of leaving your hat and coat behind. Then, one quick look around the room told you precisely how boring the party was likely to be; if you had a hat and coat you had to stay to the end to collect them, but I soon learned that without them you could make your way swiftly upstairs and escape through the bathroom window in no time at all. I got to know a lot of bathrooms like that; the best was undoubtedly Greer Garson's. It was all done in pink marble, and had a huge glass wall which opened onto a private garden. It was the biggest production for the smallest audience that Hollywood ever achieved.

Whenever they were in Hollywood, the Laughtons lived at the Garden of Allah, an exotic bungalow hotel which Thomas Wolfe told Scott Fitzgerald he could not believe would exist 'even in California'. Scott's pupil and lover, the English actress and journalist Sheilah Graham, once built an entire book around the Garden's guest list, noting in particular the hotel's fascination for the British:

Evelyn Laye and Frank Lawton got married from there, with Herbert Marshall as best man and Gloria Swanson as matron of honor; Olivier rented a bungalow for three months, and had to give it up after a week when Garbo sacked him from *Queen Christina*; Heather Thatcher came out to stay with the daughter of P.G. Wodehouse and all the papers noted with amazement that she wore a monocle; Herbert Wilcox stayed there when he was in love with Dorothy Gish and gave a party and said to her 'Well, what do you think of this hotel, then?' and Dorothy thought for a minute and replied, 'It's a lie!' When Hugh Williams was sacked from Paramount after making five films, three of which ended up in a critic's Ten Worst Films of 1934 list, the studio rang him at the Garden and said as he was going back to London would he like to take with him 2,400 publicity stills they had left over.

In 1959 the Garden of Allah, by then the property of the Lytton Loan and Savings Company, was bulldozed to make way for yet another tower block; they did, however, leave a small glass-framed model of it by the side of Sunset Boulevard, just across from that other great home of the Hollywood English, the Château Marmont. By the time I went looking for the model in the middle 1960s, it too had disappeared without trace.

One result of the increasing number of 'British' films now being made by almost all Hollywood studios (even RKO and Warners, home of the all-American gangster classics, had begun filtering in the occasional English subject) was that a kind of accuracy began to develop. No longer did the followers of Elinor Glyn have to rush around sets removing spittoons from medieval banquet scenes. Even the *Illustrated London News* noted this change with something like relief in April 1935:

Hollywood is rapidly Anglicizing its output to such a degree that it is no longer surprising to find chapters of English history, slices of London life, or chronicles of British enterprise emerging from its studios with scarcely a jarring note either in setting or in accents. Those timbered Tudor mansions that represented to the American mind the ideal home for the idle rich in the heart of London have practically disappeared, and along with them the transatlantic notion of our social amenities, modes and manners has been energetically revised. To use a colloquialism, America has at last 'got the hang of us' ... careful international casting and expert advice have, between them, succeeded in establishing a British School in California ... after such achievements as *Cavalcade*, *Bengal Lancer*, *David Copperfield* and *Clive of India* it behoves us to pay a tribute to American powers of assimilation.

A nation of immigrants, and a film community many of whose leaders had at some time had to pass through London, could reasonably be expected to cope with England on screen rather better than the British ever managed to cope with America; this did, however, lead to a lot less fun for film critics, who could no longer point out in print that the River Thames did not flow immediately beneath the walls of Buckingham Palace and that beefeaters seldom went on traffic duty. It also fuelled the continuing hatred of Hollywood felt by certain native film-makers, who saw their best potential subjects and stars being too regularly sold to American studios.

Nor did the further outposts of the British Empire take kindly to having their own history told by Hollywood rather than London; Indian journalists, for example, reacted to *Lives of a Bengal Lancer* with considerable fury. K. S. Shelvankar in *The Times of India* took the view that:

It sheds a spurious, belated lustre on the romanticism of Empire, and strives to recreate the pious, serenely aggressive spirit of the Victorian age. 'Here', it says, 'are 300 millions – sheep, wolves, rebels, slaves. Protect them; punish them; but for God's sake don't leave them alone. It would be a calamitous dereliction of duty.' A film thus heavily charged with vanity and sanctimonious bombast is not likely to gratify Indian sentiment. In fact it exasperates and humiliates the Indian spectator and awakens in him violent and deeply subversive feelings; in the long run it must act as a strong incitement to sedition. ... Facile simplicities of the racial view are served up. The white man is a 'super-man', the 'native' at best an infant, helpless and apt to be troublesome. These are mischievous fallacies to circulate: they foster self-delusion in one party and hatred in the other.

Quite how far the success of Mahatma Gandhi in a fanatically film-conscious nation could therefore be ascribed to the antics of the Hollywood Raj has never been adequately assessed; so far as Hollywood was concerned, the Indian box-office figures did not make a sufficient impression on world-wide takings to cause much alarm when American films were disliked there, and the British could, of course, safely wash their hands of the whole problem since the films were only about them, not actually by them. Fifty years later, when Richard Attenborough released his film *Gandhi*, ironically it was the more conservative British who were to complain of misrepresentation on screen.

By and large Hollywood was now producing a far better England than England; as George Cukor said proudly of his 1935 *David Copperfield*: 'We shot the White Cliffs of Dover near Malibu and I have to say that our cliffs were altogether better: they were both whiter and cliffier.' In the same sense, Ronald Colman was by now more English than any of the English actors who had stayed in England, though he too was developing a wary cynicism at some of the studio system's more bizarre manifestations. When, he once recalled, Sam Goldwyn (who for a while held his contract) loaned him out to Warners for the Lubitsch *Lady Windermere's Fan* it was decreed that the cast list should read 'Ronald Colman appears by kind permission of Samuel Goldwyn'. This so incensed Lubitsch that it became a running joke on the set · 'You will now', said the great director, 'cross to the window, open it, and wave – by kind permission of Samuel Goldwyn.'

Though he was still keeping himself to himself whenever possible, Colman had become the uncrowned king of the British community in Hollywood; from the earliest days, when he and Percy Marmont would go to Christmas parties at Ernest Torrence's house and make a simultaneous dash for the tree when Torrence announced a gift for 'the best-looking man in Hollywood', Colman had outlasted the competition, becoming in turn Beau Geste and Bulldog Drummond and Raffles. Colman was, comedians apart, the first actor to suggest in talking pictures that something could actually be fun, and his sense of humour was probably as important as his charm in separating him from the run of other good-looking Hollywood Englishmen like Marmont and Torrence. Though haunted by a broken first marriage which kept him away from England to avoid unnecessary and doubtless publicity-worthy confrontations, and haunted too by a strong sense of the impermanence and unreality of Californian life, Colman eventually found lasting marital happiness in Hollywood with his second wife, Benita Hume, and suitably enough it was he himself who handed the torch on to his only real heir, David Niven, who wrote:

When I first arrived in California, broke and twenty-two years old, I was working as an extra and living in the servants' quarters of the Hollywood Roosevelt hotel in a room given me by the reception clerk there, Al Weingand. . . . He also played tennis with me and beat me consistently. One day he said, 'Ronald Colman is a friend of mine and he's looking for a fourth at tennis on Sunday. Would you like to come?' Ronnie was at that time the King of Hollywood and famous as a recluse [largely because he and Miss Hume were then living together before their marriage and not keen for the press to find out]. So on Sunday I met the great man and was there all day with his chums Bill Powell, Dick Barthelmess and Clive Brook. They were marvellous to me and after a few months my career prospered and I graduated from Colman's tennis group to his supper group, which consisted in fact of all the same people. Goldwyn then offered me a small contract and Ronnie was horrified: 'The best producer by far, but a real bastard.' Goldwyn meanwhile saw me as a kind of minor replacement for Ronnie, though only because I too was British and moustached.

Something of Colman's unique popularity at this time, both inside the profession and among audiences, can be gained from the fact that when in 1935 a Hollywood magazine asked fifty actresses to name their favourite actor and also the one they thought most handsome, Colman won by a clear twenty-two votes to Clark Gable's eight and Fredric March's seven. Cedric Hardwicke, however, was inclined to take a more cynical view: 'I found a friend in Ronald Colman, who after scoring no memorable success as an actor in England was now a full-blown star complete with mansion, butler and chauffeur. "God how I love the theatre," Ronnie was given to exclaiming at least once a week, and, "Oh, for the good old days."'

Hardwicke was knighted in 1934, which was, not entirely coincidentally, also the year that Hollywood began taking an interest in him: he was perhaps the only one of the old stage knights to get regular billing as 'Sir Cedric' on screen across the next thirty years. Hardwicke had scored a considerable success in the West End as old Barrett of Wimpole Street, and though the screen version went to Laughton, he soon followed him out west: 'I had anticipated that Hollywood would be an actors' Eden: it proved to be a paradise only for the medical profession. . . . This was the only place on earth where man had attempted to build an industrial society in a sparsely irrigated and sub-tropical climate where the weather, being immutable, was denied him as a subject of conversation.'

Though Hardwicke was to spend the best part of three decades in California, where he made almost forty films, he regarded it with barely suppressed irritation both professionally and geographically: 'My aversion to sunshine left me unimpressed with the sun-drenched scene, its unearthly foliage, trees without sap, flimsy buildings without charm or with the brightly painted attraction of children's toys.'

Shaw had once told Hardwicke that Hollywood, far from being a golden opportunity, was for a good stage actor little more than 'a chance to lose all your victories', but Sir Cedric was beset almost throughout his life by heavy alimony payments (he was three times married) and thus remained in America doing essentially undistinguished work enlivened by the occasional *Hunchback* or *Suspicion*. He never really got used to Californian social customs, however:

My wife and I were summoned to the spacious halls of Pickfair as guests of honour. The invitation read 7.30 p.m., so that was the hour at which we decanted ourselves from the studio limousine. A slightly startled butler ushered us into the bar, where we waited alone for some ninety minutes. Soon after nine o'clock other guests began arriving in droves, and we filtered out of the bar into the far-flung living quarters of the house. A sweeping staircase soared into the upper vastnesses from the hall, and it was at the head of the staircase that our hostess, who proved herself charming, ultimately made her arresting appearance. The time by my wrist-watch was almost exactly ten.

Hardwicke was not deeply impressed by his own exiled compatriots either, though whether his distaste was rooted in professional jealousy of those who had got there before him and were already on lucrative full-time contracts, or simply in an awareness that his fellow Britons were in danger of turning themselves into caricatures, is not entirely clear: 'As a recruit to the English colony, whose members kept the flag flying and poured tea each afternoon at four, I paid my due respects to C. Aubrey Smith, the senior member of the colony, whose craggy manner suggested that he had just completed a ceremonial tour of all four corners of Queen Victoria's empire.'

Nevertheless, the British colony in California was tied together by the unforgettable realization that financially and in terms of creature comforts they were vastly better off under the Californian sun than they would have been doing their Shakespearian duty back home at the Old Vic: 'Before God', Ronald Colman once told his agent, 'I am worth $35 a week; before the motion picture industry I'm worth anything you can get.'

17:
Closing Ranks in Ruritania

There was now no going back; by the middle of the 1930s a generation of British stage actors led by Gielgud, Redgrave, Richardson and Olivier was dragging the British theatre into a whole new convention of classical and modern acting, one far removed from the left-over barnstorming Victoriana in which most of the Hollywood British had served their apprenticeship. Though Hardwicke, largely because of an intelligent and close association with the work of Bernard Shaw, was able to go on commuting throughout his career to the theatre in New York and London, for the likes of Aubrey Smith and Ronald Colman, who had never been especially distinguished theatrically, there was now no need or reason to risk their celluloid reputations on what they considered to be uncertain and underpaid ventures on the stage.

Accordingly they stayed in California, playing gracious and faintly envious hosts to the occasional visiting celebrity from the West End or Broadway, murmuring with ever fainter conviction of a need to 'get back to their roots in the drama' while cheerfully taking the Goldwyn shilling.

A few of the more intelligent young Americans saw through the façade – among them Vincent Price, who once told me that much of his early screen work depended on his ability to look and sound even more English than the English, despite the fact that he was in reality the son of a wealthy baking-powder manufacturer from Missouri. He had, however, studied art at the Courtauld in London and done a prolonged stage stint as Prince Albert in *Victoria Regina*, early experiences which seemed to stand him in better stead in Hollywood than any native experience he might have picked up along the way:

You have to remember that in those days the English colony really ran Hollywood. There was the old Hardwicke-Smith guard up in the hills, and then down by the beach the young renegades, Niven and Flynn, living at the house they called Cirrhosis-by-the-sea. In between there were middle-range people like Reggie Gardiner, who eventually took to sounding so desperately clipped and stiff-upper-lipped on the screen that not even English audiences could ever understand a word he said. The colony also had considerable grandeur, especially Ouida Rathbone, who behaved like some manic duchess and used to fill the swimming pool with gardenias every time Basil had a party. The smell was really appalling.

And if the colony tended to close ranks and stick together, it was at least partly so as to preserve their most valuable professional asset : the English or at the very least British accent. They all had before them the terrible warning of Ida Lupino, who, cast for a leading role in *The Bishop Misbehaves*, was replaced on the first day of shooting by Maureen O'Sullivan because Miss Lupino, having been settled in California now for four or five years, was found to be 'no longer sufficiently British'. Happily she then went on to a long and successful career starring in and directing American-American rather than American-English pictures.

Late in 1935 the *Christian Science Monitor* published some statistics on foreigners in Hollywood : the Central Casting Bureau, which in those days farmed out all the extras to the various studios, had given work to a total of 25,000 non-Americans in that year. They had come from thirty-two nations, and the largest proportion employed were Chinese, of whom 3,000 had turned up on the screen. The English came second with 2,500, followed closely by the French with 2,300. Next came Mexicans, Spaniards, Russians and Italians, with the Scots managing about two hundred and the Irish somewhat less ; the Welsh appear not to have been there at all until John Ford made *How Green Was My Valley* in 1941, and even that was cast almost entirely from the Hollywood Irish.

But the English did, of course, have a head start in terms of a shared language, even if Oscar Wilde had maintained it was the one thing that truly separated them from America ; the *Christian Science Monitor* researchers noted not only the ever-publicized cricket club but also

equestrian events and dog shows, which also attract a generous sprinkling of titled British names to give Hollywood affairs a distinction which Hollywood people like to think can only be matched in Europe. ... Several English cake shops now exist, catering almost exclusively to the English, who maintain a stricter aloofness than do most other resident aliens ; steak and kidney pies have miraculously made their appearance all over town and are sometimes even eaten by the natives ; Devonshire cream is also manufactured, but in very small quantities. The Americans prefer it whipped. Once a year, on New Year's Eve, the principal members of the British colony gather in a Hollywood café to hear the bells of Big Ben ring out over the radio, bearing out the British reputation for loving whatever is British. Billiards are now played regularly at the homes of most British stars, and officers of the British warships visiting in California harbours entertain and are entertained by a group founded by Victor McLaglen and known as the British United Services Club, comprised in large part of actors who have served in one of the branches of the British military; while on many a film set old members of the same London club [usually the Garrick], meet and fraternize.

A few months later, when news came of the death of King George V, the British colony went into deep mourning; C. Aubrey Smith flew the flag on his lawn at half-mast for several weeks and all party invitations were ostentatiously refused for at least a month, though McLaglen and the Abbey Players contingent were, being Irish, predictably less moved.

But Anglophilia had spread even through MGM, where it was one of the principal causes of dissent between the studio's two leaders, Louis B. Mayer and Irving Thalberg. Mayer, the one-time scrap merchant who had formed MGM with Goldwyn back in 1924, was always cast as the crass, money-loving Philistine while Thalberg was the poetic, sensitive creator; the fact that Mayer often made script and casting decisions which were considerably more intelligent and sensitive than those of Thalberg was a subtlety Hollywood chose to ignore, and part of the intellectual apparatus that Thalberg had to lug around the sets with him in his claim to be the poet- and thinker-in-residence at Metro was, of course, a considerable affection, not to say affectation, for all things British. Urged on by his equally pretentious wife, Norma Shearer, who chose to forget that her silent career had included such all-American gems of tastelessness as *Pleasure Mad*, *Lucrezia Lombard* and *Married Flirts*, he now began to seek out suitably high-toned scripts and rapidly happened upon Michael Arlen's *The Green Hat*, which was made over as *Riptide* with a cast featuring not only Miss Shearer but also Mrs Patrick Campbell and the inevitable C. Aubrey Smith. When, however, at the first downtown preview, Sir Aubrey was heard to intone, 'Ah, this sweet air of England; presently I shall hear the nightingale,' something distinctly closer to a Bronx cheer than a nightingale was heard from the audience.

Smith was, however, held in much greater affection by American film critics because, as Bosley Crowther explained for the *New York Times* in 1937,

he is Great Britain personified in the eyes of millions of people. Whenever he appears on the screen – his elderly figure erect, his chin up and his eyes flashing out from under those beetling brows – it is as though an invisible band were playing

Rule Britannia. No matter what his role, he remains an Englishman – the stout and unalterable type, as fixed in the cinema's vocabulary as a stock shot of Big Ben or the Houses of Parliament. He is the Bank of England, the cliffs of Dover, the rock of Gibraltar and several super-dreadnoughts rolled into one. Upon Mr Smith and the Empire the sun would never dare to set. ... None of your round-faced, florid Englishmen in bowler hat and mackintosh is Mr Smith. Rather is he of the cut of a hearty fox-hunting earl or landowning squire or at least a retired major-general in the Indian army ... and if there is such a thing as a white man's burden out in Hollywood, no one is carrying it more staunchly or with more resolution than C. Aubrey Smith.

His fellow Londoner Boris Karloff had somewhat more raunchy memories of California's Greatest Living Englishman: 'Aubrey, in impeccable snowy flannels, swooping about on the dance floor at the Roosevelt Hotel, where the cricket club held its annual dance, pausing, stage-whispering through a bristling white moustache to a fellow dancer, "My house tonight – not a word – park on another street – come in the back door" – and away he would glide.'

As early as this there was, for Smith, to be no going home: when he did again cross the Atlantic, to film in England in 1938, it was already, as he told W. J. Makin, to seek out an England that had long gone:

I find the England of today is not the England I loved yesterday. I went to search for the people and the country that I loved. One of the first things I did was to sit in the pavilion at Lord's. I had thought of that thrilling moment during the years of exile out here. And then, on that summer's day at Lord's, came the realization. Bitter. The flannel-clad figures on the pitch were as skilful as ever and were playing cricket as only Englishmen can play it. But I missed the familiar characters and the deep affection that would come to them in quiet grunts and 'Well played, Sir' from the spectators. I missed, too, the old familiar faces in the pavilion. I found myself a stranger sitting amongst strangers. That evening I went to my old club. There, a similar disappointment awaited me. All the old faces had gone. New faces, new members. Only the wine-steward remembered me. Why do wine-stewards live to such a fruity old age? In desperation I bought a car and set off with my wife to motor through the green heart of England. We crossed the Cotswolds and entered the Wye Valley. But the scenery was blurred in wetness. Rain and more rain. It became worse as we entered Wales. I even experienced an almost-forgotten twinge of rheumatism. In sheer despair, we turned back towards London. I went in search of my home village. I recalled its superb situation, on a hill in Middlesex with the spread of Bucks in the distance. Another tragedy awaited me. Gone was the old Tudor house with its beautiful weathered brick and beams. Gone the stream that crossed the middle of the lane, and was a romantic spot for all boys. Instead, there was a block of newly built cheap cottages. The whole beauty of the place had been spoiled. An arterial road straddled the distance, with more cheap houses flanking it. They call it a ribbon development, eh? Well, I hate it. It has spoiled the old countryside. I went back to London and booked my passage back to California. I wasn't sorry to leave.

Writers, too, were now leaving England in search of some time in the sun; the novelist Anthony Powell went out in 1937 in the hope of some screenwriting work for MGM, a hope not much advanced when his literary agent dropped dead on Hollywood Boulevard the day before the Powells were due to arrive. Others had rather similar bad luck, however, not least J.B.Priestley, who in 1937 joined a distinguished line of Hollywood-British authors stretching back through the 1930s to John Galsworthy, who as the decade opened had been making final revisions to *The Forsyte Saga* sequence while staying on Ronald Colman's ranch. Colman, indeed, still stood for the height of Hollywood cultural pretension: a memorably daft memo had recently been sent by Sam Goldwyn to the great Soviet director Sergei Eisenstein noting that: 'I have seen your film [*Battleship*] *Potemkin* and admired it very much indeed. What we should like you to do now would be something of the same kind, but rather cheaper, for Ronald Colman.'

Priestley had been wintering in Arizona because of his wife's health and went on to California in 1935 to work on several screenplays, from all of which he later insisted on having his name removed, presumably because they were then put through alien typewriters before reaching the studio floor. He did, however, in his autobiographical *Midnight on the Desert*, write extensively of his Hollywood impressions. Los Angeles he found 'a sprawling city which somehow suggests this new age of ours at its silliest', its inhabitants an unattractive collection of 'boosters and boomers, bogus mystics and fortune-tellers, all representative of an America I neither understand nor enjoy'. The isolation of Hollywood was what Priestley found most alarming: 'In London and Paris and Berlin, film-making has to compete with a thousand other interests and occupations; but once in Hollywood, after crossing mountains and deserts, you must get into films, stay in films, or perish. You are, as it were, wrecked on an island that does nothing but make films.'

Hollywood stars were, to Priestley, 'people born to achieve reality in a photograph' and Garbo 'as romantically inaccessible as the Grand Lama'; their community he found 'oddly tragic: not enough security, too much competition, too many intrigues ... the atmosphere was too often like that of the court of some half-crazed despot ... there is no place where you get more money, and no place where you get less value for it ... only the wildest make-believe of Hollywood can express the astonishing reality of Los Angeles'.

In one brief chapter, Priestley said more about the Californian film-making community and its problems than the many hundreds of books that have since been written on the subject. Driving at night along Sunset Boulevard, his final memory is of a flashing neon sign announcing round-the-clock availability. A doctor? A dentist? A fireman? In fact no; the sign Priestley saw advertised the services of a psychologist.

Other writers returned to London still more amazed and confused: one reported a remarkable modesty around the studios, where he had seen large signs proclaiming the offices of SMALL FILMS and LESSER PRODUCTIONS; the existence of such moguls as Sol Lesser and Edward Small had entirely escaped his attention. Others managed to come to some sort of terms with the studio system, and even do some of their best work within it. R.C.Sherriff was finally persuaded by James Whale, fully five years after *Journey's End*, to make the journey west, complete with mother, for the scripting of H.G.Wells's *The Invisible Man*. They were shooting it at Universal, where Carl Laemmle insisted on all writers clocking in at nine every morning. Sherriff's problem was that he worked best at night, and in hotel rooms rather than offices; Whale advised him to check in every morning, spend the days wandering around the sets watching others at work, have a little sleep in the afternoons and then return to his hotel for actual work every night. It kept Laemmle happy, and bought Sherriff enough time to realize that in order to write his first screenplay adequately he would have to have another look at the original Wells novel. That, unfortunately, was the one thing Hollywood appeared not to possess; they offered him fifteen earlier screen 'treatments of the property' in which increasingly desperate screenwriters had tried to shift the location to Mars or Czarist Russia in an attempt to make the story photogenic, but nobody now could find the book they had originally purchased. Sherriff finally took to combing the junk markets of downtown Los Angeles until he hit upon a secondhand copy on a barrow in a Chinese market; reading it again, he decided that it would film perfectly the way it stood. That was not, however, something he could admit to the story editor who was paying him $1,500 a week to come up with a brilliant and above all new 'treatment' of the work that appeared to have defeated so many other screenwriters over the past two years. Accordingly, Sherriff gambled on the fact that nobody at the studio had ever read the original, came up with a perfect transliteration of it in screenplay form, and was wildly applauded for having succeeded where so many had failed.

His assignment duly, rapidly and happily completed, Sherriff was packing up to return with mother to England and his mature studentship at Oxford when to his amazement he was sent for by the head of the script department at Universal. The offer was a twelve-month contract to write three screenplays at $25,000 each, and this in 1936; Sherriff politely explained about his studentship at New College, Oxford. The Americans looked at him in amazement and sent him to see Uncle Carl Laemmle in person; again, and carefully, Sherriff explained about the place that had been held open for him at New College during this Californian sabbatical. 'What do you do there?' asked Laemmle suspiciously. 'I write essays for my tutor,' explained Sherriff. 'And how much does he pay you for them?' asked Laemmle, determined not to be outbid for Sherriff's services by some goddam English tutor. Sherriff explained carefully that he was paid nothing; on the contrary, he said, he paid New College for the privilege of being allowed to study there. Laemmle was still more confused. He explained slowly and clearly to Sherriff that Universal were offering $75,000 for three of Sherriff's screenplays, and that he, Sherriff, would have to pay nothing in return. Sherriff still refused, and Laemmle bade him a sad and confused farewell, having however promised that if Sherriff would continue writing for Universal in England after his Oxford studies came to an end, he could be sure of at least £6,000 a script.

Thus, on leaving Oxford, Sherriff was able to buy himself a Rolls-Royce and a seaside house on the proceeds from his treatments for the studio of *The Road Back* and Galsworthy's *Over The River*; sadly, the arrangement then collapsed, defeated by the sheer impossibility of having Sherriff in one country and his employers in another. Instead Sherriff went to work for Korda, not returning to Hollywood again until the war and *Lady Hamilton*.

Universal's desperate attempt to hang on to Sherriff in California was largely because English writers there were still at a premium; the British box-office was now an important consideration in studio budgeting, and such London critics as the young Graham Greene had begun savaging the inaccuracies of Hollywood-London pictures made without expert help. In the 1936 *Lloyds of London* some diligent British researcher had counted ninety-two errors of history, geography or costume and it was, said Greene in the *Spectator*, 'a film in which the name of England is so freely on the characters' lips that we recognize it at once as American. These people live, make love, bear children all from the most patriotic of motives and it's all rather like London in Coronation week.' Greene was also appalled by the 1936 Cukor-MGM *Romeo and Juliet*; a solid, not to say stolid, employer of the Hollywood British, it featured not only Leslie Howard as a somewhat ancient Romeo (his Juliet, Norma Shearer, was no starstruck teenager either) but also Basil Rathbone (as Tybalt), Reginald Denny (as Benvolio) and C. Aubrey Smith and Godfrey Tearle's half-brother Conway as the heads of the rival houses of Montague and Capulet. Greene failed to understand why Friar Laurence should have been living in what appeared to be a modern luxury flat complete with a laboratory of test-tubes, and wondered why there had to be 'a balcony so high that Juliet should really have conversed with Romeo in shouts like a sailor from a crow's nest when sighting land'; he also found John Barrymore's Mercutio 'haggard with the greasepaint of a thousand Broadway nights'. Greene's experiences as a critic prepared him admirably for dealing in later years with David Selznick, who took the view that *The Third Man* might be all about buggery, and with Sam Zimbalist, who once asked him to rewrite the ending to somebody else's screenplay of *Ben Hur* on the grounds that 'there seems to be kind of an anti-climax after the Crucifixion'.

Meanwhile, not all of the Hollywood English were leading private lives of exemplary or irreproachable cricketing purity: Reggie Gardiner was by now having an exotic extramarital affair with Hedy Lamarr, and the quiet-spoken Bart Marshall, though still officially married to Edna Best, managed in the middle 1930s to conduct off-screen affairs with Kay Francis, Miriam Hopkins and Gloria Swanson. The British were much in demand, and every New Year's Eve they would still gather at the Ronald Colmans' (he having by now married Benita Hume), where Aherne, Sanders, Fairbanks Jnr (an honorary member of the colony years before his honorary KBE) and Niven would listen respectfully while the talk turned invariably to the First World War, in which Colman had been gassed, Rathbone had won the Military Cross, Marshall had lost a leg and Nigel Bruce had been severely wounded.

Apart from those New Year's Eve celebrations, one of the last great gatherings of the pre-war Hollywood English was undoubtedly John Cromwell's 1937 *Prisoner of Zenda*, which had Colman in the title role, Madeleine Carroll as the Princess plus Niven, Aubrey Smith and the

Canadian actor Raymond Massey, long on the London stage, in starry support alongside young Doug Fairbanks. It was a David O. Selznick production, and he had decided on it largely because of the world-wide publicity surrounding the abdication of Edward VIII to marry Mrs Simpson. Here too, Selznick realized, in this old Ruritanian war-horse (which had already been filmed as a silent in 1913 and 1927 and was to have two more sound versions), was the story of a king in romantic difficulties, and as the shooting coincided with the George VI Coronation an astute Selznick publicist had the entire British-born cast line up for a photograph 'sending a loyal message of congratulation to Their Majesties'. The shooting also coincided with the Hitler-Mussolini alliance ('bloody whippersnappers,' said Aubrey Smith when the news reached him on the set via the London *Times*, the only paper he ever read or believed).

The shooting was not altogether easy: the publication during it of the diaries of Mary Astor, one of the cast, caused a fair number of raised eyebrows among the diehard British, and the director John Cromwell was sending acid memos to Selznick about the fact that Fairbanks appeared on the set 'overindulged and lazy', while Colman 'never knows his lines; I don't know which of them annoys me most; also both he and Madeleine Carroll appear to have a "bad side" for the camera and as it's the same "bad side" shooting them face to face is all but impossible'. In the end, George Cukor and W. S. van Dyke were brought in by Selznick to shoot retakes.

Best of all, though, was the moment when Ray Massey was having trouble with the characterization of Black Michael and decided to take his troubles to the old master Aubrey Smith. Smith looked up from his *Times*, told Massey that in his time as a stage actor 'I have played every single part in the *Prisoner of Zenda* except that of the Princess. And you know, old boy, I'll tell you a funny thing. I never discovered how to play Black Michael either.' And with that, he turned off his hearing aid and went back to his copy of *The Times*.

18:
Up Stars, Down Stars

The British in California were now happily sub-divided into *Upstairs, Downstairs* groupings which harked back across ten years to *Cavalcade*: 'upstairs' there were the old paternal aristocrats, men like Arliss and Aubrey Smith, plus the younger bloods like Niven and Loder, the occasional old-buffer uncle like Nigel Bruce and one or two poetic misfits like Colman and Howard, all linked by a readiness to leap into uniform on every possible occasion. Women were still not much in evidence, the coming of Greer Garson and Vivien Leigh being still a year or two off. Those women who had starred in Hollywood-British pictures tended either to stay and go native, like Ida Lupino, or to return home to Britain not because they took an especial feminine dislike to California but rather because the films that were employing most British in the middle and late 1930s were still the swashbucklers or the Empire adventures, which remained a male preserve. Even after a showcase like *Prisoner of Zenda*, Madeleine Carroll returned immediately to the British cinema, where most of her work was still to be found.

But there was one sub-group which had now found useful and semi-permanent employment 'below stairs' in Hollywood pictures and they were the butlers; like their old-colonel 'masters' above, they were a uniquely British creation and therefore able, like them, to maintain a casting stranglehold over the studios. By 1937, three had cornered the market, and they were led by a six-foot-four character comedian who was eventually and profitably to give his name to Broadway's only chain of fish and chip shops. When, just before the war, Mary Pickford had cause to sack her American houseman for incompetence he was heard to scream at her from the doorstep, 'Madam, you don't want an ordinary mortal like me: the butler you are looking for is Arthur Treacher.'

When he first landed in Hollywood in 1933 after an undistinguished London stage career, Treacher was told that his height would make it impossible for him to play love scenes with American actresses; butlers were, however, expected to be larger than life and Treacher therefore became an early screen Jeeves to David Niven's 1936 Bertie Wooster in an undistinguished B feature (*Thank You, Jeeves*) scripted 'after P.G. Wodehouse', some critics said a long way after, by Stephen Gross and Joseph Hoffman and produced by Sol M. Wurtzel, who himself might almost have been invented by Wodehouse as the all-American tycoon. The film did nonetheless establish Niven as a star for the first time, and also established him and Treacher for the first time as recognizable screen types. This led to a wealth of employment carrying trays for Treacher, who was soon able to hire his very own butler and live happily almost ever after.

The second of the three great Hollywood butlers was a London lawyer-turned-actor called Eric Blore, who made his name first in the 1920s as a popular West End songwriter and then as the gentleman's gentleman whose discourse on crumpets and scones in *The Gay Divorce* (1934) set a new high for talking butlers. Astaire employed him again in *Top Hat* and *Shall We Dance?*, and both Blore and Treacher were still butling their way around Hollywood well into the 1950s, as was the third member of their domestic force, Ernest Cossart, a fractionally less elegant type.

The other great and regular employer of the British was, of course, Sherlock Holmes; one-reel Holmesian adventures shot in America had started as early as 1903, and in 1922 Roland Young, later to achieve screen immortality in the ghostly title role of the *Topper* series, was Watson to John Barrymore's Holmes. By the middle 1930s both Clive Brook and Reginald Owen had played the role in Hollywood talkies (Owen in fact graduating to the great detective after starting off as Clive Brook's Dr Watson) and then in 1939 came the start of the great Rathbone-Bruce series, one which was to contain in its last lines some of Hollywood's most direct comment on the early days of the Second World War.

But not all the English actors who went out in the late 1930s intended staying or even making the cinema their lives; Robert Morley, my father, for instance, went out in 1937 to make the *Marie Antoinette* that was his first film (and won him his only Oscar nomination) but then did not return to work in California for another quarter of a century. He had been tempted out in the first place by Ben Goetz, who was running the MGM office in London and had seen him on the London stage as Oscar Wilde, deciding then and there that Robert would be ideal for Louis XVI, a role for which Laughton had already been mentioned in some advance publicity.

There were a number of snags [recalled Robert years later], one of which was that I would have to go to Hollywood to make a test during the time that I was already under contract to do *Oscar Wilde* in New York. My agent demanded a salary of two hundred pounds a week, and told Goetz that I was anyway independently wealthy and could afford to turn down anything less than that. But my agent forgot to tell me that was to be the line, so the morning I was supposed to be leaving for New York I went into MGM and asked to borrow fifty pounds for an overcoat, and Ben had the grace to pretend he'd been fooled, though I think he already knew that I'd already been sacked from two English films, the first because the director thought me effeminate and the second because I was rude on the set to Victor Seastrom, who didn't care for insubordination. ... Anyway, I arrived in New York on the *Bremen* in my new overcoat and quite worried because my mother was always convinced that one of us was going to die while the other was in the States, but she'd never told me which of us in her premonition was to be the actual victim. Then the immigration officer threatened to refuse me admittance because one of my eyes was judged to be defective on my medical. He asked what sort of work I was planning to do. 'An actor?' he said. 'Well, I guess they're blind half the time anyway, so if you're half-blind all the time it won't really notice.' And, delighted with his own joke, he stamped my passport and I was in.

That same evening I flew for the first time. Never again in my life was I to know such excitement. In those days the flight from New York to Los Angeles took sixteen hours, and I sat with my nose pressed up against the window gazing out at the great moon and down at the limitless land beneath me. A great chain of beacons guided the pilots, and for me the greatest wonder of all was the realization that men had climbed mountains, crossed deserts, dived down into the Great Lakes and with immense labour and courage and ingenuity had seen to it that for three thousand miles these beacons were in place and kept alight. We landed to refuel in Omaha and Dallas and Salt Lake City, and the sun rose over the Sierras and at last we came back to the ocean.

Robert got the role, *Wilde* on Broadway was postponed until the autumn, and he and his life-long friend Peter Bull (also cast in the film, though, alas, only finally visible as a left shoulder in the publicity stills outside the Carlton Haymarket, his role as the royal barber having been shaved to death in the cutting room) duly arrived at MGM to join a stellar company. The title role was being played by Norma Shearer, though there had been early rumours that it would go to Marion Davies and indeed Miss Davies departed from the MGM lot, taking her caravan and her Randolph Hearst support with her, soon after the final casting was announced. John Barrymore was playing Robert's father, Louis xv, Anita Louise and Gladys George were the other women and a young Tyrone Power was cast as the Count who tries to rescue Marie Antoinette from the guillotine.

The film had in fact been set up as a vehicle for his beloved wife by Irving Thalberg, but after Thalberg's death from pneumonia in the previous year ('Isn't God good to me?' said Louis B. Mayer to his henchman Mannix at the funeral) a lot of MGM's enthusiasm for the project had somehow disintegrated. A nasty row developed about the studio shares then held by Miss Shearer as Thalberg's widow, and the two-million-dollar film became a curious kind of bargaining tool. In the negotiations, Thalberg's original choice of director, Sidney Franklin, a slow and meticulous director in the Cukor mould, was replaced by W.S. van Dyke, 'one-take Woody', a director hitherto famous for his speed in getting the *Tarzan* and *Thin Man* series through the studios and out into the cinemas in record time.

Robert's memories of the film are, however, almost entirely happy ones:

It was leisurely and de luxe; we were all treated like visiting maharajahs. Huge cars waited all day outside the stages to carry us one hundred yards to our dressing rooms. On the set there would be an orchestra to while away the waits [Miss Shearer had let it be known that she always worked better to orchestral accompaniment] and a *maître d'hôtel* would take our orders for luncheon, which would be served in our dressing-rooms as soon as we arrived back there. There was only one thing expected of us: that we should never be late. One morning I was guilty of this considerable crime. The director, who was usually the kindest of teachers and photographed me like a mad child, regarded me on this one occasion bleakly. 'To whom are you going to apologize?' he asked. 'Everyone,' I told him, and made for the ladders which led to the heights. He let me go on and I climbed and scrambled for ten minutes along the swaying cat-walks, shaking hands and apologizing to the electricians, each manning an arc light. Considering that I ruined my white knee-breeches and my ermine train it wasn't perhaps the most helpful contribution I could have made towards getting on with the job; but it was, I have always felt, the right thing to do in the circumstances.

It is always a moot point how much an actor should show off; it's part of his job in a way, but sometimes the gesture misfires, the rocket is damp and doesn't explode. That is when an actor tries the patience of the public, and everyone else for that matter. Propped outside the studio one afternoon I found a bicycle; it belonged to an MGM messenger boy but I hadn't ridden one for years and I thought it might be amusing to have a spin. I also thought others might be amused by me riding around the lot dressed in my usual Louis XVI ermine. It wasn't a great success. No one seemed to notice me except the messenger boy, who was waiting impatiently for the return of his property. He cut short my over-charming apology, my speculation as to how long it had been since I had last ridden a bicycle: 'All the stars do it, Mr Morley ... *once.*'

Soon after I arrived, Norma Shearer gave a dinner party for me and allowed me to ask the stars I most wanted to meet. Janet Gaynor, Carole Lombard, Lilian Harvey, Fred Astaire, Ruth Chatterton and Jeanette MacDonald; and as each entered I was conscious of a deep feeling of disappointment. I had grown accustomed to their faces being so much larger.

Before our picture began, there were rumours that it was to be deliberately sabotaged by the MGM front office in an attempt to persuade Miss Shearer to sell out her large stockholding in the studio and retire from the screen. ... Certainly her director, Sidney Franklin, was taken off the picture almost the night before it started and the job was given to Van Dyke, who, it was alleged, was to get a large extra sum for every day he brought the picture in ahead of schedule. Franklin had been working on the preparations for the picture over two entire years; Van Dyke had apparently not seen the script until he arrived to start the shooting and didn't seem to know much about the French or their Revolution, so when one of the innumerable MGM historical advisers came up to him on the set and told him that he'd positioned the guillotine wrong in the Place de la Concorde, he listened politely and then said, 'Fine, kid, fine, that's how it was ... and this is how it's going to be.'

But once they got to know each other he and Shearer got along famously, and he was immensely popular with all the cast and crew because he worked to an absolute timetable. At six every evening they brought him a slug of gin and precisely half an hour later, no matter what was happening, he would leave the set. His producer, Hunt Stromberg, seldom appeared at all unless there was a crisis, in which case he was always preceded by an equerry carrying a portable telephone which was plugged into a special circuit and relayed to all within earshot news of his exact whereabouts and predictions of his next destination. ... He would stay until three or four every morning cutting the picture, and it was he who decided how the various scenes were to be shot and if he was not satisfied, Van Dyke was told to shoot them again. He was also responsible for all the casting and the final script, and he was expected to be preparing two or three other pictures at the same time.

Louis B. Mayer was the redoubtable proprietor; in those days his studio was making the Mickey Rooney series about the Hardy family. 'The only ones worth a damn,' Mayer once told me, and added, 'You're doing *Marie Antoinette*, aren't you? Not your fault, but God how I hate epics.' The cinema, he told me on one occasion, had given precisely one great artist to the world: 'Greta Garbo ... unless you also count that damn Mouse.'

Our picture took six months to make, and when it was finished Mayer invited me to the first showing in the studio theatre. I sat with him and Shearer, and behind us sat the executive might of the studio, accompanied by their secretaries and/or mistresses. The picture seemed to last forever, and halfway through I began to despair not only of my own performance but of Shearer's and everyone else's as well. At last it was over and the lights came on. There was a long silence. No one said a word, although some of the secretaries ostentatiously snuffled into their handkerchieves. From behind, someone clapped three times and then stopped. 'After a film like that, LB, what else is there to say?' was the only comment I heard.

For some reason, I was convinced that Mayer was going to ask me what I thought and that I would have to tell him. So I got up and scrambled over his feet and fled for the exit. I walked out of that theatre and off the lot and along Culver City Boulevard, convinced that every car that overtook me contained some studio official deputed to capture me and bring me back to where Mr Mayer was now sitting on his throne, waiting to ask the fatal question. An hour later, I was still marching on down the endless, unpaved street, by this time frightened lest I should encounter one of the packs of wild dogs which they said were often on the prowl in those parts. I got home about five in the morning. Nobody, to this day, has asked me what I thought of *Marie Antoinette*. But I never recovered my nerve; nor have I watched myself on the screen ever again with any real enjoyment. I would undoubtedly have been a better screen actor if I had had the courage to sit through some of my own performances; but the shock of that first sight of myself was total.

The day I left Hollywood, Mayer took me to lunch in the MGM executive dining room. It was like eating in Buckingham Palace. He pointed out that they had spent a lot of money promoting me, and he wanted very much to find other pictures for me. Above all he wanted me to promise that after *Wilde* I would come back to Metro. 'When you've finished your play, Bob' – he had never called me Bob before – 'just let me know and we'll have a picture for you. In the meantime, if any other studio makes an offer for you all I ask is that you'll give me the chance to match it.' So when I finished playing *Wilde* on Broadway I sent him a telegram saying that I was free. My agent begged me not to do it, to wait until they came to me. 'I do not', I told him patiently, 'have to play hard to get with my Uncle Louis.' But of course I did. In due course I got an answer from the casting office. 'If', they wrote, 'Mr Mayer has any suitable employment for you in the future, he will certainly be pleased to get in touch with you. In the meantime Mr Mayer points out that in order to avoid duplication of effort, it is best not to approach him personally.'

My father, despite the Oscar nomination, did not work for MGM again until 1954 and then only in England. Somebody somewhere must have turned him up on the studio's casting file for 'period monarchs' because within less than a year they gave him the mad George III in *Beau Brummel* and the French Louis XI in *Quentin Durward*. He also picked up occasional offers on their way to Charles Laughton, but never considered them too seriously: *Les Miserables* did not to Robert sound like a lot of fun, and somebody told him that the *Hunchback of Notre Dame* never even spoke.

He and Peter Bull were, however, deeply impressed by the convention of the Hollywood première; though they couldn't actually stay for that of *Marie Antoinette*, they did go to the gala opening of *Snow White and the Seven Dwarfs*; another night they heard that Metro were having an opening at Grauman's Chinese Theater, so off they went, immaculately dressed, and were able on the way in to answer some questions for the listening radio audience about the progress of *Marie Antoinette*. Robert told them it was all going to be wonderful and how delighted he was to be there and the man with the microphone seemed pleased and the audience on the sidewalk clapped enthusiastically. Peter and Robert then smiled, waved graciously and followed Carole Lombard down the red carpet to the door where a man asked for their tickets. 'But this', remonstrated Peter, 'is Louis XVI from *Marie Antoinette*.' 'Unfortunately, sir, we are full,' replied the commissionaire and Robert and Peter then had to make their way back through the no longer applauding crowd and home to their flat for a boiled egg and a game of Monopoly. Hollywood was like that, too.

For Peter Bull, though, it was also full of unexpected treats:

At the centre table in the MGM commissary you could see Messrs Gable, Tracy, Powell and a lot of Barrymores and I was able to bask on the lavatory seat in Garbo's dressing-room to my heart's content ... Noel Langley was also at MGM then, muttering about being 'in prison', having to write scripts for the *Wizard of Oz* and *Maytime*, and the awfulness of MacDonald and Eddy ... We used to play a lot of Monopoly in the evenings with a man who became the literary critic of the *Observer*, John Davenport, and then there was Mary Morris, a young actress with beautiful eyes and great integrity who came out on an idiot's contract of $75 a week. The studio could never think what to do with her, as she conformed not at all to any preconceived idea of a film actress, and they used to test her bi-weekly in improbable costumes. One would meet her on a Monday wandering gloomily around the lot dressed as a French courtesan at the court of Louis the Something, and then on a Thursday she'd be portraying a very blacked-up servant from the deep, deep South ... She grew very unhappy indeed and eventually obtained her release, asking to be routed back to England from Hollywood via Siberia, which shook the MGM travel department quite a bit.

I did two days' work in the first two months of what we had now taken to calling *Marie and Toilette* on account of Miss Shearer's obsession with her screen appearance, and on the way home again I won the Blue Riband of the Atlantic for ping-pong on the *Aquitania*. Altogether it had taken half a year of my life to get my shoulder into that still outside the Empire Leicester Square: six months well and usefully spent.

19:
Scarlett Heights

By no means everybody liked or approved of the Hollywood British –
sometimes not even the Hollywood British themselves. The screenwriter
and comedy director John Paddy Carstairs, there in the early 1930s on
scripting assignments for Paramount, found the community 'loud-
mouthed, arrogant, clannish and all too inclined to regard the whole
business of film-making as a kind of schoolboy prank'; and the pianist
Billy Milton found his life there a depressing mix of disillusionment and
unemployment. The writers weren't always too happy either: Maria
and Aldous Huxley, visiting for the first time in the autumn of 1937,
found Hollywood

like a permanent International Exhibition. The buildings are ravishing, fantastic and flimsy. They are all surrounded by green lawns and huge palm-trees
and flowering hibiscus and to finish it off the population wear fancy-dress costume
or rather, in the hot weather, fancy-undress costume. ... Yesterday we had a
very intellectual dinner with Charlie Chaplin. Paulette Goddard is a very good
and handsome hostess and Upton Sinclair was one of the guests. Charlie we have
always loved and admired. He did yesterday a mimic of Mussolini making a
speech, and then of the Indians of Bali singing and dancing. But he is a sad little
man and looks ill now.

Other writers were in for Hollywood shocks, too; when Maugham went
back for a brief visit in 1938, Alan Campbell (the husband of Dorothy
Parker) gave a dinner party for him and after it Maugham, thanking him,
said that while he was in California he would very much like to meet F.
Scott Fitzgerald. 'You did,' said Campbell, 'here, tonight.' Fitzgerald had
apparently already become an almost transparent shadow of his former
self, dried out and bleached by the sun into virtual anonymity.

The end of the 1930s did, however, bring Olivier back to the Hollywood
English in something like triumph; after the fiasco of *Queen Christina* he
had stayed away for five years, refusing even to test for *Romeo and
Juliet*, since he did not at that time believe in screen Shakespeare – a

belief that his own 1936 *As You Like It* apparently did little to alter. But in September 1938 came the news that Goldwyn was to start a picture of *Wuthering Heights*; the original casting idea for Heathcliff had, inevitably, been Ronald Colman, who seemed to be the constant stumbling block to Olivier's Hollywood career; when he proved contractually unavailable, Goldwyn had told his director, William Wyler, to test Douglas Fairbanks Jr and Robert Newton. But Wyler had another idea: it had already been decided that the Cathy would be Merle Oberon, on loan to Goldwyn from Alex Korda, who had made her a star and was about to marry her, and during those negotiations Korda had sent out to Hollywood a print of an undistinguished romantic comedy he had made in the previous year with Oberon called *The Divorce of Lady X*, in which her co-star (though billed beneath the title) had been Olivier. Wyler decided that they worked well together, and flew to London to persuade the actor to give Hollywood, or rather himself in Hollywood, another try.

Olivier had, however, just started a passionate extramarital affair with Vivien Leigh, and was only interested in *Wuthering Heights* if she were cast as Cathy; Wyler explained the impossibility of that, but added that she could have the second lead, that of Isabella, and that 'she'd never get a better start in Hollywood pictures' – a prophecy that seemed to make perfect sense a full three months before the final casting of *Gone With The Wind*. Vivien turned down Isabella (the role went to Geraldine Fitzgerald), but she and Olivier's greatest friend and Old Vic colleague, Ralph Richardson, convinced him that he ought not to turn down Heathcliff: in the memorably brisk words of Sir Ralph, 'Yes. Bit of fame. Good.'

Few successful films have had a worse start. Olivier was bitterly unhappy at being parted from his beloved Vivien, and found Miss Oberon distinctly 'lacking in passion'; she was deeply missing Korda, and annoyed that Olivier seemed to have thoughts only of Leigh; Goldwyn meanwhile was furious with Wyler for hiring 'that damn ugly English actor' instead of a more glamorous Hollywood Heathcliff; and David Niven was so appalled at being cast as the milksop Edgar by a director with whom he'd already come to blows on *Dodsworth* that he risked a studio suspension of four weeks before reluctantly agreeing to take it on. His first day's shooting ran true to what he already knew would be the Wyler form: thirty-four takes of the same scene with, at the end of them, David asking, 'But Willy, what do you *want*?' and Wyler replying sadly, 'For you just to be *better*.'

What was about to happen, however, in among the Hollywood heather on that set for *Wuthering Heights* was nothing less than the cinematic education of Laurence Olivier, as he himself recalled in a 1969 interview:

Looking back at it, I was snobbish about films. Then I had the good luck – but what hell it seemed at the time – to be directed in a film by Wyler. He was a brute. He was tough. I'd do my damnedest in a really exacting and complicated scene. 'That's lousy,' he'd say, 'we'll do it again.' At first we fought all the time. Then, when we had hit each other until we were senseless, we became great friends. Gradually I came to see that film was a different medium, and that if one treated it as such and tried to learn it humbly, with an open mind, one could work in it.

Goldwyn was still not convinced, threatening indeed to close down the picture after seeing the first rushes: 'He's a mess, dirty, unkempt, stagey, hammy and awful.' Wyler, seeing something more, fought to keep him and Olivier was everlastingly grateful; when, six years later, he began to work on his own great film of *Henry V* it was Wyler whom he first begged unsuccessfully to come over to London and direct.

The rest of the *Wuthering Heights* casting was another of the great Hollywood British gatherings: not only Oberon (in fact Tasmanian by birth) and Niven and Olivier and the Irish Geraldine Fitzgerald but also Hugh Williams, Flora Robson, Donald Crisp (who had been one of D. W. Griffith's directors in the early days), plus Leo G. Carroll and Miles Mander and Cecil Kellaway, three London actors who were to be dried by the California sun until they appeared almost like parchment figures in a vast range of Hollywood work.

Predictably, Graham Greene still didn't care for any of it:

How much better they would have made *Wuthering Heights* in France. They know there how to shoot sexual passion; but in this Californian-constructed Yorkshire, among the sensitive, neurotic English voices, sex is cellophaned; there is no egotism, no obsession. This Heathcliff would never have married for revenge (Mr Olivier's nervous, breaking voice belongs to balconies and Verona and romantic love) and one cannot imagine the ghost of this Cathy weeping with balked passion; Miss Merle Oberon cannot help making her a very normal girl.

By many others, though, *Wuthering Heights* was reckoned a success, despite the fact that Goldwyn ordered Wyler to shoot an alternative ending because 'nobody wants to look at a goddam corpse as the fade-out'. Wyler refused, so Goldwyn had an assistant make the shot of Olivier's stunt double and a girl seen in double-exposure walking on some clouds – no worse a mistake, perhaps, than the Yorkshire heather which had mysteriously been allowed to grow about two feet higher than nature ever intended.

The film (billed on New York posters as 'the strangest love story ever told') won Olivier an Oscar nomination, but the prize was snatched by another English actor for another classic English novel-into-screenplay: Robert Donat for *Goodbye Mr Chips*. Olivier remained in no doubt of its value to him, however: 'Wyler taught me that if you do it right, you can do anything; and if he hadn't taught me that I'd never have made *Henry V.*'

Wuthering Heights also led to perhaps the greatest single gift that the Hollywood British ever gave to the film colony that supported them: an actress for Scarlett O'Hara. During the shooting, Olivier happened to be talking to his agent, Myron Selznick, the brother of David, about the massive talent hunt that was still underway to find Clark Gable's co-star in *Gone With The Wind*. What had begun as a huge publicity stunt had now reached a point of utter panic, with Selznick having apparently tested every single living actress in Hollywood and failed to find his Scarlett. What, asked Olivier, about Vivien? Selznick had, it appeared, ruled her out after a screening of *A Yank at Oxford*, in which she had co-starred with Robert Taylor and which Selznick had deeply disliked.

Olivier, relating all this in a letter home to Vivien from the *Wuthering Heights* set in November 1938, happened to add what a pity it was that Selznick had only seen her in that one less than wonderful film; had he seen her in the flesh, he might well have cast her, and the future Oliviers could have been working side by side in California.

That was about all the encouragement Vivien needed; already faintly put out by trumped-up Hollywood gossip-column reports of a 'romance' between Olivier and Oberon (in reality they were barely speaking on the set, not least because Oberon accused Olivier of spitting at her during takes) and having a spare three weeks before she was due at the Old Vic to rehearse *Midsummer Night's Dream*, she decided on a Christmas visit to California.

How much of what then happened was genuinely unexpected, how much of it had been planned by Olivier and Myron Selznick, and how much by Vivien herself, has been the source of considerable speculation in countless books. The facts are that on the night of Saturday 10 December Myron Selznick offered to give Olivier and Leigh dinner at Chasen's before taking them to watch his brother burn the city of Atlanta as a start to the filming of *Gone With The Wind*.

David Selznick had just let it be known that the choice for Scarlett was down to a final four: Joan Crawford, then one of the biggest stars around, Bette Davis, who was some way from the book's description of Scarlett, Paulette Goddard, who was thought lightweight, and Jean Arthur, who was generally reckoned the outsider. All that changed on the night of 10 December, as David Selznick himself wrote two days later in a letter to his wife in New York:

Myron rolled in just exactly too late, arriving about a minute and a half after the last building had fallen and burned and after the shots were completed. With him were Larry Olivier and Vivien Leigh. I had never seen her. When he introduced me, the dying flames were lighting up her face and Myron said, 'I want you to meet Scarlett O'Hara.' I took one look and knew that she was right – at least as far as her appearance went – at least as far as my conception of how Scarlett O'Hara looked.

The following Monday, Vivien was sent to George Cukor, who was then slated to direct the film, for tests; as soon as she realized she was in with a chance (though Cukor like Selznick had considerable initial doubts about her screen talent) she wired Guthrie at the Old Vic of her sudden unavailability for *Midsummer Night's Dream* and clung on in California to see what would happen.

What happened, despite the fact that Leslie Howard was unavailable so her tests had to be shot with the rather less inspiring Douglass Montgomery, was that Vivien Leigh, against all the opposition and most insider guesses, got the role of Scarlett O'Hara; and with that victory something very drastic changed in the nature of the British colony in California. For years it had been reasonably static; certain gueststars had come out from London and gone back after a single, usually rather theatrical, performance, but the old giants – Colman, Marshall, Brook, Rathbone – stayed on doing most of the work.

Now, suddenly, in a few short months before the war, the whole picture had changed: two London stage stars, each with a trail of undistinguished films behind them and a deep determination never to spend a moment longer in California than it would take to shoot a film there, had landed two of the plum roles of the decade. Thanks to Wyler and the Selznick brothers, Laurence Olivier and Vivien Leigh were now two of the hottest properties not just of the Hollywood British but of all Hollywood, and though they remained unmistakably British, Vivien was playing in a deep Southern accent and Larry was carefully avoiding the clenched mannerisms of a Ronald Colman. They had somehow broken down not only the barriers of Hollywood but also those of their Hollywood compatriots, whose colony was never to be the same again. By stressing the nearness and importance of New York and of London, by hastening back to the stage as soon as their films were complete, and by ignoring the local gossips who reckoned that Selznick would never dare cast Vivien as Scarlett while she was living with a married man, the future Oliviers managed to change all the rules by which their predecessors in California had been living since the middle of the previous decade. It was the sudden, largely unexpected success of Larry in *Wuthering Heights* and Vivien in *Gone With The Wind* that, more than the start of the Second World War, changed the identity of the Hollywood British.

But Larry's troubles on the set of *Wuthering Heights* paled into insignificance beside those of Vivien Leigh on that of *Gone With The Wind*; she didn't care for Clark Gable, whose breath smelled and whom she considered lazy and none too bright; her one friend on the set was the Anglophile director Cukor, and he was sacked by Selznick after a couple of weeks' shooting because he wanted too great a say in the final cut of the film. Selznick then brought in the boorish Victor Fleming, who Vivien thought took an impertinent interest in her breasts and saw Scarlett as a one-dimensional shrew/bitch. He, too, was replaced – some said at the urging of both Leigh and Olivia de Havilland – and the film was in fact finished by Sam Wood, though by this time Selznick had virtually taken over as director as well as producer, a dual role that many believed he had wanted to play all along.

Vivien finished her role as Scarlett at noon on 27 June 1939, and went straight on that afternoon to test again for Selznick, this time hoping to get the role of the second Mrs de Winter, since Olivier had already agreed to play Maxim in the film of another great 1930s bestseller, *Rebecca*. This time, however, Selznick was determined to deny it to her, largely because Alfred Hitchcock, whose first American film this was to be, felt even more strongly than he did that Vivien's triumph as the headstrong Scarlett was precisely what made her wrong for the mouse-quiet Mrs de Winter ... an opinion shared by both George Cukor and the screenwriter and playwright Robert Sherwood, to whom Selznick went for further advice on a difficult matter. Vivien was by now openly trying to marry the star of *Rebecca*, and her performance in *Gone With The Wind* was already well enough known around Hollywood to make her the brightest star on Selznick's contract list. Refusing her the role that both she and Larry most wanted her to play required all of Selznick's tact and another dozen or so of his immensely long transatlantic telegrams.

By the end of August 1939, both were back in Hollywood after a brief summer in England trying to get out of their respective first marriages; Vivien was now doing some final retakes on *Gone With The Wind* (still secretly advised by Cukor, to whom she had continued going for nocturnal instruction in the role long after he had quit the set) and Olivier was starting out on *Rebecca* opposite Joan Fontaine, who also counted as Hollywood British since she and her sister Olivia had been born in Tokyo to the English teacher Walter de Havilland.

Hitchcock, under a contract he had recently signed with David Selznick, brought to *Rebecca*, his first Hollywood film, an intriguing mix of the old and new Hollywood Britons: not only Olivier and Fontaine but such other newcomers as Gladys Cooper and Judith Anderson as well as (from the old guard) Aubrey Smith, Nigel Bruce, Reginald Denny, George Sanders and Leo Carroll. Originally the plan had been for Hitch to make a Selznick film about the *Titanic* (for which presumably many of the same cast could have been used), and when that fell through he was not altogether delighted with the changeover, since he found Daphne du Maurier's gothic Cornish cliffhanger 'an old-fashioned novelette lacking in humour'.

Nevertheless, with Selznick safely caught up in all the post-production details of *Gone With The Wind*, the English director was given a studio freedom unknown to any of his American predecessors and as a result he made one of the most quirkily triumphant of all the Hollywood British pictures, managing even to fight off Selznick's determination that the smoke arising from the final conflagration of Manderley should spiral up to spell out the letter R.

It was, however, Selznick as producer rather than Hitchcock as director who won the Oscar for *Rebecca*, and before that happened some hairline cracks were already becoming evident in the solidarity of the Hollywood British. Told that Joan Fontaine had just married Brian Aherne, Olivier said, rather too loudly, on the set one morning, 'Couldn't she have done better than that?' and from then on Miss Fontaine took a distinct dislike to the rest of the colony: 'They were a cliquey lot who would sit in each other's dressing-rooms swapping theatre stories and recalling old chums from their Mayfair days. . . . Ronald Colman was the self-appointed king of this tight little group, while the queen was undoubtedly Basil Rathbone's wife, who reputedly had changed her name from Ida Berger to Ouida Bergere.'

From the other side of that particular fence, Gladys Cooper noted in letters home that Miss Fontaine seemed 'curiously untalented', and it may even have been that the crafty Hitchcock fostered this chilly atmosphere in the studio to achieve precisely that level of isolation and unhappiness which the second Mrs de Winter is *supposed* to feel in *Rebecca*. But Gladys, too, had her own doubts about the Hollywood British colony she was now joining for the first time:

Larry is quite wrongly cast as Max de Winter, but he is a big draw here now since they saw him in *Wuthering Heights*, so what does it matter? The main trouble I have here is finding the studios each morning: I have rented a car, but the roads all go very straight and unless you turn off them at just the right moment, you end up in the hills miles away from anywhere within a few minutes. All the English here stick together and Basil Rathbone is getting fifteen hundred dollars for a half-hour weekly radio show about Sherlock Holmes ... it is really fantastic what people are getting out here for doing comparatively little work.

But all good things come to an end, and this one more or less did so on 3 September 1939, when *Rebecca* had been shooting for just over a month. 'That autumn morning,' recalled Joan Fontaine, 'when Britain declared war, calls to the British Consul in California were placed from every bedside phone before the morning tea ... should every male and female born under the British flag take the next plane home? Were we needed, expected, commanded?'

An understandably bemused Eric Cleugh (the job of British Consul in California never having rated very highly on the priorities of the Foreign Office) said he would be contacting London for further instructions; meantime there were films to be made and nobody, least of all the British Consul, saw much point in a mass exodus of mainly septuagenarian and sometimes First-World-War-wounded veteran character actors to defend the homeland from the Hun.

Olivier, not entirely unexpectedly, took a more dramatic view of the situation, as Douglas Fairbanks Jr recalls:

That September 3 weekend we were all spending the day on a chartered yacht off Catalina, anchored in the harbour of the yacht club there. ... Larry and Vivien weren't yet married so they had her mother as a chaperone, and there was Niven and Bob Coote and Mary Lee, my wife, and me. Chamberlain was on the radio from London ... war had begun with Germany. ... We listened grimly, each concerned with special thoughts of his own about what to do. The silence was finally broken, and not, as might have been expected, by the usually ebullient Niven, but by Larry, of all people. Without our noticing it, he had quietly and

unobtrusively proceeded to get as smashed as a hoot-owl. Then, very
and carefully, he had climbed into a dinghy and rowed away. On reachi
stern of a fairly large anchored yacht young Laurence stood up, just stead
enough not to fall into the water, and like some Cassandra in swimming shorts
bellowed to all within earshot, 'This is the end. You're all washed up. Finished.
Enjoy your last moments. You're done for. . . . Relics, that's what you are now,
relics!' Before the bemused American layabouts could reply, our Larry boy was
again rowing resolutely off towards the next yacht that had caught his bleary eye
and repeating his prophecy of doom. An hour later an official protest was delivered by the club secretary not to us but to the owner of a small sailing yacht
close by, demanding an immediate apology for having insulted other club
members. That owner was a man who still bore a passing resemblance to Larry,
Ronald Colman.

The British in California were now totally at sea.

After he had sobered up, Olivier was the first to notice a distinct chill in the California air that September of 1939:

It was a painful situation, and wretchedly embarrassing with the Americans who were, for once, our now not very enthusiastic hosts. Many of them seemed far from certain whose side they were on. There was an enthusiastically pro-German feeling in those areas of the United States containing extensive proportions of German immigrants. Milwaukee, for instance, was largely German-speaking.

Indeed in Hollywood itself, large numbers of German immigrants were employed as directors and designers, while a few, like Von Stroheim, were regularly to be seen in front of the camera; with Pearl Harbor more than two years away, and an American policy of non-intervention in the European war all but declared, the confusion among the immigrant British workers in California was considerable.

For certain actors, there was no real problem: younger men like Olivier and Niven made it immediately clear that as soon as they could disengage themselves from whatever film they were currently shooting, they would be on the first train or plane back to New York and then England and the war. For others, the situation was considerably more complex: those above the age of immediate call-up, those long settled in America with wives and children and sometimes even grandchildren, those on apparently iron-clad studio contracts with several more years to run, urgently wanted some kind of official advice which would override all local considerations. They were, after all, in an extremely exposed, albeit still physically comfortable, situation: most were actors with a public as well as a private commitment to Britain. They were actors who for years had been making very good money playing stalwarts of the Empire, sons of Victoria, colonels of the Raj; all still had relatives in Britain, as well as audiences there and in America who had come to trust them as quintessentially British. They could not afford to be caught shirking their duty.

The trouble was that nobody, least of all the British Government, seemed willing to define precisely what their duty was; indeed there was understandable alarm in Whitehall at the realization that if, as Olivier noted, 'every Englishman living abroad were to come gallantly dashing home, the public services would have to face an additional population of anything up to half a million extra mouths to feed and extra hands to find employment for'. Not surprisingly, therefore, a 'stay put' directive was almost immediately issued from the British Embassy in Washington, though if that had been as well publicized in Britain as it was in America a lot of the ensuing unpleasantness might have been avoided.

Led by Cedric Hardwicke, a number of the Hollywood British flew to Washington to find out precisely what they were supposed to be doing during the 'phoney war' of 1939/40: Lord Lothian, the Ambassador, told them briskly that they were actors on legitimate business doing good for their country by portraying 'the best of England' to world audiences. In other words they were to shut up and stay put.

Certain immediate problems then arose. The British press began castigating the Hollywood British for having 'gone with the wind up' and being deserters in their country's hour of need. Lothian's cabled reply was strong, though unfortunately it remained for years buried in a pile of Foreign Office briefings; it read, in part: 'The maintenance of a powerful nucleus of older actors in Hollywood is of great importance to our own interests, partly because they are continually championing the British cause in a very volatile community which would otherwise be left to the mercies of German propagandists, and because the continuing production of films with a strong British tone is one of the best and subtlest forms of British propaganda.' To a radio broadcast by the BBC repeating these press allegations of 'desertion', Lothian further replied: 'The only effect of broadcasts like this is quite unjustifiably to discredit British patriotism and British-produced films; neither do Americans like having British dirty linen washed for their benefit in public.' That, however, was not enough to deter a number of the British at home from settling some old scores: Michael Balcon was to make Hitchcock, who had left his studios for those of David Selznick just a few months earlier, a constant target for charges of desertion.

Hitchcock's decision to settle in America just before the Second World War was as final and permanent as had been Chaplin's just before the First World War. With his devoted wife, Alma, and his assistant, Joan

Harrison (later to marry the novelist Eric Ambler, himself an extremely distinguished British screenwriter), Hitchcock had reached the conclusion that Hollywood held the only possible future for somebody who had done everything that was to be done in and with the British cinema, and in that sense the war was for him an irrelevance. Moreover, Hitchcock, though he was to remain the most stalwart of the Hollywood British in matters of dress and his taste for roast beef, was not trading off his nationality in the way that most British actors there still were. After *Rebecca* his films took on either an American or an international setting so that with a few exceptions (*Dial M for Murder*, *The Paradine Case*) they ceased to be recognizably the work of an English director at all. Hitchcock's love of the studio setting meant that his London backdrops were very often even more unreal than those of his Hollywood contemporaries. The truth was that Hitchcock, again like Chaplin, inhabited and photographed a world of his own, one which had no more to do with Hollywood than it had ever really had to do with London.

Ironically, however, it was Hitchcock, then already past forty and unfit for military service anyway, who was singled out for personal abuse in his own country for having settled abroad in wartime. Michael Balcon wrote in a British paper in August 1940 of 'people who prefer to remain in Hollywood instead of returning home to aid their country's war efforts' and added: 'I had a plump young junior technician in my studios whom I promoted from department to department. Today he is one of our most famous directors and he is in Hollywood, while we who are left behind shorthanded are trying to harness the films to our great national effort.'

Angry and hurt, Hitchcock replied: 'The British government has only to call upon me for my services. The manner in which I am helping my country is not Mr Balcon's business and has nothing to do with patriotic ideals.'

A quite different problem faced the rest of the Hollywood British in 1939. As hired actors, they had no control whatsoever over the kind of pictures the American studios were then making, and the chances of their slipping in some patriotic epics, even if anyone could think of a suitable script, were remote. America, moreover, had acquired through the films of the 1930s an image of England that was fixed in some other century altogether. No films had been made in California featuring contemporary Britain: *Cavalcade* stopped in 1929 and *Rebecca*, though nominally modern-dress, was in fact set in a totally timeless Californian Cornwall. Men like Chamberlain and Baldwin remained largely unknown in the days before regular transatlantic travel by statesmen; most movie-going Americans thus pictured an England still ruled by old Queen Victoria, whose gallant sons were out defending the corners of the Empire from natives. The one element of truth about modern Britain that had filtered through in the last decade was the fairy-tale story of a Baltimore girl running off with a British king who many thought must have been Victoria's son. It was as if, in reverse, all British knowledge of contemporary American life had been derived from a close study of *Gone With The Wind*.

Rallying round the flag in 1939 was thus no easy matter, even for those who were most keen to be seen doing it; when war was declared Herbert Wilcox happened to be in Los Angeles shooting *Nurse Edith Cavell* with his wife Anna Neagle. For his next subject, he was told, something less overtly propagandist might be a good idea, and so he settled on the all-American *Irene*, in which Miss Neagle was co-starred, not entirely successfully, with Ray Milland. But other and more distinguished film-makers were also now heading out to California, since there appeared to be remarkably little happening in Britain in the early months of 1940 and no particular appeals had been made by a government which was apparently entirely happy to have its film-makers carrying on in California. Indeed it was Churchill himself who suggested to his friend Alexander Korda that he might be more usefully employed in Hollywood than at Denham in 1940.

Korda thus went back to the California community he had so detested almost a decade earlier and found that his feelings had not much altered; his marriage to Merle Oberon, who had been resident there since *Wuthering Heights*, was already in trouble. But Korda knew that if his *Thief of Bagdad* was ever to be finished it would have to be finished in Hollywood; moreover, Churchill knew that his old friend on his constant travels from there back to Denham would be a perfect courier for MI5, and had no hesitation in using Korda's production offices on both sides of the Atlantic as occasional branches of the Secret Service, with Korda himself being rewarded by a knighthood in 1942 for services to his adopted Britain.

It was, therefore, Korda in Hollywood who managed to come up with the first great British propaganda film of the Second World War. Using Laurence Olivier and Vivien Leigh, married at last and feeling trapped in America by their own massive commercial failure on Broadway with *Romeo and Juliet* and their own country's apparent inability or unwillingness to find them anything useful to do at home, Korda worked in an American studio but with a British writer (R. C. Sherriff) and an almost entirely British cast; and what he made was the film that Churchill himself had suggested might be a useful contribution to the war effort, if only because it too dealt with a great and embattled British leader fighting a deadly European foe. Though ostensibly about Nelson and his celebrated lady love, *That Hamilton Woman* (known in England less flamboyantly as *Lady Hamilton*) did contain a massively Churchillian speech, many believe written by Churchill himself, in which Nelson pleads with the Lords of the Admiralty not to trust Napoleon's peace overtures: 'He can never be master of the world until he has smashed us up – and believe me, gentlemen, he means to be master of the world. You cannot make peace with dictators, you have to destroy them.' There could not have been much doubt, even in California, about precisely which dictator was meant.

But despite the good and patriotic work that he was undoubtedly doing, Olivier was still not happy to be back in California, as Korda's nephew and biographer Michael has noted:

Even in peacetime, Larry had never been comfortable in the company of his fellow British expatriates in California, whose Englishness had become both a caricature and a livelihood. He described them as British by profession, character actors whose own characters had been fixed forever by a Hollywood stereotype. There was something amiably ridiculous in the sight of these robust English figures, with their tweeds, their moustaches and their regimental blazers, sitting down to tea under the orange trees and palms of Beverly Hills, engaging in cricket matches and talking of England as 'home' when most of them had lived in California for twenty years. They resembled in many ways the pukkah sahibs of an earlier generation, and Ronald Colman was frequently heard comparing Beverly Hills to Poona. The sight of Cedric Hardwicke in a deerstalker hat and Inverness cape on Santa Monica Boulevard, or C. Aubrey Smith in a blazer and straw boater on his way to the Cricket Club, no longer astonished the natives. Most of the British exiles were in fact very content to be in Hollywood – with rare exceptions, they were only modestly talented and happy enough to exchange the rigours of the English stage, the dreary tours through the provinces, the low pay of the rep, the occasional parts in minor films, for the more glamorous and substantial rewards of Hollywood.

But Olivier and Vivien Leigh were not of that number, nor indeed was Korda – which was why all three made rapid returns to Britain after the shooting of *That Hamilton Woman* was complete. Korda alone was soon to return to California, despite a Washington row which nearly caused him to be banned forever from the USA, thereby ending his wartime usefulness to Churchill and the Secret Service. The problem was 'America first', an isolationist committee which took the view that the American movie industry had been infiltrated by Jewish money and British agents and was being turned into a propaganda organization designed to drag an unwilling America into a war not of her making. *That Hamilton Woman* and the even more fervently pro-British *Mrs Miniver* were cited as the two worst examples of this new and danger-ous Hollywood trend, but Korda (who had nothing at all to do with *Mrs Miniver*) somehow became the focus for Washington attack, which would doubtless have redoubled had the senators there also known of his hazy Secret Service courier missions for Churchill. Happily, however, Washington committees even in those days worked extremely slowly; after various postponements instigated by Korda, his appearance before them was finally fixed for 10 December 1941, just three days after the Japanese attack on Pearl Harbor made the whole concept of 'America first' suddenly somewhat irrelevant.

Those British directors who could go into immediate patriotic action in California did so, and in that they were perhaps rather more fortunate than the actors, who simply had to wait and see what roles would be available for them next. A director like Hitchcock, riding high on the success of *Rebecca* and stung by Michael Balcon's ill-considered accusations of disloyalty to the British flag, made sure that his next film would contain some sort of answer. It comes in the closing moment, when Joel McCrea as the *Foreign Correspondent* is making a stirring Ed Murrowesque broadcast back to America from amid the bombs of London:

Hello, America. I've been watching a part of the world being blown to pieces. A part of the world as nice as Vermont, Ohio, Virginia, California and Illinois lies ripped up, bleeding like a steer in a slaughterhouse. And I've seen things that make the history of the savages read like the Pollyanna legend. ... I can't read the rest of this speech because the lights have just gone out. So I'll just have to talk off the cuff. All that noise you hear isn't static, it's death coming to London. Yes, they're coming here now. You can hear the bombs falling on streets and homes. Don't tune me out – hang on – this is a big story – and you're part of it. It's too late now to do anything except stand in the dark and let them come, as if the lights are all out everywhere except in America.

(*Music*, 'America', begins to play softly in the background of speech and continues through end credits.) Keep those lights burning, cover them with steel, build them in with guns, build a canopy of battleships and bombing planes around them and hello, America, hang on to your lights, they're the only lights in the world.

And with those few words it is arguable that Hitchcock did more for the 'war effort' than his detractors back home were ever to achieve in the same cause. They, however, were not to be silenced, and with every news story the pressure on the Hollywood British to 'do the decent thing' grew stronger. Though Anna Neagle made the cover of *Picture Post* for starring in *Cavell*, 'the first English film to be made in Hollywood', and generally reckoned A Good Thing (even though *Journey's End* had, of course, been made there in its entirety a decade earlier), Gracie Fields was vilified by the same British press as a coward and a traitor for settling in California a few months later when it became abundantly clear that her husband, an Italian, was in danger of being interned in Britain as an enemy alien. Elisabeth Bergner, domiciled in Britain since the advent of Hitler in her native Germany, slipped over the border into America while she was meant to be filming in Canada and was similarly vilified, as was Korda until Churchill rescued him with a few published letters. On the other hand Olivier and Leigh, working for Korda in California, attracted no hostile press coverage at all. The rule seemed to be that if you were foreign, or Hitchcock, and living in London then you had no right to move to California even before the war had started; if, however, you came into neither of these categories, then other rules might apply, depending on the whim of the journalist concerned. The denunciations of the British in America had much of the random illogicality of the later French denunciations of 'collaborators', and in certain cases caused nearly as much distress; Gracie Fields clearly still felt the pain when writing her life story twenty years later: 'Every British newspaper screamed that I had deserted my own country and taken £100,000 worth of jewellery out of England, that I was a traitor, that I'd run away. ... Questions were asked in Parliament, even.'

Writers did not escape either: Aldous Huxley had been at MGM since the summer of 1938 preparing a 'treatment' of *Madame Curie* for Garbo (a film that was eventually made six years later with Greer Garson and no screen credit at all to Huxley), and in the summer of 1939 he had begun work on the script of the Olivier-Greer Garson *Pride and Prejudice* (for which he was granted a screen credit) and moved from that to Twentieth Century-Fox for the Orson Welles–Joan Fontaine *Jane Eyre* (again credited). But by the end of 1939 Huxley had been joined in California by three other British writers – Christopher Isherwood, W.H. Auden and Gerald Heard – and early in 1940 they all came under severe British press attack following an article in the *Spectator* by the MP and diarist Harold Nicolson. How, asked Nicolson more in sorrow than in anger, could Americans be convinced of the rightness of the anti-Hitler cause when 'four of our most liberated intelligences refuse to identify themselves with those who fight'?

Nicolson's was an act others could not wait to get in on: the Dean of St Paul's published (again in the *Spectator*) a nasty little poem:

> This Europe stinks, you cried – swift to desert
> Your stricken country in her sore distress.
> You may not care, but still I will assert
> Since you have left us, here the stink is less

and Evelyn Waugh introduced into *Put Out More Flags* two left-wing poets called Parsnip and Pimpernel who disappear to America when war breaks out.

Once again the inevitable questions were asked in Parliament (Hansard: 'Will British citizens of military age, such as Mr W.H. Auden and Mr Christopher Isherwood, who have gone to the United States and expressed their determination not to return to this country until the war is over, be summoned back for registration and calling up in view of the fact that they are seeking refuge abroad?') and once again Parliament stood well aside, having no clear policy and not much idea of what to do with four British writers of distinctly unmilitary bearing even if they did return.

Others joined the battle (E.M. Forster in the writers' defence, Priestley and MacNeice on the attack, Spender somewhere in the middle) and *Picturegoer* was by now reporting some memorably daft goings-on in the film capital. Studios were, it appeared, 'bribing' our lads not to return to Britain and thereby 'sabotage' projected films worth millions of dollars, while John Loder was personally attempting to form a British Legion of Hollywood. Cary Grant announced sharply and rightly that he had been an American citizen for several years, and Merle Oberon announced that she was seriously thinking of becoming a spy. *Picturegoer* for 27 January 1940 ran a singularly nasty piece by Maurice Cowan listing all British writers, actors and directors then working in Hollywood and suggesting they all be forcibly repatriated, regardless of age, to work in British studios for army pay; quite what films they were supposed to make there was never made clear. One or two careers were, however, temporarily damaged in the crossfire: an actor called Patric Knowles made the mistake of applying for US citizenship just after the declaration of war, and was sharply reminded by the British press that he had once appeared in a soldier's uniform, alongside Errol Flynn no less, in *The Charge of the Light Brigade* and that his behaviour was therefore unbecoming in an officer and a gentleman. He was, though, still to be found playing small parts in Hollywood as late as 1973.

Even if they weren't to return to the fray, the British in Hollywood clearly had to do something about what was now rapidly developing into a distinctly unphoney war; Cary Grant announced that he would be taking on no more uniformed roles for the duration: 'Who the hell wants to be seen playing at soldiers around the studios while all this is going on?', and Alan Mowbray announced that as Chairman of the new British War Relief Fund he would be organizing a special theatrical performance at which Mickey Rooney would imitate Charles Laughton in *The Hunchback of Notre Dame*. That seems, amazingly, to have raised £2,000 for the British cause. Meanwhile, actresses were being asked to knit balaclavas for the lads at the front, though, as Joan Fontaine noted, anybody who wore one of hers would have been blinded long before contact with the enemy.

My grandmother Gladys Cooper was by now getting distinctly irritable about how well the British in California still appeared to be living:

Went to large dinner party at the Basil Rathbones' last Sunday: all rather too rich and overpowering with dinner on a white terrace and servants. The next night I dined at Roland Young's house and he only had Henry Daniell and his wife, so Henry and I gossiped a lot about England and Roly Young, who'd been filming all day, fell asleep at the table and we had to wake him up as we were leaving to say goodnight and thank you. Such a nice little man.

But Gladys, too, a woman now in her early fifties, was more than a little hurt and horrified when she discovered that it was her old London stage friend and partner Sir Seymour Hicks who had published the original 'Gone With The Wind Up' article in a British paper:

Such a ridiculous thing for the old boy to do, and so unfair to most of us. What possible good could I do back in England now? I'd just be using up valuable resources and getting in the way ... but Phil [Merivale, to whom Gladys was then married] says that if we stay out of it we shall morally have lost any right to call ourselves British subjects after the war is over, though of course all that would change if America ever entered the war and many of us here think that's what we should be encouraging as then it would all be over so much faster. ... Noël Coward and Duff Cooper and some others are already out here doing propaganda work and they want to evacuate children from the Actors' Orphanage in England out here too, so May Whitty and I are forming a committee to raise the money. ... Apart from that things are seeming rather aimless out here and we all just sit by the radio waiting for war news from Europe and every bulletin just contradicts the last, so now I have taken up gardening to keep my mind off things. ... Two days a week I go to the Red Cross British Relief Fund here and make pyjamas (you would laugh if you saw my sewing); Mrs Ian Hunter and Mrs Boris Karloff and Mrs Melville Cooper are all in my group and we are doing our best, but I fear it isn't nearly enough. ... My name still means so little out here that I'm not even much good for raising money, and when they asked for $500 from each of us for the Orphanage children and I realized I hadn't even got that in the bank I got very, very depressed ... if only I could get one good film.

Later in 1940, as subsequent letters to my mother indicate, Gladys did begin to make rather better money (notably in *Kitty Foyle* with Ginger Rogers) and her spirits began to pick up as the news from home got, if no better, at least not much worse: 'We have now got some new things called "car stickers" with a Union Jack on them and written across it ALONE AND UNAFRAID and lots of shops we've taken them to are now sticking them up in their windows so nobody in California can ever forget about England.'

21:
Home Thoughts from Abroad

Just before the outbreak of war, King George VI and Queen Elizabeth paid a state visit to President Roosevelt, and the Hollywood British gathered themselves together for one massive if eccentric showing of the flag: in a live radio broadcast back to Washington from Los Angeles Sir Cedric Hardwicke, Nigel Bruce and Aubrey Smith solemnly sang 'Three Little Fishes', Basil Rathbone and Vivien Leigh read love poems by the Brownings, Greer Garson and Leslie Howard did extracts from *Goodbye Mr Chips*, Merle Oberon paid 'loyal respects to their Majesties in these difficult times', the Ray Noble Orchestra played 'Charlie is my Darling', Brian Aherne read Rupert Brooke, Dennis King sang 'Annie Laurie', and David Niven was the master of ceremonies. Some years later, in London, he happened to ask Queen Elizabeth what she and the King had made of the proceedings. 'Wasn't it awful?' Her Majesty replied. 'The President's radio battery ran down just before you all came on.' Those of us who have heard the broadcast, now a collector's piece and happily recently reissued on record, are inclined to take the view that their Majesties had a lucky escape.

By the middle of 1941, some equally eccentric gestures of solidarity were being made on film: Basil Rathbone and Nigel Bruce, finding themselves in the middle of a highly successful run of *Sherlock Holmes* on both film and radio, decided that some of the scripts could well do with a final pro-British message. Accordingly *Sherlock Holmes and the Voice of Terror* (released in 1942) was updated to a wartime setting and ended with a throat-catching conversation between Rathbone and Bruce high on the white cliffs of Dover (or a reasonable studio facsimile thereof):

HOLMES: There's an east wind coming, Watson.

WATSON: No, I don't think so. Looks like another warm day.

HOLMES: Good old Watson – the one fixed point in a changing age. There's an east wind coming all the same, such a wind as never blew on England yet. It will be cold and bitter, Watson, and a good many of us may wither before its blast. But it's God's own wind, nonetheless, and a greener, better, stronger land will lie in the sunshine when the storm has cleared. (*Music swells to finish.*)

Nor were those the home thoughts from abroad of some Hollywood-based British screenwriter; the dialogue had conveniently been written, word for word, by Sir Arthur Conan Doyle at a similar time of national peril in 1917. And these ultra-patriotic pay-offs now became a signature of the Holmes series: *Sherlock Holmes and the Secret Weapon* (1943) ends with Watson saying, 'Things are looking up, Holmes; this little island's still on the map,' to which Holmes replies with the full Shakespeare: 'Yes. This fortress, built by Nature for herself. This blessed plot, this Earth, this realm, this England,' and fade to black. *Sherlock Holmes Goes to Washington*, also released in 1943, ends with the detective duo driving away from the Capitol down Pennsylvania Avenue:

HOLMES: This is a great country, Watson.

WATSON: It certainly is, my dear fellow.

HOLMES: Look. Up there. The Capitol – the very heart of this democracy.

WATSON: Democracy – the only hope for the future, eh, Holmes?

HOLMES: It is not given to us to peer into the mysteries of the future. But in the days to come, the British and American peoples will for their own safety and the good of all walk together side by side in majesty and in justice and in peace.

WATSON: That's magnificent. I quite agree with you.

HOLMES: Not with me, Watson. With Mr Winston Churchill. I was quoting from the speech he made not long ago in that very building.

A whole history of Anglo-American relations in the Second World War could be derived from these Holmesian postscripts in the B features that Universal was now turning out in bulk. Another of the 1943 releases, *Sherlock Holmes Faces Death*, had Holmes announcing to Watson: 'There's a new spirit abroad in our land. The old days of grab and greed are on their way out. We're beginning to think of what we owe the other fellow ... and we shan't be able to kneel and thank God for blessings before our shining altars while men anywhere in the world are kneeling in either physical or spiritual subjection ... and God willing we'll live to see that day, Watson.'

Happily, both men did: Nigel Bruce was filming right up to *Limelight* in the year of his death (1953) and Basil Rathbone up to *Autopsy of a Ghost* in the year of his (1967). But they were lucky to have found, in 1940s Hollywood, characteristically English roles which could so easily be linked to the war effort. Others had more of a problem (not least the playwright Freddie Lonsdale, who just before Pearl Harbor announced to Cedric Hardwicke that in an effort to escape the European bombing he was going to Japan: 'I'm yellow and nobody will notice it there').

When the bombs did fall on Pearl Harbor, the panic spread to California within hours, as R. C. Sherriff recalled:

England had been expecting the war for so long that when it came we hardly turned a hair. But to the Americans it came like a thunderbolt, while for those who lived on the Pacific coast it was terrifying. If the Japanese could fly in and destroy most of the American fleet at Pearl Harbor, there wasn't any logical reason why they couldn't land an invasion army almost anywhere along that totally unprotected coast. . . . One night there was an air raid alarm, and terrified people took cover under tables in their flimsy wooden houses; for more than half an hour some guns in the vicinity put up a ramshackle sort of barrage, firing at each other's shell bursts until they got word that it was a false alarm. But at least it reassured people that there were a few guns somewhere. When nothing further happened, things gradually settled down again. Hollywood got its mind back on its pictures, and an old lady who had shut herself up for two weeks in her bungalow next door to ours came outside again.

Sherriff himself rapidly returned to London and a long, successful career in the British cinema and theatre; others waited out the war in California, since it had long been their only real home. For this, however, they were still not readily forgiven by the British press: Malcolm Phillips, writing in a March 1942 issue of *Picturegoer*, suggested that all British 'hero types' still working in Hollywood should be filmed only in black and white, 'since Technicolor would undoubtedly show up the yellow of their skin'. The Oliviers were now safely back at the British front and therefore escaped this particular criticism (Sir Laurence's continuing distaste for Hollywood had not been improved by one Californian cinema billing him in *Wuthering Heights* as 'Mr Scarlett O'Hara'), but others, like Milland and Cary Grant, were still getting frequent moviemagazine demands to 'come home like David Niven'. Richard Greene, later a long-running television *Robin Hood*, and Patric Knowles, both of whom went on to extremely honourable wartime military service, were among those vilified at the outset. Michael Balcon spelt it out in an interview he gave early in May 1940: 'I am surprised and disgusted by the attitude of British people at present in Hollywood; when things become tough here they desert the country and take cover in America. . . . I maintain that they should return at once to this country instead of cavorting about on the dance floors of Hollywood.'

Cautiously, for the laws of libel were even then strong, Balcon did not name anybody outright except Hitchcock and those like Niven and Leslie Howard who had had 'the decency and courage' to return, and those like Robert Donat who, though under contract to MGM, were insisting that all their work be done in England. But the situation was by no means as clear, even in the dark days of 1940, as Balcon may have thought; *Picturegoer* printed a number of hostile replies from British readers to his attack, including one which read: 'Are you happy with your part as a film-maker in this great struggle? If so, why are you so troubled for the consciences of others?' In the main, though, Balcon's supporters were the more vociferous: 'I urge', wrote another *Picturegoer* reader, 'that all films made by these Hollywood deserters be banned from British cinemas. Loyal Britishers can do without looking at the mock heroics of a bunch of cowards. The failure of their pictures over here would mean a salary cut and possibly end their miserable careers.' But in his otherwise extremely detailed 1969 autobiography, Balcon makes no mention whatsoever of what was at the time a long-running and frequently headlined press campaign largely initiated by his own interview. It is, I suppose, just possible that he too had begun to have second thoughts about its validity.

Meanwhile those Hollywood British old enough or distinguished enough to be above the fray were turning their minds to the curious change that had come over their fellow Hollywood workers now that America, too, had joined the war:

At first [wrote Cedric Hardwicke] nobody could believe it had happened. A group of us used to meet at my house in those days for Sunday brunch and bridge. Kippers were on the menu that December sabbath. I lay abed anticipating the pleasure of eating them when I heard on the radio the first incredible news of what was happening to the Pacific Fleet. I remember my reaction then was to telephone everyone I knew. I found then a reaction among old Hollywood hands which occurred time and time again during the war – they believed in photographs but not in reality ... because there were no pictures as yet of Pearl Harbor in flames, Hollywood as a whole simply did not care what was happening. If, later in the war, Japanese troops had landed on Santa Monica Boulevard, not a soul in town would have believed it until you showed them a photograph or a film of the event. Then they would have jumped around like fiends.

When, via the newsreels, Hollywood did eventually realize what was going on, the British colony suddenly found itself in an altogether new and unusually bizarre kind of employment. Up till now there had been a great many anti-Nazi films, going all the way back to Warners' *Confessions of a Nazi Spy* in 1939 and including, of course, Chaplin's 1940 *Great Dictator*; but the Japanese attack on Pearl Harbor meant a sudden increase in the demand for villainous Orientals and Middle-Europeans at all studios. The problem was that most German and Japanese nationals had long since gone home, and those few that were left were not deeply reassured to find signs springing up in Los Angeles barbers' shops reading, 'Japs shaved here – no responsibility for accidents'.

So, in a town full of good guys, who was left to play the baddies? In some desperation it was decided that if genuine German or Japanese villains were proving unavailable at Central Casting, it would be all right to use other foreigners in the roles so long as they did not look or sound too American. It was Darryl Zanuck who decided that for one particularly turgid war film he was making it might help (in the absence of the genuine Japanese, who were mainly now to be found in Californian internment camps) to have the entire Tokyo war cabinet played by Englishmen, since American audiences would then readily be able to detect by their voices that they were unAmerican and therefore likely to be baddies. Accordingly Basil Rathbone, Nigel Bruce (both on leave from *Sherlock Holmes*), Aubrey Smith, Cedric Hardwicke and Roland Young were summoned to make-up at five o'clock one morning. Dedicated technicians spent the next five hours making them look suitably slant-eyed, and they were then assembled at a replica of the cabinet table in Tokyo. Aubrey Smith rose duly to his feet: 'We are gathered heah', he declared in the ringing tones of an Indian Army Officer, 'to considah the next crushin' blows to delivah against the enemy Americans.' Sounds of undisguised hilarity from the Americans on the set indicated even to Zanuck that audiences might not be about to fall for Sir Aubrey and Sir Cedric as typical wily Orientals, and the parts were duly recast with immigrant White Russians who, if not very Japanese either, at least didn't look or sound too terribly English.

Meanwhile the British community did get itself together for one major war-picture of its own: *Forever and a Day*, released in 1943, was in intriguing contrast to the other two great tributes to the embattled British which sandwiched it – *Mrs Miniver* (1942) and *The White Cliffs of Dover* (1944). Both *Miniver*, starring the unbelievably glutinous Greer Garson, and *Dover*, starring the not-much-better Irene Dunne, were plastic attempts by Hollywood to create a never-never England about as phoney as the tweed-raincoat ads seen occasionally in *The New Yorker*.

But *Forever and a Day* was different; this was an attempt, admittedly somewhat shambolic, by the British in California to create their own film about their own country. It was in no way as obvious as *Miniver* (based on Jan Struther's novel), which had as its finale a service in a bombed English church where the vicar (Henry Wilcoxon) urged his parishioners to strive for victory while the congregation sang 'Onward Christian Soldiers' and the camera panned up through the roof to the RAF bombers flying overhead as the soundtrack changed to 'Land of Hope and Glory', thereby neatly encapsulating in less than five minutes every single cliché of the Hollywood-British war film. Nor was it as sentimental as *White Cliffs of Dover* (in which Roddy McDowall and Elizabeth Taylor as the supposedly all-English young teenagers already bore marked nasal Californian twangs), largely because it managed to avoid the worst excesses of a Hollywood screenplay.

Indeed *Forever and a Day* nearly manages to avoid a coherent screenplay of any kind at all. It was the brainchild of Herbert Wilcox, Victor Saville and Cedric Hardwicke, and was intended doubtless as some sort of riposte to the accusations of disloyalty coming from the homeland. The idea was that all British writers, directors and actors resident in Hollywood would give their services free, and all profits from the film be donated to deserving war charities.

Though Wilcox (and Anna Neagle), in fact, returned to London at an early stage of the proceedings, having shot one short sequence, Saville, Hardwicke and Bob Stevenson persevered with the project, even persuading RKO to donate studio space and technicians on minimum rates since they were the studio with at that time the most to spare – in the event of a raid, as well-known local posters of the day advised, 'Head for RKO: they haven't had a hit in years'.

The problem, which was to become a familiar one to countless devisers and producers of subsequent all-star charity shows on stage and television, was that every star wanted to do his or her bit regardless of what anyone else was doing. Accordingly, and mercifully, to avoid the 'stage door canteen' cabaret approach then endemic to American films of this nature, a rough plot-line was devised tracing the fortunes of one London house from 1804 to the Blitz. Twenty-one writers (among them Sherriff, Isherwood, Lonsdale, C.S. Forester, John van Druten and James Hilton) were then invited to come up with short sequences set within the house at various times in its history, and a cast of truly stunning stardom was shot in twos or threes as they became available from other paid projects. The cast list is therefore a roll-call of the Hollywood British in the middle of the war: Anna Neagle, Ray Milland, Claude Rains, C. Aubrey Smith, Dame May Whitty, Edmund Gwenn, Ian Hunter, Jessie Matthews, Charles Laughton, Cedric Hardwicke, Reginald Owen, Ida Lupino, Brian Aherne, June Duprez, Eric Blore, Merle Oberon, Una O'Connor, Nigel Bruce, Roland Young, Gladys Cooper, Richard Haydn, Elsa Lanchester, Sara Allgood, Robert Coote, Donald Crisp, Herbert Marshall and Victor McLaglen.

The posters announced '70 – Count 'Em – 70 of Hollywood's favourite stars', and to make up the numbers a few Americans like Ray Bolger and Edward Everett Horton (who anyway looked more British than most British) were allowed to slip in as well. The directors who worked on various sequences included René Clair, Edmund Goulding, Hardwicke himself, Frank Lloyd, Stevenson and the original Wilcox and Saville. Never in the history of Hollywood endeavour can so many have been assembled for so little. Cinema managers were advised to be 'very careful about the billing' since it was felt that customers who had come to see their favourite star and then only saw him or her for a matter of seconds might not take kindly to the arrangement. *Time* magazine thought the storyline understandably somewhat breathless, but noted to the delight of my family that 'Gladys Cooper (as a war-bereaved mother) is startlingly good in a film which bears all the traces of having been composed by a well-intentioned but mediocre committee'.

Even the British, for whom the whole thing had been devised, seemed remarkably ungrateful: 'One of the most brilliant casts of modern times', wrote James Agate, 'has been assembled to bolster up one of the poorest pictures.' Charity, it would seem, did not even begin at home; nevertheless, $1,000,000 was raised by the film for war funds in Britain and America.

22:
Writing on the Cinema Wal

Some indication of the strength of American feeling for Britain in 1942, or perhaps just of the strength of a really good weepie, can, however, be gained from the track record of *Mrs Miniver*: though featuring relatively few of the Hollywood British (Garson's co-stars were Walter Pidgeon, Teresa Wright and Richard Ney) it was stylishly directed by Wyler, grossed $6 million on its first American release and took four of the year's top five Oscars (Noël Coward won an Oscar nomination for his equally British *In Which We Serve*, which had the added advantage of being made on home territory and with rather less sentiment). Moreover, President Roosevelt told Wyler that his film had greatly lessened any political opposition to increasing US aid to Britain; similarly when Margaret O'Brien appeared as the lovable child in *Journey For Margaret* (also 1942 and about an English girl being evacuated to America) the demand for comparable evacuees was heard from California to Long Island. Even when Anatole Litvak wanted to make a different kind of war film, one which would feature a dour Yorkshireman (implausibly played by Tyrone Power) who decides to desert from a war which is, he thinks, being fought only to preserve an outdated British aristocracy, he was sharply told to tack on to *This Above All* a happy ending in which Power returns to the fray for the love of a good woman (Joan Fontaine). Another semi-pacifist picture, *The Hour Before Dawn*, scripted by Isherwood, was abandoned by Paramount even before it reached the studio floor, and Isherwood turned instead to an equally doomed life of Buddha.

In Britain, even *Mrs Miniver* couldn't win them all; though several critics (notably C. A. Lejeune) echoed the American enthusiasm, the film critic of the *Sunday Pictorial* found it

full of ghastly caricatures meant to represent the workers of Britain, while at the other end of the social scale the Minivers themselves are portrayed as the backbone of the country – the comfortable, easy-going middle class. A few years ago ᴜu may remember how this class saved Britain from disaster by putting Baldwin into power and applauding Munich. ... While Mrs Miniver and her ilk drifted uselessly around village flower shows and vicarage tea parties, nine out of every ten men in Jarrow were out of work ... and now we are asked to applaud this useless baggage resurrected from the Court Page of *The Times* to represent a nation at war while the woman who created *Mrs Miniver* (Jan Struther) announces that she plans to wait out the rest of the war in America.

The war seemed somehow to confirm rather than destroy the Hollywood British; the playing fields of the University of California campus at Los Angeles still reverberated to the sound of leather on willow as Aubrey Smith, who had once played cricket with the immortal W. G. Grace, took Bruce and Karloff out to bat. News of the war was, of course, reasonably available on American radio, but Smith would believe nothing until it had been printed in his fortnight-old copy of *The Times*, which still somehow arrived from London bearing reports of fresh disasters. The colony was diminished now, of course: the Oliviers had gone, and Niven, and Leslie Howard, who left murmuring gentlemanly apologies about the 'unutterable rubbish' that he had just helped transfer to the screen in the shape of *Gone With The Wind*. But those that were left behind took their war duties no less seriously: Nigel Bruce would creep up on film sets behind unsuspecting young British actors not yet in uniform and murmur, 'Going back to do your bit? Jolly good show. You'll join the RAF, I suppose? Or the RN, what? Or the Army, perhaps? By the way, here's your ticket to London. Nothing to pay. It's the least we old-timers can do, what? About the picture you're making now? Not to worry, old boy; we've organized an immediate release for you. Goodbye, old fellow, and good luck.'

The American war correspondent Quentin Reynolds, visiting California straight from a London blitz in 1940, found himself surrounded by old English actors wondering what to do; he could not bear to remark on Herbert Marshall's missing leg, or Nigel Bruce's lameness, or the general old-age of all concerned; nor could he bring himself to tell them that London had enough troubles at the moment without having to deal with their return as well. He merely told them to go on collecting the war bonds; Laughton raised a million dollars in one forty-eight-hour radio marathon, and Cary Grant handed over his entire $140,000 cheque from *His Girl Friday*.

Whatever reservations some elements of the British press may have had about the element of cosy middle-class propaganda that was oozing

out of the sprocket holes of films like *Mrs Miniver*, it needs to be noted
here that not one single anti-British film (with the possible exception of
Drums Along The Mohawk, which dealt with the War of Independence)
was allowed to escape from Hollywood between 1939 and 1945. On the
contrary, films like *A Yank in the RAF* (1941), *A Yank at Eton* (1942) and
A Yank on the Burma Road (also 1942), terrible though they undoubtedly
were, had the specific propaganda intent of reminding mid-western audiences that they and the British were now to be as one, whatever their
previous differences of nationalist opinion might have been.

By mid-September 1942 Charles Laughton was intoning the
Gettysburg Address (as he had in *Ruggles of Red Gap*, in which he played
the British butler who tames an American rancher) on the steps of the
Treasury building in Wall Street for yet another British war-bond rally,
while Greer Garson was lending her name to a newly built tank in
Arizona with the distinctly un-Miniver line, 'Hitler, here comes trouble.'
But a few months later, in a mysterious plane crash which has never
been satisfactorily explained, the Hollywood British were to lose their
most charismatic leader.

With the one exception of Ronald Colman, who went to his grave more
than a decade later convinced that a knighthood had been denied him by
his decision to remain in California throughout the war (a theory called
into some question by George VI's knighting of Aubrey Smith in 1944),
Leslie Howard was beyond doubt the ideal of the screen Englishman; as
C.A.Lejeune once noted, 'He had a passion for England and the English
ideal that was almost Shakespearian.' Contracted to return to film in
England just before the outbreak of the war (his agent let it be known
that the return was 'solely for reasons of patriotism'), Howard would in
fact have been among the first to go anyway. His view of the Germans
was 'to fight them to the last ditch', and in the early isolationist months
before Pearl Harbor it was Howard who broadcast back to the US most
often, trading his celebrity value there for the chance to urge America
into the war.

As his most constant and intelligent observer, Jeffrey Richards, has
written, Howard spoke then and in his last films 'of the quiet spirit of an
England roused to action by a monstrous evil'; his classic screen image
was of the aesthete deeply angered when Nazi submariners destroy his
books and pictures, a role he played in *49th Parallel*, and suitably enough
it was he who spoke, anonymously, the epilogue to Coward's *In Which We
Serve*. He was the Scarlet Pimpernel who became Pimpernel Smith,

getting first the aristocrats out from under the guillotine and then the Jews out from under Hitler, and he it was who came to personify a particular anglicized blend of nation, Empire, mysticism and war in his first broadcast back to the US from a Britain at war:

I can't explain the mystery of the call that comes to people from the land of their birth – I don't have to explain it to you, anyway. The call of Britain seems particularly potent, doesn't it? Look at the way they've come hurrying from the four corners of the earth, especially as that call comes at what must be the most critical moment of our whole long history. Most of you, I'm sure, will know what I mean when I speak of the curious elation which comes from sharing in a high and mysterious destiny. The destiny of Britain we cannot know for certain, but we can guess at it, and pray for it, and work towards it as we find ourselves singled out of all the nations of the world for the rare honour of fighting alone against the huge and ruthless forces of tyranny.

The chances are that Howard in the end gave his life to those forces, since his plane was shot down over the Bay of Biscay by two German fighters on 1 June 1943 when he was returning from a lecture tour of Spain and Portugal with a man who looked very like (and may by the Germans have been taken for) Winston Churchill. But by then Howard had made his great contribution to the war effort, not only with *Pimpernel Smith* but also with *The First of the Few*, both films made by him as director as well as star and both films vastly better than such contemporary Hollywood efforts as *Mrs Miniver* or the *Sherlock Holmes* updates.

Anyone who would like to think of Leslie Howard as one of the Hollywood British has to face the fact that all his best screen work, from *The Scarlet Pimpernel* through *Pygmalion* across ten years to *Pimpernel Smith*, was done in England. With the exception of *The Petrified Forest*, in which he transferred his starring role to the Hollywood screen from Broadway, his work in California was, as he himself said of *Gone With The Wind*, 'colourful rubbish'. And ironically, in going home to make *First of the Few* and *Pimpernel Smith*, it was actually Howard himself who showed Hollywood, at a time when nobody else bar Coward seemed to have the money or the will, precisely how faithful films about the British ought to be made. As a result, the Hollywood version of life in Great Britain was to become an early casualty of war. By 1945, a leader-writer on *The Times* was already feeling nostalgic for it:

What a loss it is. Never again to see that enchanted or at any rate transmogrified land, wrapped almost all year round in a dense fog – that will indeed be a deprivation. It was a land which we had all learned to love, for not only had glimpses of it redeemed many a bad film from dullness but it had a quaint, dreamlike charm all of its own. Its House of Commons (in which Sir Aubrey Smith almost always sat, often as a Duke), though generally rather smaller than our own, was infinitely more animated as well as being better lit; it is indeed scarcely possible to recall a session which was not rendered historic by the denouement of some major international crisis. Its policemen, barely discernible as they patrolled the fog-bound streets, resembled our own; but their helmets were slightly different, they never took their thumbs out of their belts, and the only traffic they were called on to regulate was an occasional hansom cab. Its aristocracy were, though not particularly powerful, numerous and, though stupid, generally condescending; they often had beautiful American daughters. They lived in castles of the very largest size and were much addicted to sport, particularly foxhunting. This was normally carried on at the height of summer (fog being perhaps less prevalent at that season) and though much of the densely wooded and often semi-precipitous country appeared unfavourable to the sport as we know it, the rather small packs never had a blank day. The lower orders, a cheerful lot, wore gaiters in the country but in London, being mostly costers, dressed in a manner which befitted this calling. The Army, except of course in war-time, consisted almost entirely of senior officers, most of them in the Secret Service. There were two universities, one at Oxford and the other at Cambridge. Cricket and football were not much played and – possibly as a consequence – there was a great deal of crime. But it was a wonderful place, and the only general criticism which can be levelled at the inhabitants is that when, as frequently happened, they met an American they betrayed an almost complete lack of understanding of the American Way of Life.

All of that was about to change. Just as the war altered British social life by introducing vast numbers of women to the concept of work outside the home, so was it also to make it impossible for the Hollywood dream of England to continue turning up on celluloid. Indeed, one crucial problem for the remaining Hollywood British as the war drew to its close was precisely what they were to do from now on. The demand for films about the Empire declined as rapidly as the Empire itself, and the newer forms of Hollywood movie (the big-band musical, for instance, or the Bogart-Ladd police thriller) seemed to have precious little need of the British. Even the great *Casablanca* had, from the old guard, only used Claude Rains, and then in the role of a French police chief; though the new Bogart thrillers were admittedly to give gainful, if brief, employment to the gargantuan Sydney Greenstreet, whose first film (*The Maltese Falcon*) was made in 1941 and his last only nine years later.

But Sydney Greenstreet, great though he was in every possible sense, was not exactly the kind of Hollywood Englishman likely to endear himself to Rathbone or Aubrey Smith: the thought of his vast, evil bulk on a cricket pitch is curiously implausible.

The new wartime immigrants from London were, in fact, of a very different kind: often below military age, or simply female, they were as often as not evacuees from Europe who happened to land up in California and once there took to acting as a lucrative local pastime. The one who was to emerge as leader of this new generation was the London-born daughter of American parents who, like her lifelong friend Roddy McDowall, had been evacuated to California well before her twelfth birthday.

Unlike McDowall, however, who had already emerged as a child actor in such English films of the late 1930s as *Just William*, Elizabeth Taylor only won an MGM contract because her art-dealer father happened to find himself on auxiliary fire-watching duties with one of the studio executives, who let it be known that for *Lassie* they were in need of a child with an English accent; and she only then went on to win the coveted *National Velvet* role because another English evacuee child in California, destined for political stardom, Shirley Williams, was scratched from the final race.

Though both Taylor and McDowall worked a lot with, and grew to love, the old British colony in California, they had one unique experience denied to any of their predecessors: apart from acting at MGM they were also being schooled there, in the classrooms that had been built on the lot for an earlier generation of native children like Temple and Garland and Rooney. And try as hard as they professionally did to retain their Englishness, they found it virtually impossible not to grow into all-American teenagers. By 1947 Elizabeth Taylor was plausibly playing a daughter to Irene Dunne and William Powell in *Life With Father*, while as early as 1943 the all-American colt *Flicka* was coming home to Roddy and his folks. Taylor and McDowall were, in fact, not the last of the Hollywood British, but the first of the Hollywood transatlantics, an altogether new breed of jet-travelling internationals whom the old cricketing guard found almost as alien as the Americans themselves.

While the young McDowall and Taylor were making a lucrative living in the *Lassie* movies, *National Velvet* and *My Friend Flicka* (the English always were meant to be especially good with animals), one of the greatest rows ever to involve the Hollywood British was breaking out in

London. It centred around the always controversial figure of Errol Flynn; born in 1909 in Tasmania, the son of an Australian professor whose special subject was the mating habits of whales, he had started off as an actor in English repertory theatres and graduated to Hollywood in 1935 to play a corpse in a *Perry Mason* B thriller. Though a friend of David Niven, Flynn was generally not much liked by the Hollywood English, who found him altogether too unreliable both as an actor and as an ally in the British cause; indeed one recent biographer, desperate to find a new sales pitch for yet another life of Flynn, managed to bill him as 'Nazi spy, international criminal, compulsive thief, committer of manslaughter, smuggler of gold, guns, drugs and lover of Howard Hughes and Tyrone Power' (both of whom, it added in an only faintly reassuring footnote, 'were also bisexual').

But what really annoyed the British at home was in fact none of that: rather was it his apparently single-handed capture of Burma from the Japanese. The problem arose because of an otherwise undistinguished 1945 Raoul Walsh picture called *Objective Burma* in which Flynn was starred with a tough all-American cast for a grittily 'realistic' study of the fighting in the Burmese jungle. Local critics in Los Angeles and New York found this unobjectionable enough; indeed the *New York Times* thought it 'one of the best war films yet made'. When, however, in October 1945 the film hit London, all hell broke loose; rising to his feet in the House of Lords, Lord Denman remarked that 'in this film Mr Flynn, aided by a score of American paratroops and some natives, undertook almost single-handed and with no mention of British involvement the conquest of Burma'. It would have made as much sense, noted his lordship, to have had Tommy Handley and the cast of the BBC radio series *ITMA* capture Okinawa unaided by Americans. The American public, he added 'is not to be blamed if it gets a rather distorted view of the British war effort. The truth is that we have been making war while they have been making imaginary films of imaginary wars.'

So great was the outcry in the London press that Warners had rapidly to withdraw their film from circulation and issue a public apology. It did the studio, and indeed Flynn, very little lasting harm but the row over *Objective Burma* signalled another drastic change that had come over the cinema during the war. Audiences, even in Britain, were far more travelled than ever before; moreover, with a film industry made strong by the war, a film industry capable at last of turning out its own classics of war and peace thanks to a new generation of directors like Carol Reed and David Lean and Anthony Asquith (none of whom ever showed much more than the faintest indication of wishing to work in Hollywood), the British no longer had to take the American output on trust or sufferance. Audiences, as well as critics, began subjecting Hollywood films to harder critical scrutiny than ever before. The British filmgoer, and the British cinema, had grown up and grown independent of Hollywood in the five years from 1939 and things were never going to be the same again, a point noted by David Niven in a highly intelligent column written for the *Daily Express* shortly after his return from the war to California in 1946: 'The British film industry was pampered during the war years, whereas the Hollywood industry was hampered ... there were no "reserved occupations" in the American film industry. Actors, producers, cameramen, directors and technicians were without exception called up for service. In England, however, producers, actors and key technicians were all 'reserved' so long as they remained actively involved on a particular film. In Hollywood, men like Frank Capra, William Wyler, John Ford, George Stevens, John Huston and Garson Kanin as well as actors like Jimmy Stewart, Robert Taylor, Tyrone Power, Henry Fonda and Melvyn Douglas were all away for three years or more.'

In Niven's view, now that the Americans were back in the film business there would be true transatlantic competition once more; but in fact the war had changed those rules too. By 1946 British film studios were more than capable of producing British films; what they wanted from Hollywood, not entirely surprisingly, was American films to help keep cinemas flourishing for the showing of native products as well. The Hollywood British film was, therefore, now in trouble, and no better indication of this could be found in 1946 than Ernst Lubitsch's *Cluny Brown*. This was a minor, some might say inoffensive social satire about an anti-Fascist Czech professor (played for no discernible reason by Charles Boyer) who comes to live with an upper-class English family, where he falls in love with a Cockney parlourmaid, played equally implausibly by Jennifer Jones.

The film was set some time between Munich and the outbreak of war, and Lubitsch was clearly aiming at a satire on *Ninotchka* lines, dealing this time with the upstairs-downstairs rather than East-West crossing of the romantic barricades. The fury that the film unleashed in the British press, though somewhat less than that surrounding *Objective Burma*, was enough to warn Hollywood off all but the most safely Victorian of British pictures for years to come – and this at a time when the world market for Hollywood had been destroyed by the growth of strong independent national cinemas from France to Brazil, making British box-office figures unusually important.

'Kippers fried in cream,' shrieked the *Sunday Graphic*, 'an anchovy laid across a strawberry ice – any other simile that conveys complete and awful wrongness is needed to describe Hollywood's idea of life in the stately homes of England. Cars are too big, riding clothes too unridden-in; even when a quiet dinner-party by candlelight is attempted, the ancestral dining-hall is still flooded with the flat glare of a score of studio arc lights.' The *New Statesman* thought that the names of the film's writers (Samuel Offenstein and Elizabeth Reinhardt) were enough to convey its awful unEnglishness, while the *Sunday Express* ('we deserve to be told') demanded: 'How is it that British-born actors and actresses can get mixed up in a film presenting such an absurd travesty of life as this, full of caricatured aristocrats and adenoidal chemists and self-conscious "characters" and upper classes all seen as amiable half-wits, while the lower orders are smugly servile morons ?'

Seeing perhaps the writing on the cinema wall, Sir Aubrey Smith (then on a penultimate visit to his native land two years before his death at eighty-five) felt obliged to issue a formal apology for his part in the film; perhaps, he suggested, J Arthur Rank ought to take retaliatory action 'by making an inaccurate film set in America'. Others of the Hollywood British involved in *Cluny Brown* included Margaret Bannerman and the celebrated actor and eccentric fish mimic Richard Haydn, whose long California career stretched from *Charley's Aunt* in 1941 across three decades via *The Sound of Music* to *Young Frankenstein*. He was also a director, notably of the Bing Crosby *Mr Music*, and author of the brilliant *Edwin Carp* diary; living up on Amalfi Drive, he remains to this day one of the last, if also the most reclusive, of the British colony.

This was now the high season for Hollywood mockery in the British press; hot on the heels of *Cluny Brown* came *Ivy*, a period thriller by Mrs Belloc Lowndes produced for Universal by William Cameron Menzies, the American director who'd had such a triumph a decade earlier in England with Korda's *Things To Come*. Now, however, British critics found him guilty of a film 'set', noted Virginia Graham, 'in Edwardian times, which enables Miss Joan Fontaine to emphasize the smallness of her waist and carry a parasol, and in an England where it appears the coach-and-four was still much in evidence and scions of country families talked about theousands of peounds'.

Margaret Lockwood and Phyllis Calvert were already managing these things a lot better for Gainsborough, with the result that the new young British in Hollywood, actors like Peter Lawford, who a decade earlier would never have been out of Indian army uniform on screen, now found themselves making Judy Garland musicals like *Easter Parade* as all-American juvenile leads rather than hanging around waiting for the call of the celluloid bugle.

The women (with some exceptions) were also having an easier time of it: with the decline in sporting and military British period pictures in Hollywood had come a sharp increase in the number of romantic weepies, which meant that a whole new post-Garson generation of actresses like Deborah Kerr and Jean Simmons were now to take charge of the Californian British; the Memsahibs had at last arrived.

23:
The Memsahibs Arrive

Before Greer Garson, the history of British actresses in Hollywood had been erratic and often unsatisfactory; there had been no female equivalent of Ronald Colman, no constant romantic leads, and nor had there even been a regular colonel's lady to partner the likes of Aubrey Smith. The pioneer Englishwomen out there in the early 1920s and 1930s, actresses like Dorothy Mackaill, had been obliged to 'play American' in films like *No Man Of Her Own*; and though Edna Best had a brief Hollywood spell, she too was always regarded as an outsider, a distinguished visitor to the sets from New York or London stages.

Even by 1939, when Gladys Cooper first arrived for *Rebecca*, nobody really knew what else to do with her. Still too young to play the cranky old ladies cornered at that time by Dame May Whitty and Edna May Oliver, she was also too old and far too independent to be 'made over' as an American. A great star of the London stage for more than twenty years (she had run her own company at the Playhouse), Gladys found that she was rapidly reduced to small character roles not because Hollywood thought of her in any sense as a failure but simply because the roles that had once been hers (such as the one written for her by Somerset Maugham in *The Letter*) were now being played on film by the likes of Bette Davis. It was only really as she aged into her sixties that MGM began to take an interest in the long-term contract they had given her in the middle of the war; then she could safely be typed as 'old English dowager', and regular employment was hers from then on.

Similarly Lilian Harvey, probably the greatest British film star to work abroad in pre-war years, found after her huge German success that Hollywood had not the faintest idea how to cast her, while actresses like Diana Wynyard and Isobel Jeans would occasionally be invited out to repeat a London or Broadway stage role for the camera, but again very definitely on a visitor's visa only.

One English actress who might have stayed and prospered in the

Hollywood of the 1930s was Elizabeth Allan, who had the bland good looks that MGM favoured and which got her the lead opposite Colman in *A Tale of Two Cities*; then, however, she was either courageous or unwise enough to sue the studio over a role that had been promised to her but was eventually given to Rosalind Russell in *The Citadel*, and that put an end to that. Jessie Matthews and Anna Neagle, two of the biggest stars of British films in the late 1930s, only made fleeting Hollywood appearances (including the inevitable *Forever and a Day*), and Merle Oberon achieved the unique distinction of playing many English roles in Hollywood without ever appearing in them to be especially English.

Cicely Courtneidge, another big star of British films immediately before the war, made one brief and disastrous trip to Hollywood in 1937 for *The Imperfect Lady*, a title which proved all too apt, as she later recalled:

Louis B. Mayer sent for me. I was shown into an enormous room rather like the audience chamber in Buckingham Palace and away in the distance I could just see a little man sitting at a huge desk. It seemed ages walking to meet him, but when I got near he rose from his chair very politely – a nice change from some of the other people I'd met at the studio – and said, 'Good morning, Miss Courtneidge, I am sorry to hear you're unhappy with us.' So I told him the producer they'd given me seemed to know nothing at all about me and Mayer said hadn't he seen any of my English pictures and when I told him no the fun really started. I never saw that producer again, they sacked the director and found me another, a lot of new authors arrived and started doing rewrites and the film was still terrible.

Indeed Miss Courtneidge's distaste for Hollywood was such that when her husband, Jack Hulbert, was offered a Hollywood musical at about the same time, he got as far from London as New York, decided there that he really couldn't face all the trouble that doubtless lay in store, and promptly returned home on the *Aquitania* instead of getting the train to California.

Others, too, didn't even try to work in Hollywood: June, later Lady Inverclyde, a considerable star of the West End musical stage between the wars, simply went out in 1930 to have a little holiday with Jack Buchanan while he was filming there:

The train journey from New York was hell on wheels, for air conditioning did not then exist and when we reached the torrid desert of New Mexico the air rushing through the open window was like blasts from a white-hot furnace, laden with dust, sand and soot from the engine. All one could do was hang wet towels in front of the inadequate electric fan, lie half-naked on one's bed and sip lemonade in which the ice had melted too swiftly to have much effect. But on the fourth night, as we spiralled into California, the temperature dropped and in the morning I saw well-irrigated pastures, lemon ranches, orange groves, walnut orchards, wind-breaks of tall feathery trees, little houses painted white, yellow and blue as in the South of France. ... Beverly Hills was then a charming little semi-rural city. ... Remembering those weeks, my mind's eye becomes crowded with world-famous faces: Mary Pickford, a diminutive figure in white beach-pyjamas; her husband Douglas Fairbanks with the torso of a Greek god and the high spirits of a lad; Joan Crawford, their plump young daughter-in-law, with huge hungry-looking eyes and a heavily painted mouth; John Gilbert, beginning to drink himself to death after the dual tragedy of losing Garbo and discovering that his high speaking voice was ill-suited to talkies; Charlie Chaplin, surprisingly good-looking without his famous tramp costume and funny little moustache; Ronald Colman, so exciting as an actor and so comfortably prosaic in real life; Kay Francis dashing into the midst of a formal dinner party in studio makeup and a shapeless woollen sweater; Grace Moore, always the diva in emeralds and diamonds; Jeanette MacDonald with her brilliant titian hair and chronic dyspepsia; Constance Bennett, slender as a sylph and with a Parisian taste in clothes; and of course Garbo, whom I was invited to meet at a small dinner party given by one of her few friends, Salka Viertel. 'Please do not dress up,' warned my hostess, 'and do not tell anyone you have been invited. Greta loathes meeting strangers and might not come.' ... She appeared at the door, however, motionless in white trousers, a white polo coat, the brim of her white witch's hat tilted over her forehead, and because the famous dark glasses were missing I saw her eyes boring into mine. Salka rushed forward crying, 'Greta, darling.' But Greta darling turned on her flat heels and vanished into the darkness with her hostess in hot pursuit. Shamelessly we bent our ears to catch a few words of the low-voiced altercation in the garden. Presently footsteps were heard but Mrs Viertel reappeared alone and, pointing an accusing finger at me, said, 'You stupid girl, it's all your fault. I told you to stay on the couch where Greta would not be able to see you.'

Unaccustomed to such exotic social traditions, Lady (June) Inverclyde soon returned to the rather more familiar life of the West End, and others who followed in her footsteps fared little better on the Hollywood circuit, though Cecil Beaton did at last succeed in befriending Garbo and by 1948 was walking with her up in the Hollywood hills:

In that house down that mountainside [Garbo pointed out to him] John Gilbert once lived and one night he had become drunk and pointed a revolver at her and she had fled out into the night and gone into some stranger's house ... but they had been nice people and the story never reached the newspapers. ... As we walked a number of alarming dogs ran out to greet her, and then after fondling a pet donkey she said, 'There must be nice people who live here, so close to nature – people can exist like this in California if they want to, oblivious of the movies and Louella Parsons.'

Garbo had not been inside the gates of MGM for six years when Beaton persuaded her to join him there for a private screening of *Anna Karenina*. That always most Anglophile of studios was Greer Garson's territory now, and it was she who, along with Madeleine Carroll, had opened up a path for British actresses in Hollywood in a way that, curiously, Vivien Leigh's success in *Gone With The Wind* never had. For Leigh had been playing an American, and though the film won her both an Oscar and a long Selznick contract (the latter in fact soon to be a problem, since Selznick then forbade her to play Ophelia to her husband's film Hamlet because he deemed the Shakespearian role 'inadequate' for his star after Scarlett O'Hara) it did not suggest to the studios the potential usefulness of British actresses.

The real achievement of *Mrs Miniver* was to make a superstar out of Greer Garson at a time when British actresses had seldom achieved satisfactory billing above the title. By 1946 she was big enough at the box-office to share the posters with Clark Gable on his return from the war; the film itself was a formless shambles called *Adventure*, but its poster slogan ('Gable's Back and Garson's Got Him') was to become almost as famous as 'Garbo Laughs'. Garson, indeed, went from strength to strength, undeterred by the fact that her Oscar acceptance speech for *Miniver*, running as it did to all of thirty minutes, was the one that prompted new rules governing Academy Awards night. Moreover, she cleared the way for other British actresses, so that by the time Deborah Kerr arrived from England soon after the war it was not just to be a ritzy stage lady out on a brief visit like Diana Wynyard a decade earlier, nor yet to be an eccentric comedienne in the way that both Bea Lillie and Elsa Lanchester as Englishwomen had found screen success. Rather was it to sign an MGM contract, having worked for that studio in England; intriguingly, the film that brought her to Mayer's attention in Hollywood was a Robert Donat marital comedy of 1945 called *Perfect Strangers*, in which Miss Kerr was featured with Glynis Johns. Watching the two of them together on screen, Mayer opted for Kerr rather than Johns as the one more likely to have a solid Hollywood future.

Kerr started in California in 1947 opposite Clark Gable in a mindless little advertising satire called *The Hucksters*; she joined Metro when the studio still had not only The King but also Tracy, Hepburn, Garland, Garson, Turner, Gardner and Esther Williams on their contract books, and her initial reaction was worthy of a schoolgirl hockey captain: 'I always wondered what it would be like. You come six thousand miles and then suddenly, by gosh, wallop, you've shot your first Hollywood scene. It's like having a tooth out.'

Kerr's survival in California, like that of Audrey Hepburn and the 1950s generation, was based on her ability not to appear over-English on screen unless this was specifically required by the script; though she did a lot of Hollywood-British epics like *Julius Caesar* and *Quo Vadis* as well as an appalling remake of *Zenda* (in the Madeleine Carroll role) she truly made her American name playing Burt Lancaster's nymphomaniac married lover in *From Here To Eternity*, a role for which Joan Crawford had been originally envisaged and one which allowed Miss Kerr to escape altogether from the long screen shadow of the Union Jack, a feat never quite achieved by such followers as Julie Andrews. Kerr also managed, unlike Greer Garson, to avoid ending up as a Mother Superior in *The Singing Nun*.

Set, however, against individual success stories such as those of Deborah Kerr and Greer Garson in the 1940s or Jean Simmons and Audrey Hepburn in the 1950s, was a general Hollywood uneasiness about precisely what to do with the British on screen. In truth, the only interest Hollywood had ever had in Britain was to do with her imperial or royal past; occasionally and reluctantly in the war years the studios had updated themselves as far as *How Green Was My Valley* or *Rebecca*, but even then they were films set in the safely remote and timeless territories of the Welsh Valleys or Cornwall. The idea of coming to terms with 1940s British politics, a man like Attlee, the Education Act, or indeed the Welfare State filled Hollywood not so much with terror as with deep apathy. A traditionally highly conservative group of studio moguls had a certain respect for a Napoleonic wartime leader like Churchill, who could anyway be conveniently related to history via the Marlboroughs, but no interest at all in the smaller men who followed him into high office; nor did they much like the sound of Socialism, something only one step removed in their vocabularies from a McCarthyite terror of Communism already rampant in Hollywood by 1947.

Now that the war had made the sagas of Empire impossibly dated, what instead were they supposed to film about Britain? The coming of transatlantic air travel, of television, of relatively rapid communications made London seem suddenly closer to Los Angeles geographically as well as socially. Americans who had been forced for the first time to travel on armed service in the war began to travel abroad on business or pleasure in peacetime; the Britain they found was no longer shrouded in Victorian fog, nor did it resound to the clatter of horses' hooves on cobbled streets, though five short years earlier the amazement of many GIs at this discovery had been considerable. Suddenly, audiences knew what Britain looked and sounded like, and with post-war austerity and rationing that was nothing especially wonderful – certainly nothing worth immortalizing on the silver screen.

Moreover Hollywood studios were now in direct competition with Elstree, Pinewood and Denham for actors, writers and directors, and, more important still, for screen time at British cinemas; London was fast becoming a rival film production centre, not a place filled with ladies clutching parasols as they gazed out of the Tower of London at the calm waters of the River Cam. To most Hollywood eyes, London by 1947 was as real, as mundane and almost as close as Chicago, and how many great films had there been about Chicago?

Thus far, Hollywood British films had always belonged to certain distinct and clearly defined categories: middle-class patriotism (*Cavalcade, Mrs Miniver*); imperial glorification (*Lives of a Bengal Lancer, The Sun Never Sets, Gunga Din*); Anglo-American relations (*Ruggles of Red Gap*); upper-class ideology (*White Cliffs of Dover*); sport (*A Yank at Oxford*); First World War heroics (*Journey's End, Hell's Angels*). None of these categories made any real sense by 1947 and, with the exception of a few untypical throwbacks, the era of the British film in Hollywood was drawing to its close.

Hollywood continued to exert a powerful influence and attraction, however: the English were still drawn to it for reasons admirably explained by J. B. Priestley writing in the *New Statesman* in 1947:

The film world is the last of the fairytale worlds. The people in it spend their time searching for Aladdin's ring and lamp. One wave of the right wand and you are suddenly transported from a back room in Bloomsbury into a suite at Claridge's. Mysterious characters from Central Europe emerge from obscurity, are seen smoking eight-inch cigars in the most expensive restaurants, and putting the very waiters under contract before melting like snowmen. Girls who have been living on baked beans in students' hostels are suddenly discovered smiling over their mink at Cabinet Ministers in the foyer of the Empire, Leicester Square. Success is a mushroom a hundred feet high. There is a magic formula –

and now Smith has it ('Get after him'), now Robinson ('That's the chap we want');
but they are all, of course, really waiting for Rumpelstiltskin. There are hundreds and hundreds of sensible, conscientious craftsmen in this business,
technicians all neatly organized into societies and unions, but nevertheless the
fate of these fellows still largely depends on what is happening to the seven-
league boots, the cloak of invisibility and the woodcutter's youngest son. When I
used to hobnob with very important film producers, Caliphs of Baghdad, for a long
time I could never understand why they were always taking telephone calls from
Cape Town, Melbourne and Portland in Oregon. Finally I came to the conclusion
that these calls helped them to believe somehow that they were real. Who would
telephone a subjective phenomenon, a sorcerer's illusion, from Portland,
Oregon? Nearly all film money is fairy gold. I have known men who toiled for
years in the glittering mines of Beverly Hills only to discover in the end that they
owned nothing but the dead leaves of bogus oil shares. Nearly all those fabulous
sums about which we read in the press seem to wither away. Five hundred pounds
a week in films are worth fifty pounds a week anywhere else. Perhaps most of it
goes to pay off witches and leprechauns. But this magical influence cuts both
ways. Bankers and presidents of insurance companies, who would not invest a
couple of hundred pounds in a weekly review, in book publishing or in the theatre,
will be lured into the crystal castle of the films, possibly by Puss-in-Boots, and
will begin writing cheques for millions. . . . Hollywood, assisted by the magazines
and some sections of our own Press, has floated us from Fifth Avenue and Miami
to Bel Air and Santa Barbara, from duplex apartments to night clubs with everybody riding around in sixty-horsepower automobiles. You catch these dream
glimpses of American life when you are young and impressionable, sitting relaxed
in the cosy dusk of the film theatres, and then the trick is done. I doubt if
Americans themselves realize that it is this dream way of life, this mirage of
slender smiling girls and tall broad-shouldered young men falling in and out of love
surrounded by every possible luxury, that has captured most of the world's
younger generations. It is not the Constitution or high production, the Supreme
Court or the living standard, but Metro-Goldwyn-Mayer and Paramount that
have planted the stars and stripes everywhere. The real American invasion has
been led by Myrna Loy, Ginger Rogers, Fred Astaire and Donald Duck. . . . It is
the Marx Brothers who have successfully challenged old Karl. The chief hope
America has given Western Europe is Bob Hope.

Once, the British had conquered California; now, as Priestley noted
here, the marching was all being done in the opposite direction. The age
of the perfect gentleman had begun to pass already: Ronald Colman was
going off into the radio and television series about a genial college professor (*Halls of Ivy*) that was to occupy his declining years; Clive Brook
had gone home to the British theatre he came from; Rathbone, Herbert

Marshall and Claude Rains worked on through the 1950s, but as often as not now playing nondescript villains of no particular national allegiance. Most symbolic of all, on 20 December 1948, the day before he was due to start work at MGM on the role that he once said he wanted to play more than any other, Old Jolyon in *The Forsyte Saga*, Sir Aubrey Smith died of double pneumonia at the age of eighty-five. It was, suitably enough, the author of *Lost Horizon*, *Goodbye Mr Chips* and *Random Harvest*, James Hilton, who spoke at a Hollywood memorial service after Smith's ashes had been flown home to Hove in Sussex:

Aubrey's years, because there were so many, take us far into the past. When he was a small boy there were a few people still living who had seen George Washington and many who had fought at Waterloo. ... There ran in Aubrey's blood a stream direct from Chaucer's and Shakespeare's England, sweet as an English apple, strong and straight and humorous and full of the generous sportsmanship that has made the very word cricket come to mean so much more than just a word. ... He became, very modestly (and hardly himself realizing it), in some sense an ambassador of and between the two countries he loved. He *was* England to a great many – perhaps an older England, but an England rich in dignity, graciousness and good will. Certainly no one could ever have known him, either in life or on the screen, without liking England better afterwards, and no one ever did more, without words or preachment, to bring the English and American spirit closer to the same heartbeat of humanity. That unforgettable face, those strong, sensitive features, became somehow a symbol of character in a world in danger of losing it, and when towards the end the King made him a knight it was the fitting thing – because that mingling of strength and gentleness which is the true knightly essence had been Aubrey's all along.

Early in the year, before Smith's death, the English writer who was to give him another and less affectionate kind of immortality had arrived in Hollywood for the first and last time: 'Reached Pasadena at 9 am,' reads Evelyn Waugh's diary for Thursday, 6 February 1947, 'and were met' (Waugh was accompanied by his wife Laura) 'by a car from MGM. We drove for a long time down autobahns and boulevards full of vacant lots and filling stations and nondescript buildings and palm trees with a warm hazy light. It was more like Egypt – the suburbs of Cairo or Alexandria – than anything in Europe. We arrived at the Bel Air Hotel – very Egyptian, with a hint of Addis Ababa in the smell of the blue gums. The flabby manager had let my suite to a man suffering from rheumatic fever – a prevalent local affliction – and we have a pretty but inadequate bedroom and bath.'

Waugh was in Hollywood to negotiate the possible filming of

Brideshead Revisited, but took such an immediate dislike to MGM and the English playwright Keith Winter, who had been assigned to do the screenplay, that the plan came to nothing. The novelist's time in California was not, however, wasted, as his diary for 7 April reveals:

We saw a highly secret first performance of Charlie Chaplin's brilliant new film *Monsieur Verdoux* and went to a supper party at his house later, which comprised mostly Central-European Jews. We also went over Walt Disney's studios. I was thus able to pay my homage to the two artists of the place. We antagonized most of the English colony, who were guiltily sensitive of criticism. Randolph [Churchill] came for a rather disgusting two days – excellent on the [lecture] platform but brutishly drunk in private. I found a deep mine of literary gold in the cemetery of Forest Lawn and the work of the morticians, and intend to get to work immediately on a novelette staged there.

Waugh's understandable fascination with the baroque horrors of Hollywood's most famous cemetery (one which had already featured in Aldous Huxley's 1939 *After Many A Summer Dies the Swan*) was duly increased when he discovered that its church had a copy of *National Velvet* enshrined in a glass monument. His diaries indicate that further filmland treats included dinners with Anna May Wong and Merle Oberon, though Miss Oberon seems to have been the novelist's only other social contact with the exiled British he was about to satirize so savagely in passing, while carrying out a still greater demolition job on the American way of death.

He eventually turned down an offer of $125,000 for the film rights in *Brideshead,* and could not wait to escape from California back to England's coldest post-war winter: 'I was not in the least anti-Semitic before I came here. I am now. It is intolerable to see them enjoying themselves.'

Back in England, Waugh started work almost immediately on *The Loved One,* and there can be no doubt that in its opening pages those two ageing knights of the realm, Sir Francis Hinsley and Sir Ambrose Abercrombie (later played on film by Robert Morley and John Gielgud), rocking gently in 'chivalric bond' as, whisky and sodas in hand, they survey the cricketing of the Hollywood British, are in fact the twin shades of C. Aubrey Smith, who died just three months after the book's London publication.

24:
Playing with Fire

With the passing of Sir Aubrey into the pages of *The Loved One*, a whole
new generation of the Hollywood British had started to appear, if not on
the cricket pitch then at least in the studios. Actors like Stewart
Granger, James Mason and Michael Wilding were now coming out to join
a more raffish breed of English actor, one that Americans, long used to
the suavities of Colman and Niven, did not really understand. 'They
were', in the view of the English-born American columnist Geoffrey
Bocca,

savage and rowdy, given to physical violence and often drunk. Some were dirty in
their personal habits. Most were graduates of the J. Arthur Rank Organization.
James Mason, for one, was quickly described by one columnist as 'the rudest man
in Hollywood'; his irascibility reached a peak in 1952 when he smacked William
Saroyan across the face for chattering during a movie. Edmund Purdom fought
out his best love and hate scenes in public with his ex-wives. Anthony Steel lashed
out at several of those who came within hitting distance. Of Stewart Granger,
Sheilah Graham wrote that he was the pin-up boy of the publicity girls at MGM,
'but only because they have pinned up his picture with a knife through the heart'.
Robert Newton drifted through several alcoholic years in post-war Hollywood,
while Rex Harrison fought such a bitter feud with Californian journalists in general and Louella Parsons in particular that he left, raging, and did not return for
years. These new arrivals drove Thunderbirds instead of Bentleys. They read Los
Angeles papers instead of the London *Times*, and they wore Wilshire Boulevard
sports shirts instead of old school ties. They did not seem to like Hollywood very
much, but they clearly liked it a damn sight better than they liked England. They
were Englishmen all ... but no longer willing or able to create, in Hollywood, a
little corner that was forever England. ... The roots sunk by post-war Britons
were to be shallow, and at the first wind of trouble they blew away. When the
movie industry in Hollywood began to slump, they quit. They sold or sublet their
houses. Those who still had friends said goodbye and moved to Rome or Switzerland. Some quietly let their American citizenship lapse and resumed British
nationality. Through the 1950s they were still in demand, however, to man the

now CinemaScopic ramparts of the Khyber Pass or to eat grapes while ordering the Christians to the lions; to play light comedians, silly asses, pirates; brave but slow-witted army officers who infuriate the American heroes; any parts that suggest Decadence or Decay. Only the English can do these things.

But, added Bocca, by the end of the 1950s 'they were to be doing these very things at Cinecittà or on location in Yugoslavia. A way of life was ending, and the accents of Lord's and Oxford, Boodles, the Green Room Club and the Mess of the Rifle Brigade were to be silenced along the Sunset Strip.'

That process was to take a while, but the first signs that things were changing came, with an awful historical suitability, from the man who was the first and longest-lasting of the Hollywood British. On 7 December 1947, almost thirty-five years after he had first started to work in California, and fully five years before he was finally to be driven out by the McCarthy witch-hunts, Charles Chaplin wrote a letter to a British newspaper which they headlined simply 'Why I Hate Hollywood'.

Trouble had started for Chaplin during the war when an actress called Joan Barry and her mother brought a successful paternity suit against the comedian; in court the prosecution counsel called him 'a grey-haired old buzzard, a little runt of a Svengali and a lecherous old hound who lies like a cheap Cockney cad'. The case, though distinctly dubious in its evidence, did Chaplin a lot of public harm in America, where the image of the friendly little tramp was suddenly overtaken by something apparently much more sinister. Matters did not improve when he appeared before a San Francisco meeting for Russian War Relief and addressed the delegates as 'comrades', nor when it appeared that his 1947 *Monsieur Verdoux*, the film Evelyn Waugh had so much liked, was making distinct connections between war, murder and big business.

At a press conference for the film, Chaplin came under direct personal attack for the first time outside a court of law; a reporter from a paper representing Catholic war veterans demanded to know how it was that Chaplin, after living and working in the US for the best part of four decades, had never in fact taken out American citizenship? 'Because', said Chaplin simply and sadly, 'I am a citizen of the world.'

That was not, however, a concept recognized by Chairman J.Parnell Thomas of the House unAmerican Activities Committee, a politician later to achieve the memorable distinction of being sent on fraud charges to the very same prison to which he had condemned some supposedly unAmerican Hollywood screenwriters. Chaplin was duly ordered to explain to the Committee a lifestyle apparently 'detrimental to the moral fabric of America', one which had included such unimaginable sins as writing a letter to 'the well-known Communist Pablo Picasso'. Chaplin declined to make any such appearance; he did, however, make his feelings extremely clear to the British:

I have made up my mind to declare war, once and for all, on Hollywood and its inhabitants. I do not like grumbling – it seems to me conceited and futile – but since I have no longer any confidence in Hollywood in general or in the American cinema in particular, I am determined to say so. The hostile reaction here to *Monsieur Verdoux* was simply because I cannot and will not think like everybody else; it was because the 'big noises' of Hollywood still think they can get away with anything. But soon they will lose their illusions and begin to perceive certain realities. This is what I say: I, Charlie Chaplin, declare that Hollywood is dying. It is no longer concerned with film-making, which is supposed to be an art, but solely with turning out miles of celluloid. I may add that it is impossible for anyone to make a success in the art of the cinema any more if (like me or Orson Welles) he refuses to conform with the rest, if he shows himself to be an 'adventurer' who dares to defy the warnings of cinematographic big business. Hollywood is now fighting its last battle, and it will lose that battle unless it decides once and for all to give up standardizing its films – unless it realizes that masterpieces cannot be mass-produced in the cinema like tractors in a factory. I think, objectively, it is time to take a new road, so that money shall no longer be the all-powerful god of a decaying community. Before long, I shall perhaps leave the United States, although it has given me so many moral and material satisfactions. And in whatever land I go to end my days, I shall try to remember that I am a man like other men, and that consequently I have a right to the same respect as other men.

Chaplin stayed in Hollywood to make his last great masterpiece, *Limelight*, for which on the advice of the playwright Arthur Laurents he cast a young London actress called Claire Bloom; for her, dimly aware of the hostility that was then surrounding Chaplin in the place he above all others had made the film capital of the world, it was still a remarkable experience:

The arrival on the set of Buster Keaton was greatly anticipated by us all. He hadn't been in films for many years and was to appear with Chaplin in the final theatre sequence. ... Keaton was fifty-six when he made *Limelight*, but gave the impression of having suffered through a life twice that long. From his lined face and grave expression one would have thought that he had neither known a light-hearted moment nor was able to instigate one. His reserve was extreme, as was his isolation. He remained to himself on the set until one day, to my astonishment, he took from his pocket a colour postcard of a large Hollywood mansion and showed it to me. It was the sort of postcard that tourists pick up in Hollywood drugstores. In the friendliest, most intimate way he explained to me that it had once been his home. That was it. He retreated back into silence and never addressed a word to me again. In his scene with Chaplin, however, he was brilliantly alive with invention. Some of his gags may even have been a little too incandescent for Chaplin, because, laugh as he did at the rushes in the screening room, Chaplin didn't see fit to allow them all into the final version of the film.

Photographs of homes were apparently being shown on sets all over Hollywood that year; the actress and mimic Florence Desmond, who had not been over-delighted to discover on her first trip out to Hollywood that her contract with Paramount actually meant playing two shows a night on stage at one of their cinemas, was now back in Hollywood to make *Three Came Home* with Claudette Colbert. One morning, tiring faintly of Colbert's considerable condescension to an English character actress, Desmond drew from her purse pictures of the two hundred acres of Sussex she then owned. It made, apparently, a considerable difference to the way she was then treated on the set.

But for Chaplin, *Limelight* really was to be a final American bow; in September 1952 he set sail from New York to attend its London première. When he had been two days at sea, the American Attorney General announced that he had ordered an enquiry into whether Chaplin should be allowed back into the US. The reason, said the Attorney General, was that Chaplin 'has been publicly charged with being a member of the Communist Party, and with grave moral charges, and with making statements that would indicate a leering, sneering attitude towards a country whose hospitality had enriched him'.

Almost to a critic, the American press chickened out of giving any credit at all to the greatness of *Limelight*, and the appalling Hedda Hopper leapt cumbersomely onto the McCarthy bandwagon, which was now rolling alarmingly fast: 'No one can deny that Chaplin is a good actor. He is. But that doesn't give him the right to go against our customs, to abhor everything we stand for, to throw our hospitality back in our faces. . . . Good riddance to bad company.'

In fact Chaplin was only too delighted to be out of America: 'Whether I re-entered that unhappy country or not was of little consequence to me,' he wrote later; 'I would have liked to tell them that the sooner I was rid of that hate-beleaguered atmosphere the better, that I was fed up with

America's insults and moral pomposity, and that the whole subject was damned boring.'

Everything Chaplin had ever earned was in American banks, and he was understandably terrified that, having confiscated his re-entry visa, the McCarthy panic might spread to confiscating his worldly goods also. Accordingly, on landing at Southampton he issued a pompous holding statement to the effect that he would be happy to return and face whatever charges could be levelled against him. In the meantime he sent his devoted wife Oona speeding back to California by air to close up the house, pay off the staff and clear out all the Chaplins' American bank accounts. They then settled happily in Switzerland for the last twenty years of Chaplin's life, though in October 1972, to the amazement of his daughter Geraldine (who advised against it until she realized how much the statue meant to him), Charlie returned to Hollywood, an old and fragile man, to collect the honorary Oscar that a shame-faced film community had finally and too late decided to bestow on him for services to the cinema. He died a few months later, still thoroughly at home in Switzerland.

Whether made wiser by the Chaplin experience, or merely because of an innate lack of interest in local American politics, the rest of the Hollywood British seem to have steered well clear of the McCarthy turmoil; none of them disgraced themselves by 'naming names', and most managed to claim some sort of visitors' exemption which enabled them to skirt the whole sordid witch-hunt without damaging their chances of studio employment. Meanwhile Britain was the one to benefit as exiles (notably Joe Losey) began for the first time to flow in the opposite direction. The director David Lean, who was never to work in Hollywood and whose multiple Oscar-winning location epics of the 1950s and 1960s, from the *Bridge on the River Kwai* through *Lawrence of Arabia* to *Dr Zhivago*, were in fact to replace the old notion of the Hollywood British picture, neatly encapsulated much British thinking about the film capital in 1948: 'You go out to Hollywood, you buy a magnificent house and you build an even more magnificent swimming-pool. Then you have to pay for it. They want you to make films you aren't really keen on, but that swimming-pool must be paid for. So you do the bloody film. In England we have nothing but rain and austerity, so the only thing left is to make good films.'

Even Cedric Hardwicke, one of the most constant and loyal of the Hollywood British, was beginning to have his doubts about the change in

Californian tastes and film-making habits; returning there to make a picture after a short stage break in 1950 he wrote: 'I felt like a Proconsul recalled to duty in Rome just on the day that Nero was starting to play with the matches.'

Later arrivals, like James Mason, who got there in 1948 to find himself castigated in an article in the menu of Romanoff's Restaurant for his rashly sarcastic comments on Hollywood dining habits, always viewed Hollywood with considerable mistrust. Though more intelligent and talented than George Sanders, Mason shared many of Sanders' attitudes to the rubbish that he was required to wade through in the course of being a film star. Even when he did get respectable work, such as playing Brutus to the Cassius of Gielgud and the Antony of Brando in John Houseman's MGM *Julius Caesar* in 1953, it was only to find Shakespeare's story being billed on the posters as 'Greater than *Ivanhoe*'.

It was this *Caesar* that took Gielgud to Hollywood for the first time: 'All right, kids,' he once heard an assistant director there exhorting a crowd of recalcitrant extras, 'it's hot, it's Rome and here comes Julius.' On another occasion, Gielgud recalled: 'I was waiting to go on the Rome street set with a whole menagerie of sheep, dogs and pigeons which had been brought in to make the city look more lively. ... One of the pigeons, which had been perched on a pillar, suddenly jumped off and began walking around the floor of the studio. A hefty cowboy who evidently looked after all the animals dashed up and yelled at the bird, "Get back, get back, don't you want to work tomorrow?"'

This *Caesar* was for Gielgud what *Wuthering Heights* had been fifteen years earlier for Olivier: an introduction to the possibilities of serious film-making after years of unhappiness in front of the cameras, and from then on both the leading knights of the British theatre were to make regular and profitable sorties to Hollywood for guest-starring roles in everything from period epics to spy sagas. Neither of them however, showed the faintest inclination to stay in California for more than a day after the shooting ended, especially as a play was usually awaiting them in London. Hollywood remained for them both a place to make quick money, which would enable them to spend more time on something really interesting in the British theatre. The idea of making a permanent life there never occurred to either of them, any more than it did to Redgrave, Richardson or their classical heirs, men like John Neville and Paul Scofield (who had, intriguingly, been before Brando the original casting idea for Mark Antony).

Other British actors of less theatrical distinction were, however, still more than ready to give Hollywood a try on a long-contract basis; the problem was that though the studio system was to survive intact into the late 1950s, producers grew more and more uncertain of precisely how to use their London imports. If an actor as strong and intelligent as James Mason had arrived there in 1938 instead of 1948, he would have been given a coherent programme of work which would clearly have established him in audience eyes as, perhaps, a latter-day Herbert Marshall. Instead, Mason was shunted around from picture to picture with no real continuity, so that even when he did strike lucky with something like *Caesar* he would then be shoved straight back into a period swashbuckler like *Prince Valiant* or a hand-me-down remake of *The Prisoner of Zenda*, which was shot with a copy of the original permanently showing on the set so that camera angles and performances could be meticulously copied.

Nor did Rex Harrison fare much better in California: he, indeed, ended up as Saladin in *King Richard and the Crusaders*, a swashbuckler of such sublime awfulness that it qualifies for an entire chapter in Harry Medved's *Fifty Worst Movies of All Time*, largely for the moment when Rex has to invite an equally implausibly cast Laurence Harvey to 'share the waters of the oasis' with him.

But Harrison, in fact, started out rather better in Hollywood than that; after the war, and some distinguished work in British films, he was offered $4,000 a week and a six-picture contract with Twentieth Century-Fox if he would play the King of Siam to Irene Dunne's non-musical Anna. The film did a great deal of good, though not especially for them: Gertrude Lawrence, then in California for her only Hollywood film (*The Glass Menagerie*; she turned down the Bette Davis role in *All About Eve* on the grounds that the film was 'not nice' in its attitude to actresses), saw what Harrison and Dunne had accomplished, bought all rights in the story and commissioned Rodgers and Hammerstein to turn it into a musical for her and her *Private Lives* partner Noël Coward. When Coward refused to be a singing King of Siam, the part went to a young and unknown Yul Brynner.

Coward himself had long since decided that the Hollywood life, even in its post-war phase, was not for him; he'd written at the very end of the war a marvellous and much underrated short story called *A Richer Dust*, which neatly summarized his attitude to the British in California, ending as it does with a London-born movie star returning to his family at the end of a war he has somehow managed to avoid. 'If', says his old mother, 'anyone mentions your tubercular lung, do remember that we had to say something.'

Not that Coward was averse to the occasional flying visit : returning to Beverly Hills from his triumphant cabaret season playing to what he called NesCafé Society at the Desert Inn, Las Vegas, in July 1955 he suddenly and surprisingly found himself the flavour of the month in Hollywood too :

I am certainly the belle of the ball again, and there have been red carpets everywhere. All the studios are vying with each other for my services and all the agents are tying themselves in knots. Mike Todd showed me his new Todd-AO process, which is really tremendously exciting and the colour also. Paramount want me to do a picture with Danny Kaye and *The Sleeping Prince* and/or anything I bloody well want on my own terms. MGM want me to play the Prince in *The Swan*. Twentieth Century-Fox are sitting with their fingers crossed. The entertaining has been incessant – on Tuesday night Cole Porter gave a small dinner, Claudette [Colbert], Fred Astaire, etc. After it, Cole and I had a lovely, rather pissed-up heart-to-hearter. On Wednesday Merle Oberon gave a glamorous dinner for me, really everyone there and the dinner most nice. The Kirk Douglases, the Jimmy Stewarts, the Joe Cottens, the Van Johnsons and Marlon Brando, who was gentler and nicer than I expected. He is a handsome creature. . . . Friday was the Bogarts' turn. A barbecue party by the pool. Really great fun, although it got a bit nippy and I was delighted to get indoors. The same familiar glamorous faces. On Saturday Frankie Sinatra gave a tremendous rout for me at Romanoff's in the private room upstairs. He is such a charmer and I love him . . . he sang like a dream. I sang less alluringly, but everyone expressed great enthusiasm and Charlie Vidor tore off his amethyst and gold buttons and links and gave them to me. I protested mildly and pocketed them.

In the event it was Olivier who did *The Sleeping Prince* and Alec Guinness who did *The Swan*; Coward himself did, however, start on a lucrative film career, though none of the seven movies he made over the next fifteen years was actually shot in Hollywood. For one of them, Mike Todd's *Around The World in Eighty Days*, he received a Bonnard, while Colman got a Cadillac. 'And all that for just one day's work?' asked an incredulous journalist. 'Not at all, madam,' replied Colman, 'for a lifetime of experience.'

25:
Staying On

By and large, the women of the post-war British colony in Hollywood were a lot happier than the men; while Olivier and Harrison were forever escaping to the Broadway or London stages, their wives Vivien Leigh and Lilli Palmer (and others, like Ann Todd, not necessarily married to actors) seemed to find in the California sun a kind of freedom and enjoyment which they missed back home in England. For Lilli Palmer, Lubitsch's Hollywood ('a village full of professionals in desperate search of an audience') was a social round of 'Hoagy Carmichael or Eddy Duchin at the piano, Judy Garland singing "Over The Rainbow", Walter Huston doing his "September Song", Danny Kaye trying out his new act, Charlie Chaplin reminiscing. Once, Basil and Ouida Rathbone gave a party where the walls were covered with thousands of gardenias. I touched and smelled my way all along their walls; there wasn't a single paper flower.'

In fact, she did some rather more distinguished work in Hollywood (notably *Body and Soul* with John Garfield) than Harrison in those early days, and it was left to him to notice that actors in California were somehow not like actors he had known in the London theatre: 'There we always talked about acting; in Hollywood nobody did. They all talked like very rich, well-informed ranchers. They were themselves – he was Gary Cooper, he was Clark Gable, he was James Stewart – they didn't have to act, they just were.' ·

It was while the Harrisons were in California in those late 1940s that the film colony was struck by two tragedies very closely affecting the Hollywood British. At a party given by Tyrone Power one night, guests started to play a game of hide-and-seek. David Niven's young wife, Primula, fresh out from England and the mother of their two young sons, pushed a door open on the ground floor, not realizing that it gave on to a flight of cellar steps, and fell to her death.

A few months later, Harrison was having an affair with a twenty-nine-year-old American actress called Carole Landis, then at the end of her fourth marriage. Items were appearing in the Hopper and Parsons gossip columns enquiring 'Which actor from London whose name begins with an H is carrying on with a local glamor girl whose name begins with an L ?', but that was about par for the course among Hollywood journalists of the time, and the whole affair might have disappeared into decent obscurity had Miss Landis not then decided to take a large number of sleeping pills, and with them her own life, a few hours after dining with Rex.

Leland Hayward, then the Harrisons' Hollywood agent, explained to Lilli Palmer the trouble they were now in, according to the prevalent morality of the film community in July 1948:

Suicide was a very shocking thing in Hollywood, he said, more shocking than in any other part of the world. And since the community couldn't attack the person who had died, the object of its violence and irrational wrath was the person who was thought to have the suicide on his conscience. There had been occasional suicides in Hollywood (amazingly few, considering the hysteria and lack of self-control that were constantly crashing against each other in that place) but in every case it had meant the end of the 'guilty' survivor's career. Suicide was a slap in the face to Hollywood's image as the world's serene, Utopian paradise. It was played up rather than hushed up. And never forgiven.

The British community rallied round, however (this was after all their first scandal since the William Desmond Taylor affair of 1922), and accompanied Harrison to the Forest Lawn funeral, where Rex found himself 'at the back of the chapel surrounded by small boys who were chewing gum and reading comics'. He then bought himself out of what was left of his contract with Darryl Zanuck and moved swiftly back to Broadway, where fortunately his American reputation was saved by a considerable stage success as Henry VIII in *Anne of the Thousand Days*. By 1952 he and Lilli Palmer were back in Hollywood filming *The Fourposter*; Leland Hayward had taken an unnecessarily gloomy view of their survival prospects after all.

By now there were more British actors leaving Hollywood every year, for Switzerland (like Mason, Kerr, Hepburn and Aherne) or France (like Niven) or just England and peaceful retirement, than were arriving there, and Americans seemed to spend most of the 1950s advising the Hollywood British to go home, as if they too realized it was all over for them. Even a young Bryan Forbes, out in California in 1951 trying to get his start as a film actor and writer, was given a one-way ticket back to

London by the director Raoul Walsh: '"Go now," he said, "go tonight. I know this town very well. If you stay here you'll become a bum. Don't go back to the house, don't pack, don't do anything. Just blow." He drove me straight to the airport and we drank together until the plane took off.'

What perhaps Walsh had also realized was that it was no longer enough in Hollywood just to be British; the old days, when Basil Rathbone had got by on what Dorothy Parker once called 'just two pro-files pasted together', or when Herbert Marshall had made a career out of reminding film critics like Graham Greene of 'national characteristics one does not wish to see exported, characteristics which it is necessary to describe in terms of inanimate objects – a kind of tobacco, a kind of tweed, a kind of pipe – or in terms of dogs, something large, sentimental and moulting that confirms one's preference for cats' – those days had by now gone forever, vanished into the middle 1950s.

Even Michael Wilding, who'd been in almost constant if less than wonderful Hollywood work through the early 1950s, found himself abruptly (and perhaps not altogether coincidentally) fired from his studio contract when it became known that his then wife Elizabeth Taylor had left him for Mike Todd. Wilding became instead an agent, until one of his clients, Edward G. Robinson, pointed the way home:

I hear tell you were once a big star in England. I also know that Hollywood has treated you shamefully. But that isn't the purport of my message, which is to tell you that already the great talents are rebelling against the tyranny of the studio tycoons, going to France, to Germany, to Timbuctoo – any place that will give them a say in the parts they play and a cut of the profits. Two years from now, television will have taken over and be making rubbishy films on the back lots where Garbo used to tread and Gene Kelly sang. ... Don't wait for those death throes. Get the hell out of this goddam town and go back home where you belong.

The year was then 1957, and Robinson had his Hollywood calculations about right.

Wilding took the advice; others managed to hang on a little longer. One of the most consistently successful Hollywood couples of the 1950s, Jean Simmons and Stewart Granger, survived almost to the end of the decade having apparently avoided most of the obvious pitfalls. Neither was confined to totally English roles, both had achieved the occasional critical success amid the routine rubbish, and some good money had been made by them both, not least by Simmons on the unusually long shooting schedule of *Spartacus*. 'And what', one of the children of Peter Ustinov (also in that epic) was asked at the time, 'does your daddy do for a living?' '*Spartacus*,' replied the child. With Laughton and Olivier also in the cast, that 1960 slave circus was to be one of the last great gatherings of the Hollywood British. Laughton, recalled Ustinov, 'would sit morosely around the set waiting to have his feelings hurt', while Olivier 'was the Vestal Virgin to Laughton's Hollywood whore, and yet whereas Laughton feasted his eyes on the work of great painters as he emerged dripping from his pool of contemplation, Larry fretted at arithmetic and tried to pick holes in the bills of the supermarket'.

Ustinov, like Niven, was to become one of the great chroniclers of the late Hollywood British, never happier than when catching John Gielgud on a late-night television interview in St Louis, Missouri, where he happened to be playing his solo Shakespeare show at the time:

'One final question,' the interviewer said. 'Sir ... Sir Gielgud ... did you ... oh you must have had ... we all did ... at the start of your very wonderful ... very wonderful and very meaningful ... let me put it this way ... did you have someone ... a man ... or ... or indeed, a woman, at whom you could now point a finger and say Yes, this person helped me when ... ' By now Sir John had understood what was being asked of him and he prepared to answer, disguising his dislike of all that is pretentious by a perfect courtesy. 'Yes, I think there was somebody who taught me a great deal at my dramatic school, and I certainly am grateful to him for his kindness and consideration to me. His name was Claude Rains.' And then, as an afterthought, John added, 'I don't quite know what happened to him; I think he failed and went to America.'

But things had changed a bit there since the great days of Claude Rains; even the stars who had been taken out in the 1950s precisely because of their original Englishness soon found themselves having to seek out other kinds of roles simply because British films as such were no longer being made much in America. Jean Simmons, for example, had her major successes of that decade in such all-American screenplays as *Guys and Dolls*, *The Big Country* and *Elmer Gantry*, while Stewart Granger, before their marriage ended in 1960, found his Hollywood career disintegrating through such rubbish as *All The Brothers Were Valiant* and *North to Alaska*.

True, Metro were still interested in the occasional swashbuckler or Court drama but now, for something like *Quo Vadis?* or *Beau Brummel* or *Quentin Durward*, they would go to Europe and recruit local theatrical talent in London, Paris or Rome. As a result, British actors in Hollywood began to realize they were missing out on almost all fronts, a feeling first expressed by James Mason, writing in the *Films and Filming* of November 1954:

I became acutely conscious when I was in England recently that I had missed an awful lot by specializing in movies. My contemporaries who stayed in the British theatre had become robust, resourceful stars, basking nightly in the glow of audience approval, a comfort not extended to movie actors. It is a life-giving glow; it stimulates an actor's inventiveness and gives him courage. It intoxicates and liberates. ... In London it is not difficult for actors to enjoy the best of both worlds. The drive to the theatre in the West End or the movie studio in the suburbs is equally convenient. An actor can alternate the one with the other. He can specialize in the live theatre and fit a movie into his programme when pressed for money to meet his income tax demands. Or he can specialize in movies and take a theatre engagement whenever he begins to feel unloved. For the actor in New York things are not quite so good. If he wants to make a movie he has to travel three thousand miles to a place he affects to despise. And his life in the live Broadway theatre is much more of a gamble than it is anywhere else in the theatrical world. But the actor who *never* mixes movie acting with stage acting is the one everyone should be sorry for, and he is generally to be found in Hollywood, where it is almost impossible for him to know if he is any good or not. The good are no good unless they are successful, and the successful are scared and mistrustful of an achievement for which they cannot confidently take much of the credit. ... I apologize for writing the biography of such a fellow, for that is primarily what I am.

Mason was intelligent enough to realize that he had, in fact, reached Hollywood at a time of considerable change: actors of roughly his generation who had relied on the old officer-and-gentleman image, men like Edmund Purdom and Peter Lawford, were having to lose the Sandhurst accent and acquire something more acceptably mid-Atlantic, while the very reason that had brought most of them to Hollywood now ceased to exist. If epics like *Quo Vadis?* (and later the remake of *The Charge of the Light Brigade*) could now equally easily be made with Hollywood money but on location in Rome or Madrid, there was really not much point in a California address. Even a writer like Christopher Fry, who twenty years earlier would have had to follow Sherriff and Walpole out to Hollywood, was able in the 1950s to write biblical epics without leaving Europe, and David Lean was able to steer clear of any studio city for such later epics as *Lawrence of Arabia*. Moreover, the most successful of the Hollywood British had ceased to be particularly or even noticeably

British at all. In post-war films Cary Grant played Americans as often as not, and it has always to be remembered that in terms of longevity and economic success the single most successful man in the entire British community in Hollywood this century had made his fame and fortune by virtually never appearing on stage or screen as English – Bob Hope.

Mason (who in the 1950s more usually appeared in the gossip columns as half of a double-act completed by his then wife, Pamela, a formidably vociferous ex-actress who became a doyenne of the colony and later acquired her own television chat show) was an astute observer of the Hollywood British in their immediate post-war phase, as a Chris Pettit/David Pirie profile for *Time Out* has made clear:

> For the English, life was pretty much the same as in any colony. The climate was better than at home, the standard of living higher and the temptations of inertia greater. According to disposition, one either counted one's blessings and settled down, or one kept up appearances by doing things well without appearing to take them too seriously. David Niven, Rex Harrison and George Sanders all practised that ironic detachment that so often hides a deadly earnest or, in Sanders' case, increasing despair. 'Are you much in demand, old man?' Sanders would enquire of Mason with deceptive casualness. Mason was, more than Sanders ... though they once made plans to build houses for wealthy widows in Los Angeles from designs by Mason.

'In those days', Mason wrote later, 'the main body of us Hollywoodites did not rapidly spiral upwards or downwards, we sort of stood still until suddenly overcome by inertia.' He also believes, according to Petit and Pirie, 'that had he settled for playing the professional Englishman, like David Niven, he might have been a bigger star' (in fact he only got *A Star Is Born* after Bogart and Cary Grant had turned it down, and *Lolita* after Coward and Olivier had declined).

Others, too, were beginning to realize that in an era of Brando and James Dean, Marilyn Monroe and Lana Turner, there was not a great deal to be said for being discreetly British. The gentlemen actors were packing up and going home again, having, in the words of one of the best of them, Roland Culver, had 'a thoroughly enjoyable time. The years I spent in Tinsel Town did little to enhance my reputation as an actor but for much of the time I lived in a charming house' (in fact Gladys Cooper's on Napoli Drive), 'had dear friends and was able to indulge in several sports I enjoyed: swimming, riding and golf. I do not regret my stay; neither did I regret leaving sunny California to return to my proper milieu in the London theatre.'

Nor were the playwrights from London finding Hollywood quite as lucrative or attractive a destination as had their predecessors in the 1930s; William Douglas Home noted in a 1957 *Spectator* article that:

It is, of course, traditional for British authors to lead a life of semi-contemplation during their first visit to Hollywood. Mr Evelyn Waugh, it will be remembered, reclined to some advantage on Forest Lawn. I, in my small way, contemplated the celluloid city from the fairways of the golf course at the Bel Air Country Club. Yet even from that distance I was able to detect the cloud of smog that hovered ominously over Culver City, stifling the breath and clogging up the wind and bringing spiky tears into the eyes of those who work beneath its shade. ... There sits the writer (as often as not the original author in person), the artist, stripped of his natural functions, denuded of his *raison d'être*, lying drained at the feet of a looking-glass producer who has usurped his role as creator: 'Widen the theme', 'Turn the tennis-star father into a female nightclub singer in Paris', 'Cut out the ambush in Algiers and make it Christmas Eve in Hamburg with a baby being born upstairs and sign up Clifton Webb', 'Change the air hostess into a Scots shepherd and sign John Wayne', 'Cut chapter two to the end, switch the scene from a Trappist Monastery to Monte Carlo and get Lollobrigida and Marilyn Monroe to play the leads'. .... As I looked down on Hollywood from the Bel Air Country Club it seemed to me that the battle was still going to the producers, and the writers were still underneath. But these days battles are no longer being won. All that remains is bankruptcy, disillusionment, internecine strife and smog.

A few others were managing to hang on, clubable actors like George Melville Cooper and Robert Coote, whose acting ambitions had never been tremendous and who were happy now to pick up the few 'old colonel', 'faithful friend' or 'responsible gentleman' roles that had once been taken by their elders and betters. Others would come out for single support-star engagements (Flora Robson specializing in eccentric housekeepers and queens) before beating a hasty retreat to Britain where the real work now lay. Others again managed a year or two of romantic stardom, like Edmund Purdom, before being buried forever under the sheer weight of dead scripts and their own cinematic inadequacy.

The women were, perhaps, still having an easier time of it; as Alexander Walker, writing in the *Birmingham Post* in June 1957, put it:

Hollywood, which has – rightly – long since ceased to look to our butter-faced actors for its leading men, still acknowledges that ours is the only land to look to when in search of what I call the 'head girls'. That chin-up, shoulders-back look, the discipline of the crocodile line, the aplomb to plough through the most

astoundingly witless dialogue as if it were the termly hockey report and therefore
to be taken seriously, the purity of character without the primness of manner, the
angelic features with the hint of iron in the jawline: these are things that no
where grow under California's sun. ... Studios lucky and rich enough to acquire
the services of Deborah Kerr or Audrey Hepburn or Jean Simmons behave like
provident finishing schools and reserve the right roles for their wards. In general,
career-girl parts are out: no stenographers, fashion models, gossip columnists or
chorus beauties – all the great avenues which, films teach us, are of advancement
in American society. Occasionally a head girl, through sheer will power, will
break the bounds and startle the school by her example, like Miss Kerr in *From
Here To Eternity* allowing the sea and Burt Lancaster to possess her simultaneously. But such rebels are soon brought back into line. Their really OK roles are
the girls with vocations: schoolteachers, nuns, bookshop assistants, Salvation
Army lasses (commonly known as Dolls), housemasters' wives, Anglo-Indian
nurses, foreign princesses – though these are on the way out – any of Shaw's head
girls and any of Shakespeare's too, if Greer Garson is not herself available. These
are the lamps that Miss Simmons and Co. keep tended; all over Europe they are
going out, but in Hollywood studios they burn brightly still.

Not for much longer, however. By the early 1960s there were few
definably English women on the Hollywood screen, even Audrey Hepburn
having gone over by then to glossy mid-Atlantic comedy thrillers like
Charade. Predictably, that wily survivor Cary Grant was already there
waiting for her arrival.

As for the empire-builders, they disappeared so fast that by 1956 Mike
Todd had to do most of his casting and shooting of *Around The World in
Eighty Days* in London, while by 1965 for *King Rat* Bryan Forbes actually
had to import to Hollywood a large number of British actors (among them
Tom Courtenay, James Fox, Denholm Elliott, Alan Webb and
Sir Guy Standing's grandson John) to play the wartime British
soldiers in Changi.

Except for such occasional British blockbusters as *Separate Tables*
(1958) or *My Fair Lady* (1964), usually of West End or Broadway origin,
the era of the Hollywood British film was well and truly over. Intriguingly, even some of the stars who were to top American box-office charts
in the 1960s and 1970s had to do so by way of England; Roger Moore,
after an extremely lacklustre leading-man career in Hollywood during
the 1950s, only rose to the heights of Bondage via a British television
success as *The Saint*.

Herbert Lom, making his first Hollywood film (*The Big Fisherman*) in
1959, wrote sadly back to London of the current status of the British there:

Actresses like Margaret Leighton, who is working on *The Sound and the Fury*, are looked upon as great artists by the people making pictures, but they doubt that they can sell a film on names like that. The only three women who seem to count at the box office are, however, all English by birth – Audrey Hepburn, Jean Simmons and Elizabeth Taylor. But as far as the public is concerned, Britain is considered a nice little island where they make pictures that America shows at midnight on television. Most Americans seem to have heard of our most popular screen actor, but his name is variously pronounced as Alec Gwines or Alex Guinness.

Something intangible had gone forever, as John Mortimer (then on his first visit to Hollywood as a screenwriter) noted for the *Observer* in September 1966: 'The city of dreams is also now the city of Watts, of ex-film actor Ronald Reagan hoping to gallop right into the governor's residence. It is a city of acute conflict where the dreams are not only on celluloid but also on LSD soaked into illicit lumps of sugar obtainable in a friendly neighbourhood delicatessen. And the deep-sleeping palace of the old Hollywood seems about to change.' Or else to disappear altogether. Yet there were, amazingly enough, one or two British reputations still to be made there, and even one last scandal.

26:
The British Empire Strikes Back

By the autumn of 1966, even my grandmother had decided it was time to pull up her Californian roots after a quarter of a century and head home to Henley-on-Thames. The writer Gavin Lambert, who in both fiction and journalism has been the most eloquent chronicler of Hollywood in decay, went to see her on her last day in the house at 770 Napoli Drive, which had already been sold to Marti Stevens:

Colman, Aubrey Smith, Nigel Bruce, the cricket eleven – they'd all gone by now, and Gladys Cooper seemed the last of the colonial settlers in Hollywood; she knew it was all over, and I think she was keen now to get back to her family in England, where she knew she could still get work in the theatre. She had no patience with decay or loneliness, or failure, and she was not one to stay around after the party was over. She'd belonged really to MGM at the height of that studio's Anglophilia, and now that was all over and Hollywood had become a youth industry, the old colony simply couldn't survive. I think she was very wise to get out when she did – otherwise she'd just have ended up like Helen Hayes doing parodies of herself on television forever. Gladys was a very cool lady, and she knew when to stop something in her acting as in her life. . . . She understood about restraint and she also managed to keep her head well above the rubbish that she was often given to do on the screen. She kept her head and her distance, and that was what made her as an actress and as a woman.

Gladys was to live and work on in England for another five years, but when she did die, just a month away from her eighty-third birthday, it struck me that she'd had no better obituary than Lambert's and nor had the colony in California, of which she was for so long, if not the dowager, then at any rate the den mother.

But a new generation of British actors still had to come to terms with Hollywood; though it was no longer necessary to take up residence there for any longer than it took to make a single film, it was not quite yet a place that could be financially or artistically ignored by any but the most exclusively theatrical of players.

The situation was now geographically much more complex than ever before; the collapse of the old studio structures, the rise of the independent producer and the still more important rise of creative tax lawyers to discover hitherto unforeseen advantages in filming abroad, had led to a state of descriptive confusion in which entire 'Hollywood' productions could now be shot in Reykjavik or Johannesburg. Thus an actor like Richard Burton, who in 1950 had been told by Olivier to make up his mind between being a household word and a great actor and had chosen to be a household word in Hollywood, was finding by 1960 that most of his film work was being done anywhere but Hollywood. He and Elizabeth Taylor may well have become the ruling King and Queen of the American film industry for a brief period in the late 1960s, but, unlike Mary Pickford and Doug Fairbanks, they ruled in fact from abroad – from Rome or London or South America or wherever the tax breaks and local union conditions happened to be best for the making of movies. There was no longer a resident Hollywood royalty of any but the most derelict kind: the celluloid-crowned heads had gone into a Swiss tax exile much as, three decades earlier, had the real crowned heads of Europe when the war blasted their thrones away. London journalists out in the California sunshine on expenses to interview the British colony were suddenly reduced to writing about Joan Collins and David Farrar; wherever the party now was, it surely wasn't in Hollywood. Even the circus seemed to have left town.

Some traditions died harder: visiting hell-raisers like Richard Harris would occasionally be photographed punching up some local gossip-columnist or nightclub owner, usually with perfect justification, but an indication of the rapidly declining importance of a Hollywood career even for a film star can be gleaned from the fact that Peter O'Toole, whose film career started in 1959 and who had become a worldwide star with *Lawrence of Arabia* two years later, only made his first film in Hollywood in 1982. By then he had made thirty others, several, like *Becket* and *A Lion in Winter*, among the highest post-war moneyspinners.

It was Burton himself who later noted: 'I went out to Hollywood in 1953 with a multi-million-dollar contract from the Old Vic and came back ten years later with £2,000 and half a house in Hampstead.' Others, too, were realizing that the big-money days of Hollywood were long since over: Burton's Hollywood films have always been among his least distinguished, and he and Elizabeth Taylor were, ironically, the two who drew the gossip columnists away from California, so that Rome and

London suddenly became, by the mid-1960s, the place for journalists to hang around in the hopes of an on-the-set interview.

Others did, however, still feel obliged to make the occasional trek out west: Laurence Harvey and Peter Sellers did much of their worst work there, Harvey 'demonstrating conclusively that it is possible to succeed without ever evoking the least audience interest or sympathy, and to go on succeeding despite unanimous critical antipathy and overwhelming public apathy' (David Shipman), and Sellers finding in 1962 that he had already left it too late, as Alexander Walker explains in his definitive biography: 'A visit to the studios was an additional depressant. Sellers there saw his childhood screen memories mouldering away, untended and uncared about, on the back lot – Esther Williams' swimming-pool, Mickey Rooney's home town. He hated Hollywood as if it had committed an almost personal assault on him by failing to care about his nostalgia.'

Some of the older hands were, however, managing to survive: Robert Douglas, after a useful career in second-lead roles of the Robert Coote bluff trooper variety, started to make a lucrative second life as a television director, while Angela Lansbury, descendant of a Labour politician, began commuting back to Broadway when the film opportunities started to dwindle. Others, too, managed to live through the years when Hollywood was coming apart at the seams. Peter Finch, the Australian actor who had a starry London stage and film career (and a much-publicized affair with Vivien Leigh), not only survived a musical remake of *Lost Horizon* (which was so breathtakingly bad that even John Gielgud in a funny hat announcing that he was a monk from 'a nearby llamasery' couldn't retrieve it) but then went on to make the last and very best film of his entire career, *Network*, in the heart of the old film capital shortly before his death of a heart attack in the foyer of the Beverly Hills Hotel in January 1977.

By then, there had grown up in post-war Hollywood a second generation of British actors' children, Hayley and Juliet Mills, and Vanessa and Lynn Redgrave, though it was noticeable that the two who returned to European careers fared professionally rather better than the two – Lynn and Juliet – who settled in Californian homes and fought their way through the local television jungle. And, of course, there was always Julie Andrews, who after a spectacular start in Hollywood musicals with *Mary Poppins*, given her by Disney in 1963 after Warners had insisted on Audrey Hepburn for her *My Fair Lady* role, went on through *The Sound of Music*, an all-time moneymaker, into a series of rapidly more catastrophic screen musicals until she ended up in frenetic comedies as a kind of surrogate Mary Tyler Moore.

Others had even more painful experiences: Sarah Miles, on the strength of considerable British success in the 1960s, went out to California after *Lady Caroline Lamb* only to get involved in a nasty press scandal similar to Rex Harrison's, when a young man commited suicide apparently motivated by unrequited love for her, whereupon she and her career disappeared for several years into the Hollywood Hills.

As the 1970s turned into the 1980s there was a sudden and bizarre demand in Hollywood for very small English television comedians, notably Dudley Moore and Marty Feldman, but this too looked somehow unlikely to last forever, especially as Feldman died abruptly on location in Mexico at the end of 1982. Though it seemed for a while that there might still be a home somewhere in the Beverly Hills for clean-cut, old-fashioned British heroes of the Leslie Howard variety, the relative failure of Michael York to do any good there after *Cabaret* suggested that his was a type no longer of especial interest to American film-makers or their audiences.

Dirk Bogarde, with whom York had done some of his best screen work in Joseph Losey's British film *Accident* and with whom he was to stumble through Cukor's appalling American *Justine*, had already reached the sensible conclusion that Hollywood was no longer for the British. 'The day I arrived there to play Franz Liszt', he once told me with only the very faintest poetic licence, 'the D fell off the HOLLYWOOD sign.'

There was, however, still a certain amount of British acting to be done in Hollywood. Younger players like Anthony Hopkins, struggling to emerge from the shadows of O'Toole and Burton, would go out to put in ritual appearances in what were often only television movies. One or two elder statesmen like Wilfrid Hyde White found a lucrative twilight playing genial family solicitors in comedy series, bringing with him to the small screen wonderfully urbane reminders of the day when timing and dignity and a decent ability to shoot shirt cuffs rather than hard drugs had been what Hollywood acting was all about.

If the dream has ended, along with the empire and the colony that once gave the Hollywood British a reason for existence there, British success stories can still be found. The greatest, of course, is Michael Caine, the only British actor who can truly be said to have inherited the kingdom of Cary Grant and who has done it forty years later by precisely the same route, managing on arrival in Hollywood to lose his Cockney origins without acquiring any especially American tendencies.

Caine remains, like Grant, comfortably and totally mid-Atlantic; his work in America has admittedly been a lot less interesting or impressive than the work he did before going there, but unlike any of his contemporaries he has settled totally and happily into the California life. Where Sean Connery and Roger Moore have always hastened back to Europe, Caine has settled with his family into a Beverly Hills palace once owned by Barbara Hutton and complete with its three bathrooms plus Jacuzzi. There he lives what he himself has described as 'a fortress life', peering out through binoculars at the millionaires around him and telling himself that he can never be too rich or too thin.

Though Caine's private life has become totally Californian, his working life more often starts with a drive to the airport than to one of the local studios; the key to his considerable success is his utter lack, now, of a class or a continent. He happens to be English and to live and sometimes work in Hollywood; but to Ronald Colman or Aubrey Smith, he would seem as alien as a space invader.

It is only the British, out on brief visits from home, who seem to notice or care about the way Hollywood has let itself run to seed: the way that the local Sardi's has become a Mexican porno movie complex, or that Central Casting is now a pool hall, or that the Bank of America stands where once were the Fox Studios. We are the only ones who seem surprised that the studio where in 1913 de Mille and Lasky and Goldwyn made Hollywood's first full-length film is now a parking lot for Macdonald's, or that you can be mugged on Sunset Boulevard in daylight, or that any half-way intelligent American movie star now lives in Carmel or Connecticut and commutes.

Yet the British still hang in there. Whether working as television scriptwriters or used-car salesmen, they have benefited from a last-ditch discovery by the Americans – prompted largely by television screenings of such series as *Brideshead Revisited* and *Upstairs, Downstairs* – that there is still a market for what is left of the stiff upper lip. Where once American cinema screens were filled with Ronald Colman explaining the honour of the regiment, now American television screens are filled with Alistair Cooke explaining the complexities of *The Forsyte Saga*. In the opinion of Bart Mills,

As the proportion of the American film and television budget that went towards titillating teenagers increased in the early 1970s, so the number of adults in the audience who felt abandoned also rose. In significant numbers they then discovered the Public Broadcasting System, a television network whose principle from the first was that it was better to have a toffee up your nose than beans in your ears. English accents became familiar to the viewers of the BBC classic serials, relayed on PBS.

Ironically, this breakthrough came at the precise moment when the 'Hollywood England' notion of big-budget American pictures shot in Britain had spectacularly failed to make the grade, or indeed Lord Grade. Suddenly, everyone seemed to discover that the British could appear in American movies without having to explain why they were British. Thus did Dudley Moore appear as a New York millionaire in *Arthur*, John Hurt as a Californian cop in *Partners*, Michael Caine as a homosexual Broadway playwright in *Deathtrap*. On television Glenda Jackson played Patricia Neal with no trace of an American accent and, when Lynn Redgrave went into the long-running *House Calls*, there was not the faintest attempt to explain away her still marked English accent by suggesting that she was out in America on some kind of hospital exchange system. With the coming of television tapes from London into their homes American audiences for the first time ceased to care about whether an accent was American or English, and ceased to search for any corresponding explanation of it in the plot. Suddenly it just didn't matter any more.

With this discovery, the Empire began to strike back at last. A roll-call of the British residing in Hollywood in January 1983 found Dudley Moore, Michael Caine, Anthony Hopkins, Lynn Redgrave, Jane Seymour, Jacqueline Bisset plus, in a new subdivision, pop stars Rod Stewart and Tom Jones. Then there were artists such as David Hockney, screenwriters like Dick Clement and Ian le Frenais, and record producers like Peter Asher as well as innumerable hairdressers, estate agents, secretaries and head waiters. The company which checks the voting figures for the annual Oscar ceremony is British run, the curator of the great Getty art collection was until recently British, and a reporter for the *Mail on Sunday* recently counted twenty-four cricket clubs, eighteen soccer teams, four bowls teams, three darts leagues and even an annual Highland Games tournament all within the greater Los Angeles area. He also found the *Queen Mary*, two local British newspapers, a weekly radio show devoted to the Goons, scores of British 'pubs' selling imported Watneys and Guinness, and a large number of non-star actors who still reckon, in Michael

Caine's celebrated assessment, that 'it's better working here than back home in England, where you make one film for yourself and the next two for the income tax inspector'.

Probably the most significant contribution made by the British to the American cinema since the war has been a gift of directors. Ever since Tony Richardson went to California in 1960 to make *Sanctuary*, a generation of younger British film directors has followed Hitchcock's tracks across the Atlantic, finding there the kind of production budgets still largely unavailable at home. Some simply went native while in America (Michael Winner's *Death Wish* films are not noticeably the work of a British director); others brought an often elusive but still faintly 'foreign' flavour to such apparently American subjects as *Deliverance* (John Boorman) and *Bullitt* (Peter Yates).

A third group, led by John Schlesinger, created films which were specifically commentaries on America made by an outside observer (*Midnight Cowboy*, *Day of the Locust* and then *Yanks*, one of the few films made by a British director about Americans on foreign soil). Others have had rather less success on the other side of the Atlantic: Karel Reisz, after *The Gambler* and *Who'll Stop The Rain?*, had to return to British territory to secure the triumph of *The French Lieutenant's Woman*, though, admittedly with an American actress in the archetypal Victorian romantic lead. Ken Russell seemed with his US-made *Altered States* to be at last escaping a run of over-the-top biographies of British composer, but it has really been the David Puttnam team who in the 1980s have most successfully straddled the ocean. Men like Alan Parker (*Bugsy Malone*, *Midnight Express*, *Fame*, *Shoot the Moon*), Ridley Scott (*Alien*) and Michael Apted (*Stardust*, *Agatha*, *Coal Miner's Daughter*) now find that in Hollywood, as in London, they are likely to be getting first call on both scripts and budgets. In that sense, Puttnam's Oscar-winning *Chariots of Fire* simply confirmed not just that the British were coming (as Colin Welland put it in his 1982 acceptance speech), but they had now arrived both as directors and producers, as well as actors and writers.

Things were very different for the British in California when Tony Richardson first arrived there in 1960 hot from his Royal Court and British film success, and they had not much improved when three years later he set about filming Evelyn Waugh's classic Hollywood British satire:

The film of *The Loved One* [wrote Waugh in a letter to Nancy Mitford] is a great

Jne of the few occasions when Peters [his agent] has let me
years ago to a mad Mexican for a paltry sum with the
would never be produced, but that Alec Guinness (who was to
it have an agreeable jaunt together to Mexico. The next thing
that an American company had bought the rights from the
Mexican ... were producing an elaborate travesty. No redress.

The 'mad Mexican' was, in fact, Luis Buñuel, not that the name
would have meant much to Waugh. When the property finally fell into
Richardson's hands, he decided with Christopher Isherwood to update
the book to the space age and have the Forest Lawn bodies sent into
the stratosphere; the result was a fair old shambles from which one or
two actors managed to emerge with a certain precarious dignity still
intact and which gained Richardson a postcard from Waugh hoping
that the film would never reach his local Odeon in Taunton.

Richardson had anyway arrived in Hollywood far too late to see
much of the colony that Sir Ambrose and Sir Francis went out to bat
for:

Apart from Vanessa trying to give one disastrous English fish-and-chip
party during the filming of *Camelot* [Richardson told me recently] I can't say
I've ever been aware of a very British presence in California. I myself have
always felt vastly more at home here than I do in England, though there does
still seem to be a certain eery fascination with the British accent. It still
carries a certain cachet, though that applies equally to telephonists and film
directors in Beverly Hills. I was never happy with the studio system, but that
luckily was cracking up already: the Zanucks and the Selznicks were monstrous money-makers with no definable love for movies, and though they took
me up socially when I first arrived, I soon learned to steer well clear of them
and their ideas of film-making.

There's still a kind of California high society, the end of the ossified Palm Beach
West world, but it's easily possible to avoid that and to live in California exactly
the kind of life you want to live, something that I never really found possible in
England. I don't feel the isolation in California that many from London seem to
notice: I don't actually think that the local newspapers or radio or television are
any worse than they are in Europe.

But there are no real colonies left in California: the French and the Germans no
longer exist here as screen stereotypes any more than the English do, which is why
young actors have a much tougher time breaking into Californian filming than they
probably did twenty years ago. It's not enough to be English; you have now to be
English and have done something at home that makes you valuable. You have to be
'brought out' here if you are going to survive.

There's also still a desperate kind of fashionability: if your last film is a hit, they really do ring up and ask you to parties for about a month. If it's not, they leave you alone and pretend they think you've gone back to London.

There's also a lot less work here than there used to be, so you don't get the big novelists coming out from Europe to work on screenplays; most of the employment is in television, and there's very little work there for the English unless they lose the accent and integrate and accept a lot of very mediocre scripts.

But most of the myths about Los Angeles are, in fact, untrue: it has some of the greatest second-hand bookshops in the world, wonderful music, and it's probably the only city in the world where you can live totally out in the open air. No wonder the British, brought up in rain and cloud, find it an awakening; everything is somehow so much easier and more equal under the sun.

At the end of February 1983, for the first time in history, a reigning British monarch landed in Hollywood; sadly, however, by the time Queen Elizabeth II arrived for her royal tour of the few surviving film studios, most of her loyal subjects there had died, retired, returned home, gone into television soap operas or given up the business altogether to sell secondhand Rolls-Royces. True, there were a few actors left, but somehow they were no longer recognizably the Hollywood British; even Julie Andrews had by now taken to appearing in transvestite musicals, while Michael Caine would have been employed by Aubrey Smith as, at best, an under-gardener.

Yet Her Majesty arrived to find Dudley Moore and Sir John Gielgud keeping the flag flying in *Arthur* (symbolically, it was Moore who played the master and Gielgud the servant), while her royal visit came neatly sandwiched between two of the most successful Oscar ceremonies the British had ever enjoyed. In 1982 they took home four Oscars for *Chariots of Fire*, while in 1983 twice that number went to *Gandhi* in the name of world peace. Yet neither film had been made within five thousand miles of California and neither employed any of the surviving Hollywood British – even Sir Richard Attenborough in a film career spanning forty years and sixty movies as actor, writer, director and producer had virtually never worked there.

All was not, however, totally lost: Her Majesty arrived in torrential rain to the news that *Mrs Miniver* was due for a remake, and Greer Garson herself was located and brought in for the Los Angeles banquet – she at least was still living in the vicinity, unlike James Mason, who had to be flown in for the occasion from his home in Switzerland. Other stars lined up on the converted television set of *MASH* by the Queen's hosts,

Twentieth Century-Fox, included such notably unEnglish entertainers as Zsa Zsa Gabor and Perry Como.

However, the British contingent did manage to occupy one entire top table: Joan Collins was there from her television success in *Dynasty*, Jean Marsh from *Upstairs, Downstairs*, Samantha Eggar, Dudley Moore, the Michaels Caine and York, Julie Andrews, Tony Richardson and pop singers Elton John and Rod Stewart. Some of the other guests looked, thought Clive James, as if they had risen from the grave for the occasion but that, on 28 February 1983, was about the extent of the Hollywood British. Nevertheless, how proud Sir Aubrey Smith would have been that Her Majesty was at last setting foot on the soil where he had spent so many years as her father's and grandfather's celluloid ambassador. And for the Queen herself, apart from Zsa Zsa's bright purple fur coat and Frank Sinatra's hair transplants, the evening was probably not too shocking; Her Majesty is, after all, more than accustomed to whole areas of her empire being reclaimed by the natives.

Index

Tortellini w/ Peas
Vinaigrette
Vinegar, lemon, salt
garlic, oil

Fried Ravioli
+ Bl cheese dill